MARCO ⊕ POLO

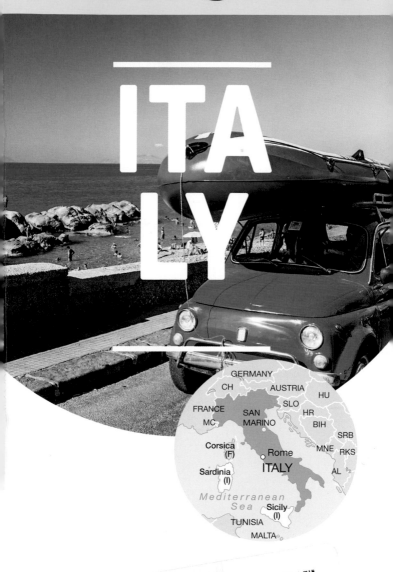

ITALY

GERMANY
CH   AUSTRIA   HU
FRANCE   SLO
MC   SAN   HR
MARINO   BIH
Corsica   SRB
(F)   Rome   MNE   RKS
Sardinia   ITALY   AL
(I)
Mediterranean
Sea   Sicily
(I)
TUNISIA
MALTA

T0150571

THE TOURING APP

shows you the way...

including routes and offline maps!

GET MORE OUT OF YOUR MARCO POLO GUIDE

IT'S AS SIMPLE AS THIS

1 go.marco-polo.com/ita

2 download and discover

GO!

WORKS OFFLINE!

SYMBOLS

 Insider Tip

★ Highlight

⬤⬤⬤⬤ Best of...

 Scenic view

 Responsible travel: for eco-
logical or fair trade aspects

**PRICE CATEGORIES
HOTELS**

Expensive over 150 euros

Moderate 100–150 euros

Budget under 100 euros

Average prices for a double
room without breakfast.
In the high season there
are sometimes significant
surcharges.

**PRICE CATEGORIES
RESTAURANTS**

Expensive over 16 (12) euros

Moderate 10–16 (8–12) euros

Budget under 10 (8) euros

Prices are for a main meal or
(in brackets) for a plain pasta or rice dish (from about 3
euros)

CONTENTS

MAPS IN THE GUIDEBOOK
(186 A1) Page numbers and
coordinates refer to the road
atlas
(U A1) Coordinates for the
city map of Rome inside the
back cove
(0) Site/address located off
the map

Coordinates are also given for
places that are not marked
on the road atlas

(*A–B 2–3*) refers to the
removable pull-out map
(*a–b 2–3*) refers to the
additional map of Rome on
the pull-out map

INSIDE FRONT COVER:
The best Highlights

INSIDE BACK COVER:
City map of Rome

The best MARCO POLO Insider Tips

Our top 15 Insider Tips

INSIDER TIP Market stroll for the senses
The market hall of the *Mercato Orientale* in Genoa awakens all your senses (photo right) → **p. 41**

INSIDER TIP From "little mouse" to Spider
The collection of the *Museo dell'Automobile* in the Fiat city Turin includes the first "Topolino" from 1936, the Fiat 500 from 1957 and cult cars from Alfa Romeo and Lancia → **p. 47**

INSIDER TIP *Mare e Monti* on the Golfo di Policastro
Southern Italian summer between mountains and sandy bays, *borghi* and beautiful hotel villas: the 26 km/16 miles long dream coast of *Maratea* on the Golfo di Policastro in Basilicata → **p. 130**

INSIDER TIP Hearty snacks and perfect cups of coffee
A traditional pleasure: the buffets and coffee houses in Trieste, the *Pasticceria Pirona,* for example → **p. 61**

INSIDER TIP Meander through reeds and water lilies
When the Mincio River reaches the old town of Mantua, it opens up into three lakes, which can be explored *by boat* (photo above) → **p. 80**

INSIDER TIP Between camellias and rose gardens
The most beautiful view of Florence is from the café loggia in the romantic *Giardino Bardini* → **p. 87**

INSIDER TIP Ancient art in front of steel turbines
Wonderfully lit statues from the vast array of treasures of the Roman empire, set against the backdrop of the disused power station *Centrale Montemartini* in Rome → **p. 114**

INSIDER TIP Slumber in caves
The *Sassi di Matera* caves were once homes for the poor; today they provide the fascinating stage for charming hotels such as *Sant'Angelo* → **p. 130**

BEST OF...

FOR FREE

● *Sound of the Dolomites*
Soloists from the Berlin Philharmonic Orchestra or Italy's famous cellist Mario Brunello shoulder their instruments and hike to cave and mountain venues in the Trentino Dolomites. Accompany them at *I Suoni delle Dolomiti,* and you can enjoy marvellous renditions by professional musicians completely free of charge → p. 60

● *Cascata del Molino hot springs*
Spa resorts have the monopoly on most of Italy's thermal springs, but in some areas such as *Saturnia* in Tuscany, you can still enjoy a hot spring in natural surroundings (photo) → p. 104

● *Magna Graecia in Metaponto*
Along the coast of Southern Italy, you can visit the archaeological sites of ancient towns built by the Greeks in the 8th century BC during their colonisation of Italy. The ruins of the ancient city of *Metapontum* are particularly impressive → p. 132

● *Cavern town of Matera in Basilicata*
You do not have to pay a penny to enjoy history when you wander the streets, terraces and steep stairs carved into the rock of the ancient *sassi* settlement scattered on a rocky slope and marvel at the many rock churches with their wonderful frescoes → p. 130

● *Via Appia Antica in Rome*
The ancient route led from Rome to the Adriatic. This Roman road in the large archaeological park is a fine example of the Roman Empire's excellent road network – and there is no entrance fee → p. 116

● *Procession and fireworks*
Traditional festivals – such as the *Trasporto della Macchina di Santa Rosa* in honour of Santa Rosa in Viterbo in September – offer a free display of Italian joie de vivre, in the form of open-air concerts, fireworks and a magnificent procession → p. 171

◖◗◖◗◖● Dots in guidebook refer to "Best of..." tips

● *To the mountains*

Italy not only has the longest coastline (7600 km/4722 miles in total) in Europe but also the highest Alps, one example being the protected *Gran Paradiso* massif in the Aosta Valley (4016 m/13,180 ft high peak) with inviting meadows and forests bursting with wildlife → p. 38

● *By the lake*

The lakes in northern Italy are so beautiful that you may find it difficult to decide which of these jewels with their mild climate, verdant vegetation and spectacular waterside villas is the most beautiful. Perhaps *Lago di Como* with its enchanting little lakeside towns such as Bellagio and Varenna? → p. 76

● *Delta landscape*

Italy's longest river, the *Po,* projects into the Adriatic between Chioggia and Comacchio and branches out into endless streams and channels. The unique charm of this flat lagoon landscape makes it ideal for cycling → p. 63

● *Magnificent palaces*

The powerful maritime republics, town states and principalities accumulated great wealth, and their legacy includes magnificent palaces, such as the *rolli* in Genoa (photo) → p. 39

● *Art and faith in Assisi*

In the homeland of the great saints, art has also taken its inspiration from faith, as is clearly visible in Giotto's frescoes about the life of the patron Saint Francis of Assisi in the *Basilica di San Francesco* → p. 97

● *The breath of Antiquity*

2000 years ago the harbour of Rome; today the ruined city of *Ostia Antica* in the shade of large pines gives you a taste of ancient Rome → p. 119

● *Lidos*

No matter where you are staying along the Adriatic or the Liguria, Tuscan or Calabrian coast: summer in Italy – in August at least – is spent at the beach, more precisely at the lido, the traditional Italian sandbar covered in loungers and umbrellas, for example at the *Lido di Venezia* or in *Rimini* and around → p. 63, 83

BEST OF...

● **In the dripstone caves**
It is cold and damp below the Earth's surface, but you will not get wet during your excursion deep below the rocks. There are large dripstone caves all over Italy with fascinating formations of stalactites and stalagmites; the largest cave is the *Grotta Gigante* near Trieste → **p. 61**

● **Aquarium in Genoa**
The diverse underwater world in the country's largest aquarium provides a perfect excursion when it is raining on the Ligurian coast – sharks and penguins will provide hours of entertainment (photo) → **p. 166**

● **Galleria Vittorio Emanuele II in Milan**
Under the glass-domed roof of Italy's largest and most elegant shopping arcade, you can wander over skilfully laid marble floors past elegant boutiques and bookstores and then enjoy a view of the cathedral square as you sip on an espresso → **p. 72**

● **Rome's main churches**
Rome's four main churches, which naturally include *St Peter's Basilica*, are so large and packed with art treasures that you can use the rainy weather to explore them at your leisure → **p. 114**

● **Napoli Sotterranea**
The city of Naples is built on tuff (volcanic) stone. Over the centuries, its inhabitants have created an underground world of cellars, large cisterns, subterranean places of worship and catacombs, and today these offer a fascinating *underground tour* → **p. 140**

● **Designer outlet centre Serravalle**
Searching for a bargain in the rain? Spend a relaxing day exploring the more than 170 shops in the country's largest outlet village → **p. 32**

RAIN

RELAX AND CHILL OUT
Take it easy and spoil yourself

● *Hay bath in South Tyrol*
Lie down in the warm, damp hay! At *Hotel Heubad* in Völs am Schlern, essential oils extracted from the mountain herbs that grow on the Seiser Alm in South Tyrol penetrate the body, and relax and refresh you in a most agreeable way → **p. 54**

● *On the Brenta Canal to magnificent villas*
An opportunity to relax and see something at the same time? Then take the Burchiello excursion boat from Padua to Venice and cruise past the beautiful Venetian villas that line the water's edge → **p. 56**

● *On the piazza*
Where better to relax than in a pavement café on an Italian piazza – sip an espresso and watch the hustle and bustle in front of the breathtaking palazzi and church architecture, e.g. in *Cremona* or *Ascoli Piceno*
→ **p. 80, 92**

● *On the seafront promenade*
It is the town of Reggio di Calabria that has one of Italy's most beautiful *lungomare*: take a stroll and enjoy the sunset! → **p. 134**

● *Fango therapy in the Euganean Hills*
Owing to their past volcanic activity, the hills of Padua are rich in minerals and mud that has healed and relaxed many generations over the centuries. Now it is your turn – in *Abano Terme* → **p. 57**

● *An inspiring trail*
There is hardly any other trail that provides such a breathtaking panorama as pleasantly and easily as that offered by Trieste's rocky coast on the Adria near Duino → **p. 61**

● *On the Cilento beaches*
You can enjoy the beautiful sandy beaches along this piece of largely unspoilt coastline just south of Naples (photo)
→ **p. 145**

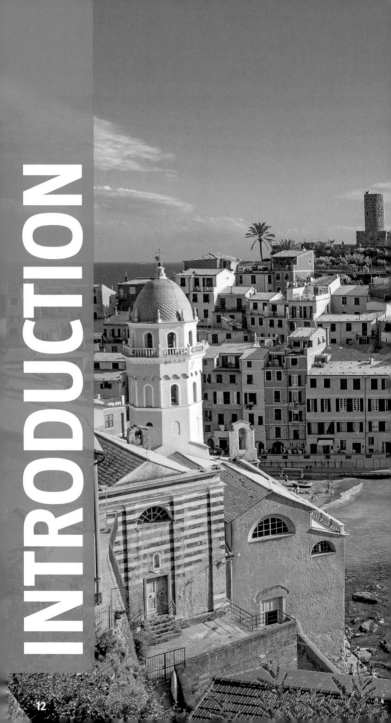

INTRODUCTION

DISCOVER ITALY!

When you arrive in Italy, the first thing you should do is to go to the piazza; it is the sitting room, hub of urban life and stage for the Italians all rolled into one. Sit down in the café with the best view, order a cappuccino, a Campari or even a local aperitif and simply watch the Italians. You will no doubt see a few elderly men standing talking with great gusto about everything and anything (football included of course). And if it is market day in winter, there will a lot of ladies in mink intent on creating a *bella figura*, which is far higher up their list of priorities than animal rights. Groups of young people will go past, *gesticulating wildly*, all fashionably dressed and clutching the ubiquitous *telefonino*.

A trip to Italy can be an expensive pleasure. The prices for hotels and beach life are often hefty, especially in touristy regions. Nonetheless, many restaurants offer *inexpensive lunch menus*, and flexible online booking makes it possible to find reasonable rates even in what are otherwise high-priced hotels. What is more, in the last few years – if one ignores the usual rip-offs and poor service that can be experienced anywhere in the world – hotels and restaurants have improved. A lot has happened

Probably the most famous steps in Rome: Scalinata Trinità dei Monti (Spanish Steps)

in the hospitality industry: in coastal towns and in the medieval hamlets, *locande*, small, individually run and tastefully furnished guest houses are opening; while in the large cities, there is a choice between **charming boutique hotels, chic design hotels** or comfortable B & B rooms, often in beautifully restored town houses. City trips in self-catering apartments are also gaining in popularity.

In the evening, people meet for an **aperitif at the bar**, in the town quite often in the luxury hotels, in the summer by the sea in beach areas that turn into lounge bars when the sun goes down or provide DJ facilities for the beach party. New stylish shops selling clothes, shoes and **original designer pieces** are opening up everywhere; they often use the spectacular setting provided by an old town palazzo.

There is always a good reason to improve and renovate districts and buildings that have seen better days. For the holy years 2000 and 2016, half of Rome was given a

From 1000 BC
Highly developed art and technology of the Etruscans

8th–5th century BC
Greeks establish over 40 towns in the south of Italy

4th–1st century BC
Rome rules throughout Italy and in the Mediterranean region

5th century
Teutons, Lombards, Vandals and Huns invade Italy

11th century
The Normans capture Campania, Apulia and Sicily

14th/15th century
Formation of independent duchies, town and maritime

facelift and the infrastructure modernised for the millions of visitors; the same goes for Milan for the Expo 2015. There are also new additions: contemporary art projects and ultra-modern museums in Rome and Venice, spectacular *art underground stations* in Naples. In Turin, once dominated by Fiat, there have been successful efforts made to bring the town *into the post-industrial era figura* with ambitious cultural projects. In the fascinating harbour city of Genoa, many of the palazzi and magnificent museums have been spruced up. This attention to *old town centres* contrasts with the sometimes depressing sprawl of the suburbs and the often surprisingly crude architecture. And despite the fact that Italians are taking environmental protection more seriously, for example by introducing better sewage plants, setting up nature reserves and increasingly bringing agriculture in line with the criteria of organic farming, it is still shocking to see the rubbish left behind on some beaches, in the woods and by the rivers – especially, but not only, in the south.

It is the Italians themselves that criticise their country the most, especially when things do not work as they would like them to.

In the evening people meet for an aperitif in the bar

Traffic chaos, lack of parking space in the cities, bad service, crowded trains. The Italians can despair about themselves and their country. As when the factories close in August, and with them a lot of the restaurants and businesses in the large towns, and *all of Italy sets off for the seaside*. Chaos and high prices are the inevitable result. Naturally, there are reserves that provide service to those who do not go off on holiday and for the solitary, intrepid tourists. And, of course, it is lovely to be able to enjoy these deserted towns without all the traffic and noise.

This provides the cue for why people love to keep going back to Italy: the leaning tower of Pisa, shimmering olive groves, Michelangelo's David, the gondola ride along the Canal Grande, *romantic coastlines* such as the Cinque Terre or the Costa Amalfitana… The Italians continue to be friendly, generous and open people, even if their life is by no means full of the pleasure and indulgence expressed in the famous dolce vita! In fact, statistics show that they actually work more than the English, French and Germans.

Italy is essentially a *mountainous country* and has to accommodate over 60 million people in its hills and valleys. In the north, much of the Alps belong to Italy: the south-facing massifs of the Central and Western Alps, whose foothills run down to the *large lakes*, and the Southern Limestone Alps which include the Dolomites.

> **Italy is predominantly a mountainous country**

Bordering this area is the Po Valley, a broad plain, which stretches from Piedmont down to the Adriatic coast. Travellers tend to pass through here quickly. Flat, humid and plagued with mosquitoes, it is not your typical Italian landscape, yet towns such as Parma, Mantua and Ferrara are well worth a visit. Poplars and dykes line the *landscape along the Po River*, which flows into a nature reserve at the delta leading to the Adriatic – a place of great beauty with its ponds, tributaries, sand dunes and many different bird species.

In terms of climate, northern Italy has a predominantly continental climate, which means that in winter Turin and Milan can often be just as cold as London or New York, although the proximity to the south is evidenced by the higher summer temperatures. The Riviera sheltered by the Maritime Alps and the Ligurian Apennines is well known for its *mild winters*. Behind Liguria, the Alps meet the Apennines, which run over 1200 km/746 miles to the southern tip of Calabria. While it can get very hot in the summer in the hills of Tuscany and Umbria, the climate on the coast is more moderate. In Campania, the Apennines even offer an *active volcano* – Vesuvius on the Gulf of Naples. Listed as a Unesco World Heritage Site, the nearby

1922–1943
Fascist dictatorship under Benito Mussolini

1946
Italy becomes a republic

1970–1989
"Years of Lead" with terrorist attacks from left and ring-wing extremists

1994–2011
Alternating governments under the right-wing millionaire populist Silvio Berlusconi and centre-left parties

2014
The social democrat Matteo Renzi becomes Prime Minister

2016
A series of devastating earthquakes hits central Italy

Umbria, the "green heart" of Italy: a kind of Tuscany for insiders

Costiera Amalfitana, or Amalfi Coast, offers sheer coastal beauty. Less overrun by tourists are Calabria and Apulia in the heel of Italy's boot; a beguiling combination of crystal-clear waters, mountains and inland forests especially for independent holidaymakers.

Italy covers a total area of around 116,000 square miles. About a sixth of this and half of its 760

> **Crystal-clear waters in the heel of Italy's boot**

km/4722 miles coastline belong to the islands. This travel guide only covers the mainland, however there are separate MARCO POLO guides available for Sicily, Sardinia, and Naples and the Amalfi Coast.

The diversity in the country's geography and climate, with its Alpine summits, river plains, densely forested highlands, Mediterranean hillscapes and coastline is in keeping with the multifariousness of *Italy's past*. Thus each town, each province and each island has its own history. Greeks and Etruscans were – after the large migration around 1000 BC – the first to leave their mark on the culture and history of Italy. From the 8th century BC, the Greeks founded over 40 towns in the south of Italy. The *Etruscans*, who mainly settled in the north of Lazio, in Tuscany and the Po Valley, were people with highly advanced skills in handcrafts and art. Thanks to their *surprisingly cheerful approach to death*, numerous examples of their expressive art have been preserved. Their burial towns, the necropolises, especially those in Lazio, are key tourist attractions.

During the 4th and 3rd century BC, Rome controlled all of Italy and, during the subsequent centuries, set about building a powerful empire in the Mediterranean area, in Asia Minor and Europe. *Imposing buildings* still bear witness to the representative ambitions of this former world power. They include the Colosseum that was inaugurated in AD 80 with 100 days of continuous tournaments, the gigantic Hadrian villa in Tivoli, the Baths of Caracalla in Rome, which could accommodate up to 1600 bathers, and Verona Arena with space for 22,000 spectators.

Renaissance art and culture became the benchmark of Europe

The fall of the Roman Empire took hundreds of years. Already under threat from the Alemanni, the Franconians, the Visigoths and Ostrogoths, the Huns and the Teutons, the empire was divided into a West and East Roman Empire, the latter having its capital in Constantinople. In the 5th century, Ravenna became the *residence of the West Roman Emperors*, which is why today it is one of the main cities to see in Italy. New nations invaded Italy and dissolved the Roman centralism by setting up independent duchies. During the Middle Ages, the Arabs, Normans and the Hohenstaufens controlled southern Italy. *Impressive cathedrals and fortresses* date from the Norman and Hohenstaufen period, especially in Apulia. From the 10th to 13th centuries, the Holy Roman Emperors and their rivalries with the popes of Italy left their mark on the Italy of the Middle Ages. The harbour towns prospered as a result of the crusades and trade with the orient. Even today, stately palaces in the towns testify to the self-confidence of the communities, which became independent town states in the 13th century.

In the 14th and 15th century, local principalities developed, with powerful families like the Visconti and Sforza in Milan, the Scaligeri in Verona, the Este in Modena and Ferrara, the Gonzaga in Mantua, the Malatesta in Romagna, the Montefeltro in the Marche region, but especially the Medici in Tuscany. Besides the church, they were the major art patrons driving the *Italian Renaissance*. Their art and culture became the measure for Europe as a whole. They enabled outstanding *art geniuses* such as Masaccio, Piero della Francesca, Brunelleschi, Donatello, Leonardo da Vinci, Michelangelo, and Botticelli to develop. The Catholic Counter-Reformation encouraged the *emergence of the Baroque period*, which can be particularly admired in Rome and Naples. In subsequent centuries, major European powers fought for supremacy in "the boot". This ended in 1861 with the creation of the Italian national state.

Italy's rich and eventful history has resulted in the country's vast array of *art treasures and cultural assets* – but what an enormous task it is to look after them. The Italian passion for gambling helps in this respect as a significant percentage of the state lottery profits flows into the upkeep of historical monuments. Museums have long since had longer opening times to enable more people to visit them. EU citizens *under 18 years of age* do not have to pay for their ticket at the large state museums and those aged 18 to 25 only pay half price. On the first sunday of the month, admission is free for all visitors. And many towns have introduced *cards,* tickets enabling the holder to enter the various sights and museums at a discounted price as well as to travel free on public transport.

Yet Italy's magic is by no means limited to the fine arts. Whilst in one respect the gastronomy sector is not soaring quite as high, a lot of dedicated young chefs are now encouraging a return to local specialities. Organic farming, organic grocery shops and *farmer's markets* all support this trend. Italy's *Slow Food movement* has played a leading role in this respect. At home and abroad, it actively promotes the preservation of local products, culinary traditions and environmentally conscious food production. Environmental organisations and the state are also investing an increasing amount of energy into protecting nature. The first large nature reserves were created at the beginning of the 20th century, such as the Alpine *national park Gran Paradiso* between the high peaks

Largest church in the smallest city-state: St Peter's Basilica in the Vatican

of the Aosta Valley and the Parco Nazionale dell'Abruzzo with its wild Apennine Mountains, home to *wolves and bears*. In the 1990s, the government allocated new protected areas, and today ten per cent of Italy's landscape and coastal areas are under conservation. Tourist authorities provide maps of the nature reserves, *hiking and bicycle trails*. Even those who enjoy more extreme sports will find challenging playgrounds in the mountains and the sea, ranging from rock climbing in the Alps and Apennines to *biking and windsurfing* as well as rafting down wild mountain streams.

> *Agriturismo* enjoys growing popularity

Beautifully located farmhouses offer holiday accommodation, often with horse rides, *swimming pool and guest bicycles* as well as home-produced food. This rural option, called *Agriturismo*, offers a relaxing contrast to the sightseeing tours – and it is becoming increasingly popular with holidaymakers. Thus the chances of having an exciting and enjoyable trip to Italy, a country that can boast *beautifully preserved old towns*, growing rural conservation and seemingly endless coastlines, are now even better than ever.

WHAT'S HOT

1 Temporary citizens

Authentic and relaxed way of life The organisation, Borghi Autentici d'Italia, set up the project *Comunità Ospitali* ("hospitable villages") with the intention of preserving the traditional form of village life. Rather than feel like tourists, guests are invited to become citizens, albeit temporary ones and take home with them a rich sense of local traditions and rituals, typical products, dishes and wines. The initiative *città slow (www.cittaslow.org)*, or "slow cities" similarly aims to bring a gentler pace of life and higher standards of living back to cities.

New masters

2

Art Rome's art scene is not only influenced by the museums *Museo d'Arte Contemporanea di Roma (www.museomacro.org)* and *Museo Nazionale delle Arti del XXI Secolo (www.fondazionemaxxi.it)*; private collections such as the *Fondazione Sandretto Re Rebaudengo (www.fsrr.org)* in Turin or the *Fondazione Prada (www.fondazioneprada.org)* in Milan also contribute their part. Turin's art fair *Artissima (www.artissima.it)* provides a good insight of what's going on in the art world.

3 Like the ancient Romans

On the beach Luxury laps at the gates of Rome. Guests relax on lounge beds or in hammocks on Fregene's beaches. They can also chill in *La Rotonda – Shilling Sea Point Roma (Piazzale Cristoforo Colombo | www.larotonda.it)* in Ostia, with yoga and massages areas. The guests of the *Bagno Elena (www.bagnoelena.it)* in Naples feel like they are in holiday heaven. On a wooden terrace overlooking the sea, you can sunbathe while you surf the internet and drink prosecco cranberry on ice.

Hot excursions

Volcano trekking Inquisitive travellers can learn why it is best not to wear synthetic socks if you are a volcanologist and what makes lava soil so fertile during a special guided tour to Vesuvius.

4

The certified experts from *Guide Vesuvio (www.guidevesuvio.it)* in Ercolano lead the way to the crater of the active volcano. With *Vesuviustour (www.vesuviustour.com | photo)*, it is not just about destination but also about the journey. Vesuvius fans will love the guided hike through the surrounding park. Situated to the west of Naples near Pozzuoli are the active seismic Phlegraean Fields with the Solfatara crater *(www.vulcanosolfatara.it)*; a large volcanic area with numerous fumaroles and sulphur springs which were used for their healing powers way back in ancient times.

Wind and water

5

Active Lake Garda is the Mecca of Italy's water sports fans. The steady breeze attracts kite surfers to Malcesine or Riva del Garda. Now, other locations are making a name for themselves as destinations for water sports. The still undeveloped south, in particular, offers fantastic conditions for the fast-paced sport. Kitesurfers head for Calabria with its Golfo di Sant'Eufemia in Lamezia Terme, home to the kitesurf school *Hangloose Beach (www.hangloosebeach.it),* Le Terrazze in Copanello and Punta Pellaro with its school *New Kite Zone (www.newkitezone.it)*. Hotspots for windsurfers include the Spiaggia Lunga at Gargano in Apulia or at Andora, Albenga or Imperia along the coast of Liguria *(Spiaggia d'Oro)*.

IN A NUTSHELL

BAR

The bar opens at the crack of dawn with the fragrance of fresh *cornetti* (croissants) and *cappuccini*. During the day, housewives, school children, manual workers, office employees, and passersby pop in. In the afternoon, youngsters plan what they are doing in the evening. In the towns, the cocktail hour marks the day's climax; in the villages, the men return to the bar for a last chat after dinner. In the summer, guests watch the activities on the piazza from their seats in front of the bar. From sober to shabby (sometimes quite kitschy) but nowadays also increasingly very trendy, the bar is the Italian's second home and visitors are also made very welcome.

BELLA FIGURA

In whatever situation, Italians always endeavour to present a *bella figura*, to literally "cut a beautiful figure". Presentation is what counts, especially in how one looks and how one comports oneself. Besides stylish clothing, it also means exhibiting good manners, tact and gentility. *Bella figura* is also knowing how to graciously interact with others and avoid embarrassing them in any social situation. This explains why impatience is seen as a negative trait and why Italians place more trust in beauty than in practicality. It also helps to understand why the Italian press pay minute attention to how their politicians are dressed. That image is a reflection of an individual's inner values is no surprise in a culture where gestures and

Photo: Ferrari Festival in Brindisi

Slow Food, the Mafia and saints: notes on the culture, daily life and politics of a multifaceted country

symbols are used to communicate meaning. The *bella figura* has nothing to do with a person's wealth though: all you need are a handful of selected ingredients in the kitchen cupboard ready for unexpected guests and a few stylish classics in your wardrobe.

CARS AND MOTORBIKES

High speeds appeal to the temperament of the Italians; only they could invent sleek cars such as the blazing red Ferrari from Modena. Motorcycle fans swear by the Italian cult brand Ducati from Bologna, and little girls swoon for the unbeatable racing driver Valentino Rossi. And like buzzing swarms, Vespas whizz through the narrow streets of the Italian towns. Despite the high motorway tolls and the traffic chaos in the towns, the Italians still enjoy driving. They have a nippy, nimble style, but can also be impatient and aggressive. But the fun element is not what it was, since the once typical statistics for Italy – a lot of vehicle damage but few road casualties – is no longer true. Smog has led to many of the large cities closing off their town centres to vehicles, including tourist cars. But it is possible to rent a bicycle in almost all of the town centres, generally in the vicinity of the station. Environmental awareness is thus also picking up speed on Italy's roads; driving with low-emission fuel is very widespread, car sharing is no longer a foreign concept and taxi companies use the hybrid cars Prius.

ECONOMY

In the second half of the 20th century, Italy developed from a rural, agricultural country into a highly developed industrial nation. Tourism dominates the service area while important industries include mechanical engineering, the packaging industry and food production. Traditional sectors, such as the textile and shoe industry, also play a key role in Italy's economy. These benefit from the creativity of the world-famous Italian fashion designers, but also from the so far successful structure of Italian business, which is dominated by highly specialised small to medium-sized often family-run companies. They are mainly based in the north and centre of Italy and, as flexible family-run corporations, often play an essential supporting role to the few large companies such as Ferrero (Nutella, Kinder), Benetton, Barilla and Fiat. However, things are not as good as they were. Relocation of production facilities to low-wage countries is also affecting Italy and bureaucracy, national debt and taxes are causing a heavy burden. There is a lack of investment in education and research, and the opportunities for young people are correspondingly poor. They represent 39 per cent of the 12 per cent unemployment. Despite years of subsidies, the south also continues to lag behind the rest of the country.

A major problem is the widespread informal economy, illegal employment. Yet numerous reforms have recently been launched, leading to a small decline in unemployment and moderate economic growth.

FAMILY

The Italian family still exists. However, it is no longer the large patriarchal family with several generations under one roof, but has split up into single and small family households. Added to this, the nation famous for being fond of children has seen an astounding decrease in its birth rate – and with statistically about one child per family, holds the European record for producing the fewest children. Today, immigrants from Africa, Asia and Eastern Europe help to ensure that Italy's own ageing population does not tip the pyramid on its head. The family continues to exist as a unit providing mutual support dealing with unemployment, finding work, coping with housing problems, looking after older members of the family and helping out when kindergarten spaces are not available. In the family, you can always find handymen, a doctor or a lawyer. That may in part explain why many Italians can live beyond their means despite high prices and often low wages – and why many youngsters would find it difficult to move into a home of their own.

GIOTTO

Of the many artist geniuses that Italy has produced, the painter and master builder Giotto di Bondone (1266–1337), son of a farmer from a village near Florence, has earned a very special place. During the period of powerful cities like the Florence of the 13th and 14th century, Giotto developed a new painting style, far removed from the schematic representation of Byzantine art, popular in the Middle Ages. Perspective, colour variations, motion, human characterization – in short realism. His painting thus became the starting point for the development of a typically Italian painting tradition, which led out of the "international" Middle Ages. In the Uffizi in Florence, it is easy to see this innovation when comparing Giotto's "Maestà" with that of Cimambue, Giotto's teacher who was a generation older. Giotto's masterpieces are the frescoes in the Cappella degli Scrovegni in Padua and the frescoes depicting the life of St Francis in the Basilica of St Francis in Assisi.

SAINTS

Over 90 per cent of Italy's population are Roman Catholics. The Pope lives in the centre of the capital in his Papal state of the Vatican. Particularly in the south, priests continue to have tremendous influence on politics and elections. Much of the population relies on an army of innumerable saints to give them support in their daily struggle for survival. Worth special mention is Naples's St Januarius. In May and in September, the devout meet in his cathedral, praying for as long as it takes for a vial of the saint's blood to liquefy. Millions of admirers have already made a pilgrimage to San Giovanni Rotondo in Apulia to pay their respects to the miracle healer Padre Pio (1887–1968) who was declared a saint.

IMMIGRATION

The Italians find it hard to regard their country as a "promised land" for immigrants. The idea is too deeply ingrained in their mind that you have to leave Italy to find opportunities and from 1876 to 1976, a whopping 24 million Italians actually did leave for different parts of the world. Yet, like every large industrial nation, the country has long become a goal for people from less prosperous nations, as is more than obvious from the overcrowded vessels found making their way to the south

Worship of Padre Pio: false piety or fervent belief?

Prega e spera:
non agitarti.
L'agitazione
non giova a nulla.
Iddio è misericordioso
e ascolterà
la tua preghiera.

coast: 8.2 per cent of the Italian population today comes from Romania, Albania, Morocco, China and Ukraine. It would be difficult to imagine the economy and the social fabric of Italy without them. The immigrants look after Italy's elderly and their children, run small corner shops and market stalls, work in the hospitals, trattoria kitchens and for the waste disposal companies. The factories in the north and the tomato fields in the south would have to shut down or lie fallow without the African workers.

LANGUAGES

Italy is a country of linguistic diversity. Apart from Italian and its dialects, ten other independent languages are spoken: Ladin in Friuli and the Dolomite valleys, German in South Tyrol (where it is ranked equally with Italian) and in Trentino. In some of the villages in Sicily and southern Italy, the locals speak Albanian, a legacy from the Albanian settlers of the 14th century. In Apulia and Calabria, there are villages where you will hear remnants of Greek. In the northern Italian border provinces of Trieste, Gorizia and Udine, the Italians speak Slovene and in some villages in Molise in southern Italy Serbo-Croat. Catalan has survived in Alghero on Sardinia, as has Franco-Provençal in the north-western regions of Aosta Valley and Piedmont. French is even the second official language in the Aosta Valley. Sardinian is also an independent language and not a dialect. The still highly acclaimed and much cited national poet Dante Alighieri from Florence (1265–1321) provided the basis for standard Italian with his "Divine Comedy", with its 15,000 verses. Since the 20th century, however, schools and television have ensured that the multilingual Italians can all understand each other.

MAFIA

In Italy alone, the Mafia makes around 100 billion euros a year, mainly through protection rackets, "tribute" money, drugs and illegal waste disposal. The fact that their operations stretch beyond the borders of Italy became all too clear with the murders in Germany 2006. Yet there are constantly successful results in the quest to catch the "untouchable" mob bosses, and the civilian population is contributing increasingly to the efforts. The Italian association Libera promotes throughout Italy a law-abiding culture against organised crime on a communal and regional level. Organic oil, wine and pasta, produced on land confiscated from the mafia are now being sold under the label ✪ *Libera Terra (www.liberaterra.it)*. The *Addiopizzo* movement ("goodbye to protection money") is drawing attention to hotels, restaurants and shops in Sicily where the owners are bravely resisting the extortion rackets. In Calabria, the *Ammazzateci tutti* ("kill us all") movement stages campaigns to raise public awareness of legality.

MUSICA ITALIANA

The music scene is as rich and diverse as the countryside. The north has produced incredibly popular old rockers, such as Vasco Rossi, Zucchero, Ligabue and Gianna Nannini. Genoa has a reputation for producing fine songwriters, the most famous of whom include Gino Paoli and the late Fabrizio De André, who is still worshipped by his fans. A different music trend has developed in the south, a mixture of the rhythms of traditional folk music – predominantly *pizzica taranta* from Apulia – and modern sound. Vanguards include Teresa De Sio and Edoardo Bennato, and the next generation includes groups such as Sud Sound System. Pino Daniele mixes jazz, pop and Neapolitan dialect. Anyone looking for the *canzoni napolitane* should listen to Roberto Murolo. And the Italian charts? Young Italians listen to the melodic pop of Subsonica, Le Vibrazioni and Negroamaro. Unconventional pop

by the success of the Slow Food movement, an organisation founded in Bra (Piedmont region) in 1986 with the aim of fighting the fast food industry and encouraging food enjoyment and good taste.

Apulia is the music venue in summer with its many *pizzica* festivals held in Salento

bards include Tiziano Ferro, Sergio Cammariere, Lorenzo Jovanotti, Marco Mengoni as well as – on the female side – Carmen Consoli, Laura Pausini, Giorgia and the young Malika Ayane. Many of these artists give live concerts at the numerous summer festivals and piazza events that take place throughout Italy.

SLOW FOOD

Italians guard their culinary traditions in much the same way as they do their art treasures. This is demonstrated

The movement aims to raise the popularity of seasonal and regional products and promote the fair and eco-conscious production of food. The project "ark of good taste" strives to preserve regional diversity and involves local slow-food groups - the movement has now spread to 150 countries – selecting their regional specialities. Turin's trade fair *Terra Madre Salone del Gusto* is held in years ending in an even number and odd-numbered years host the biennial Cheese festival in Bra. *www.slowfood.it*

FOOD & DRINK

Few countries can match the global popularity of Italian food. Children in the western world grow up with spaghetti and ravioli, and in the international arena the pizza is the only serious competitor of the hamburger.

The *salumerie,* the cheese shop, and the *food markets* will have your mouth watering within seconds. However, it is the simple, but ingenious, durum wheat flour pasta that is the traditional mainstay of Italian cuisine. The imagination and creativity of the Italians have produced around *250 different types of pasta*, first and foremost spaghetti, "strings of pasta" in numerous widths. In southern Italy, *maccheroni* holds sway, either thick or thin, smooth or ribbed, also *tubetti, rigatoni* or *penne.* Then,

there are the more typically central or northern Italian pasta, *tagliatelle, fettuccine* or *pappardelle,* and finally the *filled pasta* made of egg and flour dough in many forms and with different fillings, *ravioli, agnolotti, cappelletti, tortellini, tortelloni, cappellacci.* Many pasta dishes are traditionally topped with grated cheese, *parmigiano* (cow's milk, predominantly in the north) or *pecorino* (sheep's milk, generally in central and southern Italy).

A meal begins with ***antipasti,*** which include starters such as salami, ham, pickled onions, aubergines, artichokes or seafood; this is followed by the *primo* (first course), a pasta dish, soup or ***risotto;*** the *secondo* (main course) is braised or grilled meat, or fish, also often simply

Pasta is the ingenious basis of Italian food – and each region produces the right wine to accompany it

grilled, and a choice of vegetables (*contorno*). **Vegetables** provide the cue for the south, which is where the tomatoes taste particularly good as do the aubergines, artichokes, fresh *fave* (green, sweet broad beans), hearty leaf vegetables, such as *cicorie, cime di rape, friarielli* and broccoli. The meal culminates with **creamy desserts** such as *tiramisu, zabaione* or *zuppa inglese* as well as biscuits which you dunk into sweet fortified wines. In the south, people like to use the mild cream cheese *ricotta* in their desserts.

Ristorante, trattoria, osteria and *locanda* are words that won't help you choose a restaurant – is often better just to look at the ambience and menu as well as the guests eating there (are they Italians?). The once traditional **wine bar** *osteria* now calls itself an *enoteca* or, when in a more international vein, a wine bar. Fine wines are served in a *calice* (goblet) and cost from 2.50 to 10 euros a glass including regional **cheese and charcuterie specialities**. Although controversial (and not allowed anymore in Lazio), the invoice includes

LOCAL SPECIALITIES

agnello – lamb (photo left) served as a roast *(al forno)* or as a grilled chop *(alla griglia)*

arrosto di maiale/di cinghiale – roast pork is popular throughout Italy; central Italy also has wild boar

bollito misto – various cuts of stewed meat: beef, tongue, chicken, sausage, served with a green sauce *salsa verde* or fruit mustard *(mostarda)*

brasato – roast beef braised in red wine, typical in the north of Italy; it is usually served with polenta (made of finely ground cornmeal)

(insalata) caprese – the classic summer snack: tomatoes, mozzarella (preferably made of buffalo milk), basil (photo right)

coniglio – rabbit

fritto misto di pesce – battered, deep fried fish, squid rings, seafood

gnocchi – tiny potato flour dumplings served, like pasta, as a *primo* with a *sugo*

insalata di frutti di mare – a seafood salad with a lemon, olive oil, garlic and parsley dressing comprising of chopped squid, octopus and mussels

ossobuco – braised veal or beef shanks in a tomato sauce, typical for Lombardy

pesce alla griglia – fresh grilled fish: bream *(dorata)*, dentex *(dentice)*, sea bass *(spigola)*, mullet *(triglie)*, plaice *(sogliola)*, sardines and mackerel *(pesce azzurro)*

(alla) pizzaiola – stewed in tomato sauce, typical for the south

porchetta – a suckling pig roasted on the spit and seasoned with herbs

risotto alla milanese – rice dish with saffron originating in Milan

spaghetti alle vongole/allo scoglio – spaghetti with clams or seafood

trenette al pesto – narrow tagliatelle with a sauce made of basil, pine nuts, olive oil and parmesan

zabaione – light and fluffy custard cream with wine, originally from Piedmont

the **coperto**, the price for bread and cover (1.50–6 euros), which is always indicated on the menu. Others call it service. The service, unless specifically indicated as *non compreso*, is included in the price.

The restaurant kitchen tends to open between 12.30pm and 2pm and 7.30pm–10.30pm. Pizzerias usually keep their ovens running until midnight. Anyone feeling peckish during the day can buy *panini* (sandwiches), *tramezzini* (toasted sandwiches) and **sweet pastries** in a bar. Locals like to go to self-service restaurants or *rosticceria* at lunchtime, where you can generally buy tasty regional dishes. There are snack bars selling pizza everywhere, and you can get **deep-fried delicacies** at the *friggitoria*, which is especially popular in southern Italy.

Italy is a haven for wine lovers. Besides the international varieties, Italian vineyards also cultivate their own **regional varieties**, even in the alpine Aosta Valley where both dry white wine and good reds are produced. Italy's best red wines come from Piedmont, including the famous **Barolo**. Crisp white wines flourish on Liguria's terraced slopes. First-rate Lombard wine comes from Oltrepò, Franciacorta and Valtellina while Emilia-Romagna produces more wine than any other region in Italy. South Tyrol and Trentino focus on red wines while Friuli, especially Collio, is known for its **excellent white wines**. Veneto is renown for having Italy's most copious wine drinkers. Of particular note are the white Soave, the red Valpolicella and the **prosecco**, which is especially good from the area around Conegliano and Valdobbiadene.

The famous wine region of Chianti is in Tuscany; the **noble Brunello** grows near Montalcino. Of the Umbrian wines, the white Torgiano deserves special mention. The Verdicchio from Jesi and Macerata in the Marche region go well with fish. The *osteria* and *trattoria* in Lazio serve the white Frascati. Abruzzo is home to the red Montepulciano d'Abruzzo and the white Trebbiano d'Abruzzo.

Apulians are rightly proud of their **rosé wines**. The light sparking red Aglianico from Basilicata still comes from vines that the Greeks planted in southern Italy in 400 BC. The white Greco di Tufo

It need not be the 1979 vintage: Barolo

grape was already grown in ancient Pompeii; on **Mount Vesuvius' lava slopes** it is called Lacryma Christi. Calabria has strong red wines and excellent **dessert wines**, including the Moscato di Saracena. In the north, the Italians round off a lavish meal with a *grappa,* in the south, they tend to opt for the fruity **lemon liqueur** limoncello.

SHOPPING

The Italians display their exquisite taste in fine food and wine, sophisticated fashion and accessories as well as traditional craftsmanship in the country's many ateliers, markets and elegant shops.

DELICATESSEN & WINE

Culinary specialities make ideal souvenirs, e.g. extra virgin olive oil *(olio d'oliva extravergine),* or wine bought directly from the wine dealer, vineyard or local supermarket. A nice accompaniment is air-dried salami, pickled wild boar sausage, a thick slab of vacuum-packed Parmigiano-Reggiano, dried porcini, top-quality charcuterie like the *culatello,* balsamic vinegar and grappa... Recommended from the south: the lemon liqueur *limoncello,* sun-dried tomatoes and pickled vegetables such as aubergine and artichokes in vinegar or oil, especially the little Mediterranean onions *lampascioni,* a speciality from Apulia. One souvenir tip from Calabria is the *'nduja,* a fiery *peperoncino* pork sausage, which keeps well and adds real spice to a pasta sauce.

FASHION & SHOES

Top of the list are the big fashion names such as Armani, Dolce & Gabbana, Prada, Versace, Max Mara, followed by the more casual brands such as Benetton, Stefanel and Diesel. Look out for the sales *(saldi)* if you want to avoid high prices; they uusually start in January and July. Otherwise go to the outlet centres, where hundreds of shops also stock the main brands. They are laid out like villages and located near the motorway, e.g. the largest ● *Serravalle Designer Outlet* in Serravalle Scrivia near Alessandria in Piedmont with over 170 shops, in Lombardy near Brescia in Rodengo Saiano the *Franciacorta Outlet Village,* in Emilia-Romagna near Fidenza the colourful *Fidenza Village,* in Tuscany in Mugello the *Barberino Designer Outlet,* near Rome the *Designer Outlet Castel Romano* with an ancient backdrop, in Campania near Naples *La Reggia Designer Outlet.* Under the name "Diffusione Tessile" the Max Mara brand sells high-quality goods from the previous season for half the price: *www.diffusionetessile.it.* The manufacturers' outlets *(spaccio aziendale)* are more difficult to find; the tourist offices can

Cuisine, clothing and crafts: there is something for everyone in the markets, fashion boutiques and outlet centres

help with addresses. The website *www.outletadvisor.com* provides information in Italian, and an aid in English is: *www.factory-outlet-italy.com/en/FO/index.php*.

HANDICRAFTS

Tourism can be thanked for its role in helping to preserve local craft traditions. Even young people are now learning the old crafts and combining them with attractive new design ideas; beautiful modern forms and patterns can be discovered especially in glass and ceramic pieces. Woodcarving work can be found in the South Tyrolean Val Gardena and Aosta Valley. Murano is famous for its mouth-blown glass and nearby Venice does a flourishing trade in handmade masks (careful: many were made in Taiwan or China!) and marbled paper. Handmade paper can also be found in Fabriano and Amalfi. Drive to Impruneta for the nicest terracotta pots, for rustic Mediterranean ceramics to the Amalfi coast, Vietri sul Mare or Apulia in Grottaglie. Lecce's speciality is papier-mâché figurines of saints and for nativity scenes; in Naples, these are made of clay.

MARKETS

Practically every town has a market. There you will find the *moka* for making espresso, the milk frother for the cappuccino, the cheese grater, the truffle slicer, the mortar in marble or olive wood, the vinegar and oil set – all things that have been available at home for a long time, but which acquire an additional local flair when you buy them in Italy. Buy regional fruit and vegetables at the farmer's markets bearing the motto ⊙ *chilometro zero*. And at the weekly markets, every kind of clothing is for sale, including surprisingly high quality items at reasonable prices.

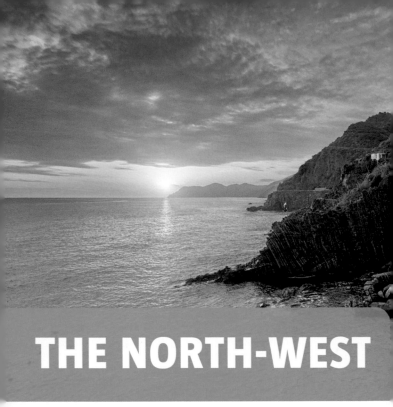

THE NORTH-WEST

Italy's "boot" starts on the south side of the Alps; anyone not approaching from the sea has to traverse the mountains. The passes used by the Romans, Alpis Poenia and Alpis Graia, are now called the Little and Great St Bernhard passes, connecting Italy to France and Switzerland.

Mountains dominate the three regions in north-west Italy: The Aosta Valley and the 100 km/62 mile-long plain through which the Dora Baltea River flows, are lined by mountain ranges that are among the most magnificent the Alps have to offer. In the north, one can see the east face of Mont Blanc (4810 m/15,780 ft), the Matterhorn (4478 m/14,690 ft, ital. Cervino) and the Monte Rosa (4634 m/15,200 ft), whilst towering in the south is the Gran Paradiso (4061 m/13,320 ft), a ski and hiking paradise. Providing a backdrop to Turin, capital of the adjoining Piedmont region, are the snow-covered peaks of the Piedmont Alps in the north and west, and in the south the Apennine hills of Monferrato, Roero and Langhe, well known for their mushrooms, truffles and excellent red wines. The Maritime Alps in the north-west and the Apennines in the south-east help foster the mild climate of the Riviera on the Ligurian coast. Though providing a stunning backdrop for the Ligurian seaside resorts, the mountains have obliged Genoa, the large harbour town, to expand 35 km/21 miles along the coast.

AOSTA

(186 B2) *(🗺 C2–3)* **Aosta (pop. 35 000) is also called "the Rome of the Alps". The well-preserved city gate Porta Pretoria, an equally intact Arco di Augusto, and especially the 22 m/72 ft high stage wall of the Roman theatre look impressive against the backdrop of the snow-covered peaks.**

This picturesque town with its lively old quarter, ideal for shopping and browsing, is the logistic and geographic centre of the Aosta Valley, the smallest Italian region with the statute of autonomy, and officially bilingual (Italian and French). Mining, energy generation (water), woodworking and the summer and winter tourism have made the Aosta Valley into one of the most affluent areas in Italy. The valley and town also thrived during the time of the Roman Empire, because of their strategic importance for protecting the Po Valley in the north-west and as the starting point for the conquest of the Gauls.

One of 40 Romanesque columns around the cloister in Sant'Orso

the former importance of the cloister in the Alpine region, one of the main stops on the Via Francigena. *March–Sept daily 9.30am–12.30pm and 2pm–6pm, Oct–Feb 10am–12.30pm and 1.30pm–5.30pm, Sun until 6.30pm*

SIGHTSEEING

SANTI PIETRO E ORSO
The cloister complex includes a late Gothic church of Romanesque origin and a crypt dating back to the Carolingian age. On the south side, between the church and the priory house decorated with terracotta is the wonderful ★ *cloister* (1133), with 40 Romanesque marble columns displaying fine stone masonry work around the capitals. Its imposing presence underlines

FOOD & DRINK

OSTERIA DELL'OCA
A courtyard leads to this friendly old town restaurant. In summer, it is lovely to sit outside; besides regional dishes such as polenta and game ragout, they also serve pizza. *Closed Mon | Via Edouard Aubert 15 | tel. 01 65 23 14 19 | www. ristoranteosteriadelloca.com | Budget–Moderate*

PAM PAM TRATTORIA DEGLI ARTISTI
Great atmosphere and good food (e.g. crêpes with mountain cheese, *crespelle*) at this popular restaurant in an old town lane. *Closed Sun/Mon | Via Maillet 5–7 | tel. 0 16 54 09 60 | Moderate*

SHOPPING

An original souvenir from the Aosta Valley is the *grolla*, a round wooden vessel with several spouts, from which locals drink a kind of coffee punch in the winter. On Jan 30/31 and in mid Aug, the *Sagra di Sant'Orso* takes place, Italy's oldest arts and crafts market. The valley's craft products can be bought all year round from the *IVAT (Institut Valdôtain de l'Artisanat de Tradition)* in the town hall *(Piazza Chanoux 11)*.

WHERE TO STAY

B & B AMBROSIA ☼ ✿
Two attractive rooms in an eco house. Sumptuous breakfast and gorgeous view of Aosta. *District of Arpuilles 94/H | tel.*

33 95 74 95 94 | www.bedbreakfastaosta. com | Budget

MILLELUCI

Slightly further out, in the Porossan Roppoz district. Romantic rooms and health centre. *31 rooms | tel. 0165 23 52 78 | www.hotel milleluci.com | Expensive*

INFORMATION

Piazza Porta Pretoria 3 | tel. 0165 23 66 27 | www.rlovevda.it, www.valledaosta-guida turistica.it

WHERE TO GO

BREUIL-CERVINIA (186 C2) (*Ø C2*)

The special appeal of this internationally renowned ski region in the Aosta region is no doubt explained by the fact that it lies at the foot of the imposing Matterhorn (4478 m/14,690 ft) in Valtournenche. A large ski area of 350 km/217 miles connects it to the Swiss side around Zermatt. Offering an amazing view and great summer skiing is the 🌺 *Plateau Rosà* glacier at 3480 m/11,420 ft, which you can reach with a glass cable car. Relaxed elegance and excellent service make the *Hermitage (36 rooms | Via Piolet 1 | tel. 01 66 94 89 98 | www.hotelhermitage.com | Expensive)* the region's finest hotel. Down in Valtournenche near *Antey Saint-André*, there is a charming hotel in an old farmhouse: INSIDERTIP *Maison Tissière (14 rooms | district Petit Antey 9 | tel. 01 66 54 91 40 | www.hoteltissiere.it | Moderate)* with a spa and a good restaurant. *www. cervinia.it*

FORTRESSES AND CASTLES (186 C2) (*Ø C3*)

There are over 130 in the Aosta Valley. Among the most important are the massive 🌺 14th century *Verrès* castle

(Easter–Sept daily 9am–7pm, Oct–Easter Tue–Sun 10am–1pm and 2pm–5pm) perched on a steep cliff and *Issogne* castle, which has a richly ornamented interior, painted Renaissance courtyard and the famous fountain in the form of a pomegranate tree. *Fénis* awaits you with a medieval knight's castle and the *MAV handicraft museum (April–Oct Tue–Sun 10am–6pm | Chez Sapin 86)*. The imposing fortified complex *Forte di Bard (Tue–Fri 10am–6pm, Sat/Sun 10am–8pm)* houses a modern designed and fascinating *Alpine museum*. Fénis and Issogne: *Easter–Sept daily 9am–7pm, Oct–Easter 10am–1pm and 2pm–5pm, in*

MARCO POLO HIGHLIGHTS

⭐ **Cloister**
Fine stonemasonry in the Santi Pietro e Orso cloister in Aosta
→ p. 36

⭐ **Mont Blanc Crossing**
Across the glacier in a cable car → p. 38

⭐ **Genoa's old town**
A fascinating mix of dark alleys and magnificent palaces
→ p. 39

⭐ **Cinque Terre**
Five picturesque – and car-free – Ligurian cliff villages → p. 43

⭐ **Reggia di Venaria Reale**
The Savoy castle near Turin is regarded as the Versailles of Italian kings → p. 51

⭐ **Sacri Monti**
Colourfully arranged figures in the Baroque pilgrimage chapels in Piedmont → p. 51

winter *Fénis closed Tue, Issogne closed Wed*

COURMAYEUR (186 B2) *(ⓜ C2)*

At the foot of Mont Blanc, this town has been a summer resort since the 19th century, as is evident from the beautiful old chalets. Today Courmayeur together with its French counterpart Chamonix offers some of the most challenging ski pistes in the Alps. The Mont Blanc tunnel connects the two resorts as does a cleverly designed series of cable cars: the famous ★ ⛷ *Mont Blanc Crossing* (valley station in La Palud, 3.5 km/2 miles from Courmayeur, *www.montebianco.com).* For one and a half hours you glide over the breathtaking silent white peaks and glacier landscape.

Experience the exclusive atmosphere of Courmayeur in the elegantly comfortable chalet hotel *Auberge de la Maison (33 rooms | Via Passerin d'Entrèves 16 | tel. 01 65 86 98 11 | www.aubergemaison.it | Expensive)* which has a fine restaurant, sauna and gym; the *Berthod* is more basic *(35 rooms | Via Mario Puchoz 11 | tel. 01 65 84 28 35 | www.hotelberthod.com | Moderate).*

Val Veny and Val Ferret, the two lateral valleys, bring you even closer to this magnificent mountain world. Arnouva, a village in Val Ferret, is ideal as a starting point for hikes and mountain bike tours from *Chalet Val Ferret,* which is only open in the summer *(7 rooms | tel. 01 65 84 49 59 | www.chaletvalferret.com | Moderate)* with a restaurant in a former barn. Courmayeur's famous guides organise adventurous mountain tours *(tel. 01 65 84 20 64 | www.guidecourmayeur. com).* The old *thermal baths (Allées des Thermes | tel. 01 65 86 72 72 | www.ter medipre.it)* in Pré-Saint-Didier have been elegantly restored – and are now a popular health oasis.

GRAN PARADISO NATIONAL PARK ● (186 B–C 2–3) *(ⓜ C3)*

Early in the morning, ibex – the emblem of this magnificent nature reserve in the south of Aosta – appear at the tree line. Even golden eagles and wolves live here below the powerful Gran Paradiso (4061 m/13,320 ft). The biodiversity is thanks to King Victor Emmanuel II; in the 19th century, this alpine region was already his protected hunting reserve. In this hikers' paradise, you will find camping sites in the middle of the countryside with a wonderful mountain backdrop, for example in Valsavarenche at the 1800 m/5906 ft high *Camping Gran Paradiso (8 wooden bungalows | Plan de la Pesse | tel. 01 65 90 58 01 | www.campinggran paradiso.it | Budget).* In the charming main town of *Cogne*, with its attractive hotels, the art of bobbin lace making continues to this day. *www.pngp.it, www. cogneturismo.it*

GRESSONEY VALLEY (186 C2) *(ⓜ C 2–3)*

The scenically varied valley extends towards the Monte Rosa massif. It was from the other side of Monte Rosa that a group of immigrants came from the Swiss canton of Valais 750 years ago. They settled here and in some of the neighbouring valleys in Piedmont. Their legacy includes the Walser-German dialect and a distinctive style of architecture. You will come across the old INSIDER TIP Walser houses at the end of Valsesia, Val di Gressoney, Val d'Ayas and Valle Anzasca. They are tall constructions; the first floor has walls of roughly hewn stone and above it is dark weathered wood. In *Gressoney-Saint-Jean* an old Walser house has been converted into the charming hotel *La Gran Baita (12 rooms | Strada Castello Savoia 26 | tel. 01 25 35 55 35 | www.hotelgranbaita.it | Moderate).* The beautiful valley offers ski-

The chamois is an agile, all-terrain native species of the Gran Paradiso National Park

ing, golf, trekking and rafting and is particularly popular with people from Milan. *www.gressoneymonterosa.it*

PONT SAINT-MARTIN (186 C2) *(𝄞 C3)*
The excellently preserved Roman arch bridge (100 BC) spans the Lys mountain stream.

GENOA (GENOVA)

(187 D4–5) *(𝄞 D4)* **A (possible) son of this town, Christopher Columbus, discovered America in 1492, yet this marked the beginning of Genoa's decline.** *La Superba* **(the proud) lost its central trading role as an international maritime power to harbours in north-western Europe.**

In 1992, celebrating the 500-year anniversary of his discovery, Columbus was commandeered into helping Genoa (pop. 597,000) to recover after being badly affected by decreasing port activities and the crisis in heavy industry. The old harbour was revitalised, and many palaces were restored as was the Teatro Carlo Felice which had been destroyed during the Second World War.

For Genoa's role as the European Capital of Culture in 2004, many buildings in the ★ old town were restored and Liguria's once typical painted façades refreshed. Wander around the lively tangle of streets and also cross the Baroque avenues of *Via Garibaldi* and *Via Balbi* to see the wonderful palaces – once residences of wealthy shipbuilders, merchants and bankers from Genoa's golden age in the 16th and 17th century – now full of art collections. Numerous aperitif bars and hip restaurants are located in the palazzi of the old town. 42 of them, called ● *Palazzi dei Rolli (www.irolli.it)*, are listed as Unesco World Heritage Sites. You reach the ☙ upper part of the town with funiculars and lifts. The ☼ roof terrace of the maritime museum in the old harbour area offers probably the most beautiful view of the town, the harbour and the sea. Genoa has become one of Italy's most appealing travel destinations.

MUSEI DI STRADA NUOVA

A newly arranged museum complex consisting of three old palazzi teeming with art treasures (Rubens, Dürer, Veronese, Van Dyck, Caravaggio and many more), precious fabrics and furnishings: *Palazzo Bianco, Palazzo Rosso, Palazzo Doria Tursi*

A popular resting spot on the steps up to the San Lorenzo Cathedral in the centre of Genoa

SIGHTSEEING

CATTEDRALE SAN LORENZO

It took centuries to complete Genoa's largest sacral building, extending from the early Christian period to the Renaissance; the *Museum of the treasury* is well worth a visit *(Mon–Sat 9am–noon and 3pm–6pm). Piazza San Lorenzo*

LANTERNA ☼

One of Europe's oldest lighthouses (12th century, 117 m/338 ft) stands in the southwest section of the old harbour and can be reached using the new promenade. History buffs will enjoy the small *city museum* at the base of the lighthouse. *Both Sat/Sun 2.30pm–6.30pm*

on the boulevard Via Garibaldi. *April–Oct Tue–Thu 9am–7pm, Fri 9am–9pm, Sat/Sun 10am–7.30pm, Nov–March Tue–Fri 9am–6.30pm, Sat/Sun 9.30am–6.30pm | www.museidigenova.it*

PALAZZO DUCALE/PIAZZA MATTEO

The square is the focal point of the Genoa district once controlled by the merchant family Doria. It is here on the *Piazza Matteo* that you will find many of the family's palazzi and the Romanesque, black and white striped church containing the tomb of Andrea Doria. The *Palazzo Ducale (www.palazzoducale.genova.it),* magnificent residence of the doge, is now a central meeting place with exhibitions, restaurants, cafés and bookstores.

PALAZZO REALE

The magnificent furnishings of this 17th century Savoy palace testify to the luxury of times gone by. Wonderful 🔆 hanging gardens. *Tue–Sat 9am–7pm, Sun 1.30pm–7pm (1st Sun of the month 9am–7pm) | Via Balbi 10 | www.palazzorealegenova. beniculturali.it*

PORTO ANTICO

The old harbour area has become a popular place for a walk, with cafés, a swimming pool, skating rink and museums such as the maritime museum 🔆 *Galata Museo del Mare (March–Oct daily 10am–7.30pm, Nov–Feb Tue–Fri 10am–6pm, Sat/Sun 10am–7.30pm | www.galatamu seodelmare.it)* containing Italy's largest submarine and the famous *aquarium* (see "Travel with kids").

INSIDER TIP VIA DEL CAMPO 29 ROSSO

In the old town in Via del Campo, at number 29r, you will find a piece of Italy's musical soul: the legendary record shop Gianni Tassio with its huge selection of songs by Genoan songwriters – first and foremost the cult figures Fabrizio De André and Gino Paoli – is now also a *music museum. Tue–Sun 10.30am–12.30pm and 3pm–7 pm | www.viadelcampo29rosso.com*

FOOD & DRINK

INSIDER TIP BAGNI SANTACHIARA

Sunbathe during the day, in the evening happy hour and fresh light cuisine not far from the town's fishing village of Boccadasse. *June–Sept daily | Via Flavia 4 | Capo Santa Chiara | tel. 33 98 61 71 67 | Moderate*

LA CUCINA DI GIUDITTA 🌣

In this light and friendly restaurant in the old town, the chefs prepare the food without animal fat, but with fresh organic vegetables, and everything is delicious. *Closed Sun/Mon and evenings except Fri, Sat | Piazza Valoria 11 r | tel. 01 02 77 00 94 | www.lacucinadigiuditta.it | Budget–Moderate*

INSIDER TIP IL PANINO ITALIANO 🌣

Delicious *panini* with Slow Food products. Superb sandwich bars *(Via Roccatagliata Ceccardi 30r and Largo San Giuseppe 23)*, also in the Sottoripa colonnade on the way to the old harbour. *Closed Sun | Via XX Settembre 68r | www.ilpaninogenova.it | Budget*

TRATTORIA ROSMARINO

Lovely modern trattoria in the town centre near Piazza De Ferrari; the kitchen offers typical Ligurian cooking that is fresh and creative. *Closed Sun | Salita del Fondaco 30 | tel. 01 02 51 04 75 | www.trattoria rosmarino.it | Moderate*

SHOPPING

You will find shops and arts and crafts in the old town lanes and elegant fashion along the *Via XX Settembre, Via Roma, Via XXV Aprile.* You should pop in to admire the abundance on display in the market hall of the INSIDER TIP *Mercato Orientale (Via XX Settembre).*

ENTERTAINMENT

Happy hour in the trendy bars in the old town, e.g. on the Piazza delle Erbe, and in Porto Antico, e.g. in *Banana Tsunami,* or along the Via Garibaldi in the museum cafés; in summer along the Corso Italia by the sea. Operas in *Teatro Carlo Felice (www.carlofelice.it).*

WHERE TO STAY

HOTEL METROPOLI

Tastefully renovated and situated right in the old town. *48 rooms | Piazza Fontane*

Marose/Via XXV Aprile | tel. 01 02 46 88 88 | www.hotelmetropoli.it | Moderate

HOTEL VERONESE
Hospitable, simple and neat, near the aquarium. *19 rooms | Vico Cicala 3 | tel. 010 25 10 77 | www.hotelveronese.com | Budget–Moderate*

WWW.COLUMBUSVILLAGE.COM
Website with numerous, often very charming bed and breakfast offers in the centre of Genoa. *Budget–Moderat*

LOW BUDGET

The grand finale of the *Bataille des Reines* takes place in the Aosta arena on the third Sunday in October. Throughout the summer, you can watch the exciting qualifying rounds between the strong black cows in the meadows and farms free of charge. *www.amisdesreines.it*

Cheap street food in Liguria: *farinata*, the flat loaf is made with chickpea flour, or the *focaccia* filled with cheese, fish or vegetables, e.g. at Antica Sciamadda *(Closed Sun | Via San Giorgio 14 r)* in Genoa.

For those who enjoy good, reasonably priced fish, the *Sagra del Pesce*, possibly Italy's most famous food festival, is held on the second May weekend in the seaside town of Camogli, in Liguria.

On dark winter evenings the installations of well-known artists, the *luci d'artisti*, light up the streets of Turin – an impressive spectacle that is free.

Via Garibaldi 12r and Via al Porto Antico 2 | tel. 010 55 72 903 | www.visitgenoa.it

RIVIERA DI LEVANTE

(187 D–E5) *(ɷ D–E 4–5)* The east coast of Liguria between Genoa and Tuscany is rocky and often steep; picturesque villages squeeze themselves into small spaces, which makes this stretch of coast even more attractive.

WHERE TO GO

CAMOGLI (187 D5) *(ɷ D4)*
The tall, sunny yellow houses, some of them displaying Liguria's typical trompe l'oeil windows, stretch along the craggy cliff walls while flights of stairs in between entice you to wander round. This attractive little coastal town (pop. 6000) was home to Italy largest merchant fleet until the 19th century. In the summer, people come to savour the Ligurian fish dishes on the idyllic terrace of *La Cucina di Nonna Nina (closed Wed | Via Molfino 126 | tel. 0185 77 38 35 | Budget– Moderate)* in the higher lying district of San Rocco. Reserve in advance!
By taking one of the boats or on foot from San Rocco further up from Camogli, you can visit the headland *Punta Chiappa* with its beautiful beaches as well as the idyllically situated monastery **INSIDER TIP** *San Fruttuoso* directly by the sea, which you can also reach from Portofino by taking a lovely walk via Monte Portofino. If you want to try the local speciality *focaccia,* a flat pizza-style bread with herbs, go to nearby *Recco,* where you can enjoy this delicious titbit in restaurants and snack bars or on the fourth Sunday in May at

Just five minutes away from a well-earned swim: the coastal path from Vernazza to Monterosso

the gourmet food festival **INSIDER TIP** *Sagra della Focaccia*.

CINQUE TERRE ★ (187 E5) (*Ⓜ E5*)

These five fishing villages are situated on one of Liguria's most gorgeous stretches of coastline, high on the cliffs (Corniglia) or at the sea set against the steep rock walls: *Monterosso,* the only village with a large beach, *Vernazza*, the largest village, *Corniglia, Manarola* and *Riomaggiore*. Above them, ripening on the steep hillside terraces, are the grapes of the DOC white wine and the heavy dessert wine Sciacchetrà. The protected mountain landscape of Cinque Terre is very popular with hikers. In the summer, the car parks located just outside Monterosso and Riomaggiore keep the confined village pleasantly free of cars; it is better and easier to visit them by train. At the village stations, information offices provide the addresses of hotels and private rooms as well as details regarding the Cinque Terre Card (a form of visitors' tax) and the hiking routes: *www.parconazionale5terre.it* Located just in front of the Cinque Terre on a broad sandy beach is the delightful coastal town of *Levanto*. From here, there is a particularly nice 8 km/5 mile ☼ *coastal path* offering a fantastic view of Monterosso, the first of the Cinque Terre villages. On the way, in a beautiful location, you pass a small hotel with 12 pretty rooms – each with its own terrace – the hotel also has a swimming pool and serves a good breakfast: ☼ *La Giada del Mesco (Località Mesco 16 | tel. 01 87 80 26 74 | www.lagiada delmesco.it | Moderate–Expensive)*.

GOLFO DI LA SPEZIA (187 E5) (*Ⓜ E5*)

The modern harbour town La Spezia – badly damaged during the Second World War – located on the gulf cut deep into the coast now has some very interesting museums: in the ☼ castle buildings of

Once destroyed by an earthquake, Bussana Vecchia is a thriving artists' colony near Sanremo

Castello San Giorgio there is the *Museo Archeologico (Wed–Mon 9.30am–12.30pm and 2pm–5pm, June–Sept 5pm–8pm)* containing the mysterious **INSIDER TIP** stone stelae found near the coast; in the town centre is a collection of old masters in the *Museo Amedeo Lia (Tue–Sun 10am–6pm | Via Prione 234)*. The old town is ideal for shopping. Along the waterside promenade, at *Dai Pescatori (daily | Banchina Revel/Viale Italia | tel. 01 87 77 08 93 | Budget)*, you can buy nicely prepared fresh fish – caught by local fishermen. The tourist office is directly opposite.

On the ☀ headland, protecting the gulf from the open sea, the enchanting little seaside town of *Portovenere* and the nearby islet *Palmaria* await you. On the east coast of the gulf is the exclusive *Lerici* on the idyllic bay *Golfo dei Poeti*, which was a Mecca for poets and artists in the 19th century. Further along, take time to wander round the ruggedly romantic cliff villages of *Fiascherino* and *Tellaro*.

SANTA MARGHERITA LIGURE AND PORTOFINO (187 E5) (*Ⓜ D4*)

On the Gulf of Rapallo bordering the Monte Portofino headland, there are some first-class resorts. The largest is *Santa Margherita Ligure;* its *Piazza Martiri della Libertà* is crowded with pubs and restaurants, and in the summer offers some of the area's best nightlife. The smallest and most exclusive one, *Portofino,* a car-free fishing village, is one of Italy's most expensive places. A luxury hotel par excellence in a magnificent location: *Splendido (64 rooms | Splendido Mare branch 16 rooms | Viale Baratta 16 | tel. 0185 26 78 01 | www.hotelsplendido. com | Expensive)*

SESTRI LEVANTE (187 E5) (*Ⓜ E4–5*)

The small town on the coast greets you with two enchanting sandy bays, the *Baia delle Favole,* which fans out in front of the colourful houses, as well as the more serene and expensive *Baia del Silenzio.*

VARESE LIGURE ⊛ (187 E5) *(ᗡ E4)*

The village, 45 km/28 miles inland in the mountains, is popular owing to the intact round old town and its reputation as a model ecological village that strives to promote organic agriculture and alternative energy *(www.valledelbiologico.it)*. Here, accommodation may be simple, but the food more than makes up for it: *Amici (closed Wed | 24 rooms | Via Garibaldi 80 | tel. 0187842139 | www.albergoamici. com | Budget)*.

RIVIERA DI PONENTE

(186–187 C–D 5–6) *(ᗡ C–D 4–5)* One seaside resort after another dots the shore as it curves round between Genoa and the French border at Ventimiglia.

The wonderful climate initially saw elegant resorts here with parks, palm-lined avenues and luxury hotels in towns like Bordighera and Sanremo. Later on, the cut flower industry and mass tourism arrived. But there are still lots of pretty towns to discover, such as *Celle Ligure, Varigotti* and *Laigueglia; Cervo* and *Noli* have lovely old districts, while *Finale Ligure* is famous for its climbing and mountainbiking areas. And up through the olive groves and chestnut woods are the tranquil mountain villages of *Dolceacqua, Apricale* and *Triora.* The hiking trail ⩘ *Alta Via (www. altaviadeimontiliguri.it)* is well marked and has places to stay; it is 440 km/273 miles from Ventimiglia to La Spezia. A 24 km/15 mile ⩘ `INSIDER TIP` bicycle track runs from Ospedaletti to Sanremo and on to Imperia, offering panoramic views, bike rental and picnic areas. *www. turismoinliguria.it*

WHERE TO GO

ALASSIO (186 C5) *(ᗡ C5)*

Of the small towns along the coast of western Liguria, it is Alassio (pop. 12,000) with its long sandy beach that best represents the mild, floriferous character of a Ligurian summer. One of the many excursions in the hilly hinterland is to the *Toirano caves.*

ALBENGA (186 C5) *(ᗡ C5)*

By taking part in the First Crusade, the free town of Albenga (pop. 24,000) managed to seal its economic growth, evidence of which is still seen today in the town with its well-preserved `INSIDER TIP` medieval centre and clock towers as well as the *Piazza San Michele* and basilica with the same name.

BUSSANA VECCHIA AND BUSSANA MARE (186 C6) *(ᗡ C5)*

Reduced to a pile of stones by an earthquake in 1887, *Bussana Vecchia (www. bussana.com)* situated north of Sanremo became an artists' colony in the 1960s, and is now full of interesting ateliers and workshops. Offering a nice contrast, *Bussana Mare* on the coast, has two restaurants which specialise in beautifully prepared fish dishes: *Gente di Mare (June–Sept daily | Via al Mare 26 | tel. 0184 514992 | Moderate)* and *La Kambusa (June–mid Sept daily | Via al Mare 87 | 0184514537 | Moderate–Expensive)*.

SANREMO (186 C6) *(ᗡ C5)*

Members of the English aristocracy used to stay here in splendid luxury hotels. One of Europe's most famous casinos opened in the town (pop. 55,000) in 1906 *(www.casinosanremo.it)* and still draws the crowds today, although now the most glamorous event is the Italian music festival in spring. Stroll through the winding streets of the old town, called *La Pigna* – it is well worth it. People like to meet on the *Piazza Bresca* with restaurants and cafés – during the day and in the evening. In palm tree-lined *Bordighera* 10 km/6 miles to the west, a good place to eat is the *Osteria Magiargè (closed Mon/Tue and July/Aug lunchtime | Piazza Giacomo Viale | tel. 0184 26 29 46 | www.magiarge.it | Moderate)*, a Slow Food tip thanks to its delicious regional and seafood cuisine.

VILLA HANBURY ⚶ **(186 C6)** (*Ⓜ C5*)
The *Giardini Botanici Hanbury* with its stunning terraced gardens – a prime example of Liguria's rich flora – is close to the French border in La Mortola near Ventimiglia. *March–mid Oct daily 9.30am–5pm (mid June–mid Sept until 6pm), mid Oct–Feb Tue–Sun 9.30am–4pm | www.giardinihanbury.com*

TURIN (TORINO)

(186 C3) (*Ⓜ C3*) **The city, traversed by the Po, is marked by the wide, straight avenues, with arcades full of inviting fashion boutiques and fragrant coffee houses** *(Corso Vittorio Emanuele)*: **elegant-bourgeois flair.**

Turin (pop. 902,000), once royal seat of the House of Savoy, became home to a huge wave of Italians from the south when the Fiat car factory was founded (1899) and a symbol of industrialised Italy. Now it represents post-industrial Italy and has blossomed into a centre for art, design, music and fair-trade food events, e.g. the 🌎 Slow Food festival *Salone del Gusto* that takes place in even years. Locals meet in the bars and restaurants of the former storerooms on the Po riverbank

WHERE TO START?
The city's core artery Via Roma starts at the train station **Porta Nuova** and links up the main squares and many good shops. West of the Via Roma is the Quadrilatero Romano, which traces the chessboard layout of the former Roman settlement. Today, much of it is pedestrianised and teeming with bars and shops. From Palazzo Reale or from Piazza Castello the route continues eastwards towards the river, to the Mole Antonelliana, the large Piazza Vittorio Veneto and to the Po waterfront. A large underground car park is near Piazza Castello: *Parcheggio Roma-San Carlo-Castello*

walls, called *murazzi*, in the town centre the *Quadrilatero Romano* district south of Porta Palatina as well as the spacious *Piazza Vittorio Veneto*. In addition to important art galleries, private foundations also display the town's interest in modern art. These include the *Fondazione Sandretto Re Rebaudengo (Thu 8pm–11pm, Fri–Sun noon–7pm | Via Modane 16 | www.fsrr.org)* or the *Fondazione Mario Merz (Tue–Sun 11am–7pm | Via Limone 24 | www.fondazionemerz.org)*. Italy's national photographic centre **INSIDER TIP** *Camera (Wed and Fri–Mon 11am–7pm, Thu 11am–9pm | Via delle Rosine 18 | camera.to)* exhibits works from national and international photographers.

SIGHTSEEING

CATTEDRALE SAN GIOVANNI BATTISTA
The Baroque *Cappella della Santa Sindone* belongs to the cathedral complex, the only Renaissance building in

the town. It is here that the Turin Shroud is kept which came into the possession of the House of Savoy in the middle of the 15th century and is now only shown on special occasions. Visitors can see infrared photographs of the image. *Piazza San Giovanni*

EATALY

The modern food centre in a former factory in Lingotto is truly a feast for the eyes: you can just look around, shop for Italian culinary delights and can eat them in the *ristorantini* or in INSIDER**TIP** *Casa Vicina (closed Sun evening and Mon | tel. 0 11 19 50 68 40 | www.casa vicina.com | Expensive)*, regarded by many as Turin's best restaurant. *Daily 10am–10.30pm | Via Nizza 230/14 | www. torino.eataly.it*

GALLERIA SABAUDA

You can admire the rich art collections of the Savoy monarchs in the side wing *Manica Nuova* of the *Palazzo Reale* royal palace in the *Via XX Settembre*. *Tue–Sun 9am–6.30pm*

LINGOTTO

An example of how to modernise former industrial buildings: today – in the old Fiat factory from the 1920s with the legendary futuristic test track on the roof – there is now an elegant hotel, a concert hall, trade fair facilities, shops and, on the roof, the *Pinacoteca Agnelli (Tue–Sun 10am–7pm | www.pinacoteca-agnelli.it)* with works by artists such as Canaletto, Tiepolo and Picasso. *Via Nizza 262*

MOLE ANTONELLIANA ☆

Turin's landmark building is a large domed edifice from 1863. At 167 m/549 ft, it is Italy's tallest architectural monument and towers above the otherwise rather flat town. From the roof there is an excep-

tional panoramic view of the town and mountain backdrop. The celebrated museum of cinema *Museo Nazionale del Cinema (Wed–Mon 9am–8pm, Sat until 11pm | www.museonazionaledelcinema. org)* also has a spectacular interior. *Via Montebello 20*

INSIDER**TIP** MUSEO DELL'AUTOMOBILE

Vintage cars, legendary models such as Topolino and Giulia, as well as luxury cars – the museum has had a facelift and the

Nicknamed "pencil tip" or "stuffed giraffe": the Mole Antonelliana

exhibits are well presented. *Mon 10am–2pm, Tue 2pm–7pm, Wed, Thu, Sun 10am–7pm, Fri, Sat 10am–9pm | Corso Unità d'Italia 40 | www.museoauto.it*

MUSEO EGIZIO

The renovation and extension of Europe's oldest and most renowned museums for Egyptian culture was completed in 2015. *Mon 9am–2pm, Tue–Sun 9am–6.30pm | Via Accademia delle Scienze 6 | www.museoegizio.org*

PARCO VALENTINO

This lovely urban park stretches along the left bank of the Po. *Corso Massimo D'Azeglio*

PIAZZA CASTELLO AND PIAZZA REALE

Right in the heart of Turin is the Piazza Castello and is the imposing *Palazzo Madama (Wed–Mon 10am–6pm | www.palazzomadamatorino.it),* once a medieval fortress, later a Baroque residence belonging to Madama Cristina of the Savoy dynasty, now a museum for ancient art and crafts; on the adjacent square is the palace of the Savoy kings, the majestic *Palazzo Reale (Tue–Sun 9am–7.30pm)* from 1660.

FOOD & DRINK

CAFÉS

Turin has the oldest and most beautiful cafés in Italy, e.g. the elegant *Torino* and *San Carlo* on the large Piazza San Carlo, the wonderfully ornate little *Mulassano (Piazza Castello 15),* the art nouveau café *Platti* on Corso Vittorio Emanuele 72, and in *Al Bicerin (closed Wed | Piazza Consolata 5)* you receive the famous little glass of *bicerin* with coffee, chocolate and cream, a wintry delight.

PASTIS

Restaurant, street café and artists' haunt in the trendy Quadrilatero Romano. *Daily 9am–2am | Piazza Emanuele Filiberto 9b | tel. 011 521 10 85 | Budget*

PORTA DI PO

Fine Piedmontese cuisine in a contemporary setting on one of Turin's most beautiful squares. *Closed Sun | Piazza Vittorio Veneto 1e | tel. 011 81 27 64 2 | www.portadipo.it | Moderate–Expensive*

DAI SALETTA

The rusic family style trattoria Dai Saletta, a Slow Food recommendation, is famous for Turin specialities such as *vitello tonnato. Closed Sun | Via Belfiore 37 | tel. 011 66 87 8 67 | www.ristorantedaisaletta.com | Moderate*

SHOPPING

You can buy the Turin speciality *gianduiotti* (nougat) in the time-honoured patisserie *Baratti & Milano* on the Piazza Castello. The huge INSIDER TIP *market* – Italy's largest – on the *Piazza della Repubblica/Porta Palazzo (Mon–Fri 8am–1pm, Sat 8am–5pm)* mirrors the ethnic diversity of the population. On Sat the *El Balon* flea market takes place in the nearby *Via Borgo Dora* and every second Sunday in the month the antiques market *El Gran Balon*.

WHERE TO STAY

COLAZIONE IN PIAZZA CASTELLO 🔾

Centrally located B & B in the stylish space of a palazzo, 3 rooms and organic breakfast. *Piazza Castello 9 | tel. 011 27 06 98 3 | www.colazioneinpiazzacastello.it | Moderate*

TOWN HOUSE 70

Comfortable city hotel in a central location with pleasant décor and excellent

Vine-covered hills and the Alps on the horizon: in the wine and truffle paradise of the Langhe

breakfast buffet. *48 rooms | Via XX Settembre 70 | tel. 011 19 70 00 03 | 70.townhousehotels.com |* Moderate– Expensive

URBANI
Near the train station, a nice clean hotel for budget travellers. *44 rooms | Via Saluzzo 7 | tel. 011 66 90 47 | www.hotel urbani.it |* Budget

Piazza Castello/Via Garibaldi, at Porta Nuova station and at the airport | tel. 011 53 51 81 | www.turismotorino.org, www.extratorino.it, piemonteitalia.eu

WHERE TO GO

ALBA AND ASTI (186 C4) (⊞ C–D 4)
These two towns have attractive centres and dominate the horizon of the Monferrato, Roero and Langhe hills to the south-east of Turin, where the wonderful red wines of Piedmont grow. These are celebrated in *Barolo* castle: in the *enoteca* you can try and buy the different wines as well as visit the modern wine museum *WiMu (Fri–Wed 10.30am–7pm | www. wimubarolo.it).* In autumn and winter, the connoisseurs flock to these hills for the truffle season in *Alba* (pop. 30,000). There is a truffle market in October. *Casetorri,* tower houses dating back to the Middle Ages, are a typical sight in Alba's old town centre. The larger town *Asti* (pop. 76,000), centre of Monferrato, also has a large medieval centre with stately squares, houses and churches.

In this famous gourmet area around Asti and Alba, you have the choice between numerous first-class gourmet establishments and a number of good trattorias. As recommended by the Slow Food movement, most of them use quality regional ingredients, such as meat from the local beef *fassone* and the good Piedmont cheeses. In Alba, for example, you can choose between the friendly *Osteria dell'*

Arco (closed Sun except in Oct/Nov | Piazza Savona 5 | tel. 0173 36 39 74 | www.os teriadellarco.it | Budget–Moderate) or one of the very top restaurants of Piedmont, the *Piazza Duomo (closed Sun/ Mon | Piazza Risorgimento 4 | tel. 0173 36 6167 | www.piazzaduomoalba.il | Expensive)*, in *La Piola (Budget–Moderate)*, on the ground floor, delicious Osteria cuisine by the same manager.

Having a nice room to go to is the perfect way to follow a perfect meal, for example vines in the *Osteria del Maiale Pezzato (9 rooms | Via Carlo Coccio 2 | Sinio | tel. 0173 26 38 45 | www.maialepezzato.it | Moderate)* with pool. It is even more rural in the B & B  *La Luna Buona (Via Lavezzato 4 | Vesime | tel. 34 86 55 95 54 | www.lalunabuona.it | Budget)* 36 km/22 miles south-east of Alba with three pleasantly nostalgic rooms and a substantial organic breakfast. The goat herd next door produces the milk for the delicious cheese. The *All'Enoteca (closed Wed Oct–*

The deer on the roof gives it away: the Palazzina di Stupinigi is a hunting lodge

in the *Locanda del Boscogrande (closed Tue | Messadio district | tel. 0141 95 63 90 | www.locandaboscogrande.com | Budget– Moderate)* approx. 12 km/7.5 miles south of Asti in Montegrosso d'Asti with seven comfortable rooms *(Moderate)* and a swimming pool. In Langhe 10 km/6 miles south of Alba, you can eat (e.g. specialities from the establishment's own pig farm), drink and sleep in a sophisticated country house style surrounded by the

May | Via Roma 57 | tel. 0173 9 58 57 | www.davidepalluda.it | Expensive) in Canale 15 km/9.3 miles north of Alba in the wine-growing area of Roero is regarded as a top address by insiders.

BAROQUE BUILDINGS OF THE HOUSE OF SAVOY (186 C3) (*∅ C3*)

Famous court architect Filippo Juvara also built Baroque and Rococo buildings in the immediate vicinity of Turin for the House of Savoy. Enthroned on a hill in the east of Turin is the monumental *Basilica di Superga (March–Oct Wed–Mon 9.30am–1.30pm and 2.30pm–7pm, Nov–Jan Sat/Sun, Feb Sun 10am–1.30pm and 4.30pm–6pm)*, which guards the tombs of the Savoy kings. The hunting lodge *Palazzina di (Tue–Fri 10am–5pm, Sat/Sun 10am–6pm)* 10 km/6 miles south-west of Turin is a stunning example of rococo architecture. The Versailles of the Savoys, the magnificent ★ *Reggia di Venaria Reale (Tue–Fri 9am–5pm, Sat/Sun 9am–6.30pm | www.lavenaria.it)* 5 km/3 miles north of Turin, was completed in its present form in 1728, and is also the work of Juvarra. You can visit the 50 rooms of the restored complex and the magnificent park. The Savoy castle *Castello di Rivoli (Tue–Fri 10am–5pm, Sat/Sun 10am–7pm | www.castellodirivoli.org)* 15 km/9.3 miles to the west is a renowned exhibition centre for contemporary art, and the avant-garde gourmet restaurant *Combal.Zero (closed Sun/Mon | tel. 0119 56 52 25 | www.combal.org | Expensive)*. Finally, 35 km/22 miles to the south is the richly decorated *Castello di Racconigi (April–Oct Tue–Sun, Nov–March Wed and Fri–Sun 9am–7pm | www.ilcastellodiracconigi.it)* with a beautiful park.

LOMELLINA (187 D3) *(𝄞 D3)*

Stretching between Vercelli, Novara and Pavia is the Lomellina plain. In the spring, the water-logged rice fields look as smooth as glass. You can try biodynamic rice at, e.g. the ⊙ INSIDER TIP *Azienda Agricola Cascine Orsine (www.cascinaorsine.it)* in *Bereguardo* in the *Valle del Ticino* nature reserve. Other sources of good risotto rice are: the *Azienda Agricola Tenuta Castello (www.tenutacastello.com)* in *Desana*. Delicious risotto is also served 9 km/5.5 miles south-west of Vercelli in *Da Balin (closed Sun evening and Mon | tel. 0 16 14 71 21 | www.balinrist.it | Budget–*

Moderate) in *Castell'Apertole* in Livorno Ferraris.

SACRI MONTI ★ ⅏

I Sacri Monti (the sacred mountains): These baroque pilgrimage sites were built in the 16th and 17th century as a bulwark against the dangerous ideas of the Reformation. They are right out in the countryside, on forested hills and mountain tops, one chapel after the other containing life-size statues enacting scenes from the lives of Christ, Mary and St Francis of Assisi. Local craftsmen made these silent yet dynamic figures out of painted plaster, clay and wood. The most beautiful pilgrimage sites are the *Sacro Monte* in *Varallo* (186 C2) *(𝄞 D2–3)* with 44 chapels, the *Sacro Monte* overlooking the picturesque *Lago d'Orta* (187 D2) *(𝄞 D2)* with 20 chapels dedicated to the life of St Francis, plus in the north of Biella the *Santuario di Oropa* (186 C2) *(𝄞 C3)*, a devotional complex with 19 Mary chapels. All of them have an excellent position with fantastic views.

SESTRIERE AND SUSA
(186 B3–4) *(𝄞 B–C3)*

Enthroned above the entrance to the Susa Valley – site of the 2006 Winter Olympics – is the impressive monastery ⅏ *Sacra di San Michele* with its wonderful Romanesque stonework on the church portal (sign of the zodiac) and a breathtaking panorama. *Susa* (pop. 7000) is a picturesque little town surrounded by high mountains with a castle, a Romanesque-Gothic cathedral and a Roman Arch of Augustus. The most popular and modern ski resort in Susa Valley is *Bardonecchia* (1312 m/4304 ft), but winter sports fans particularly like the pistes of *Sestriere* in the neighbouring Chisone valley. On the way through the valley, you will be impressed by the *Fenestrelle,* the 4000 steps leading up to the Napoleonic fortress.

THE NORTH-EAST

The Brenner Pass, the busiest crossing into Italy, is also known as the gateway to the south. At an elevation of 1370 m/4495 ft, the pass opens up the main Alpine ridge between Austria and Italy. In the pale limestone of the Dolomites, mild breezes and verdant vegetation announce the arrival of the south. Through the passes and valleys, the roads lead down as always to the Adriatic and the once legendary maritime Republic of Venice.

Throughout history, the borders in north-east Italy have been pushed back and forth. That is why people speak German in South Tyrol whilst on the other side of Trieste, the locals speak Slovenian.

BOLZANO

(188 C2) (*Ø F2*) Waltherplatz/Piazza Walther is the centre of this vibrant provincial capital (pop. 105,000) in South Tyrol. Visitors sit in the elegant street cafés with a cappuccino and apple strudel and gaze at the beautiful late Gothic *cathedral.*

Other sites include the impressive frescoes in the chapel of St John (14th century) and the cloister (15th century) of the *Dominican monastery (Mon–Sat 9am–5pm | Dominikanerplatz)* and the famous *carved altar* (around 1475) by Michael Pacher in the parish church in the Gries district. And naturally "Ötzi", the leathery mummy from Similaun in the *Museum of Archae-*

Italy's gateway: castles and mountains in South Tyrol, central Europe in Friuli, and villas and waterscapes in Veneto

ology (see "Travel with Kids"). Great shopping is possible in the centre's arcades and at the market on Obstplatz. For delicious South Tyrolean cuisine visit *Vögele (closed Sun | Goethestr. 3 | tel. 04 71 97 39 38 | www.voegele.it | Budget–Moderate)* in the centre. A pleasant family hotel is the *Magdalener Hof (39 rooms | Rentscherstr. 48 | tel. 04 71 97 82 67 | www. magdalenerhof.it | Moderate)* on the eastern outskirts of Bolzano in the countryside. Information: *Waltherplatz 8 | tel. 04 71 99 99 99 | www.suedtirol.info*

WHERE TO GO

BRIXEN (BRESSANONE) (188 C1) *(*⚏ *G2)*
About 50 km/31 miles to the north is Brixen, a cheerful little episcopal and commercial town (pop. 21,000). It has a beautiful medieval centre and a magnificent Baroque ★ *cathedral* with a *cloister (April– Oct daily 7am–6pm, Nov–March 7am– noon and 3pm–6pm)* decorated with frescoes depicting Biblical scenes (done between 1390–1510); the episcopal *Hofburg* (court palace) contains an inter-

esting Diocesan museum *(mid March–Oct Tue–Sun 10am–5pm, nativity museum Dec–beginning of Jan daily 10am–5pm).*

SOUTH TYROLEAN VALLEYS
(188 B–C 1–2) (*ɯ F–G 1–2*)

The picturesque ⌇⌇ *Ritten* plateau is the summer getaway for Bolzano's middle

Oct, tours daily 11am, 2pm, 3pm, 4pm) to the Grödnertal valley (*www.groednertal. com),* leading on to well known ski resorts such as *St Ulrich* (Ortisei), also famous for its woodcarving. Travelling via the Sella Pass past the magnificent pale grey limestone of the Sellastock massif, you arrive at the ★ ⌇⌇ *Great Dolomite Road,* one of

Brass bands and costumes; traditions are preserved with pride in South Tyrol

classes with old-fashioned hotels and villas, as is the *Seiser Alm,* Europe's largest high-alpine pasture (approx. 23 miles²), a floral paradise set against the magnificent backdrop of the *Schlern/Sciliar* mountain, Bolzano's landmark. Enjoy the health benefits of an invigorating bath in hay from untreated pastures, e.g. in *Völs am Schlern* in the ● *Hotel Heubad (43 rooms | tel. 04 71 72 50 20 | www.hotel heubad.com | Moderate–Expensive),* also available to non-resident guests.

North of Bolzano, in the *Eisacktal/Valle Isarco,* the route branches off at Waidbruck opposite the magnificent *Trostburg (Easter–*

Italy's most beautiful panoramic routes. It begins in Bolzano, continuing via the narrow *Eggental/Val d'Ega* to the Rosengarten mountain chain and Latemar, and then on to the Trentino Val di Fassa to the Sella and Marmolada mountains and on to *Cortina d'Ampezzo,* the pearl of the Dolomites, in the Veneto region, a chic holiday resort with elegant shops and art galleries. During the cable car ride on the *Freccia del Cielo (www.freccianelcielo. com)* to the ⌇⌇ *Tofana di Mezzo* (3243 m/10,610 ft), you can enjoy the breathtaking views of Adamello, the Großglockner and the Venice lagoon. After following the

Eisack valley to Klausen/Chiusa, the route continues along the *Villnösstal/Val di Funes* valley with its South Tyrolean picture book landscape.

Also popular is the *Pustertal/Val Pusteria* in the north-east with its little villages such as *Bruneck, Toblach, Innichen* and the beautiful tributary valleys with holiday farms that are ideal for family holidays, e.g. in Gsieser valley *Mudlerhof (4 apartments | Preindl 49 | Teisten | tel. 04 74 95 00 36 | www.mudlerhof.com | Budget).*

The South Tyrolean wine route starts south of Bolzano and meanders through the vineyards and wine-producing villages of the Etschtal valley past Lago di Caldaro towards Salurn; it is here that you will cross the German-Italian language border that has existed since the 8th century.

To the north-west is *Meran,* an enchanting spa town (pop. 38,000) with super-chic thermal baths *(www.thermemeran.it)* and parks full of Mediterranean plants, e.g. the *Giardini Trauttmansdorff (April–mid Nov daily 9am–6pm, in summer Fri until 10pm | www.trauttmansdorff.it).*

Above Meran is *Dorf Tirol*, once the family seat of the counts of Tirol, now a popular tourist site and home to the modern South Tyrolean state museum *(mid March–mid Dec Tue–Sun 10am–5pm | www.schlosstirol.it).*

From Meran we go on into *Vinschgau,* a sunny, dry, fruit-growing valley district which continues right through to Switzerland. The tributary valleys lead south to the Ortler glacier *(Stilfser Joch)* and in the north to the Oetztal Alps *(Schnalstal* valley) both also summer ski areas. In the Schnalstal, *Castel Juval* rises up before you *(Easter–June and Sept–Oct Thu–Tue 10am–4pm with guided tour | www.messner-mountain-museum.it),* one of the six museums set up by South Tyrol's most famous mountaineer, Reinhold Messner. A cultural highlight, INSIDER TIP *St Prokulus*, a small 8th century church in *Naturns,* contains the oldest frescoes in the German-speaking world *(Easter–Oct Tue–Sun 10am–12.30pm and 2.30pm–5.30pm, guided tours at 10am and 3pm).* Castles and monasteries adorn the valley

---

It was also here that one of the most respected Catholic saints, Anthony of Padua, a contemporary of Francis of Assisi, preached and later died. The enormous *Prato della Valle* garden square is a nice place to relax (an antique market is held here every third Sunday in the month). A great excursion tip: a ● boat trip along the Brenta Canal towards Venice past the beautiful noble villas *(www.ilburchiello.it)*.

SIGHTSEEING

BASILICA DI SANT'ANTONIO
Every year, about 4.5 million people make a pilgrimage to the tomb of Saint Anthony in this vast domed church (13th century). Donatello's bronzes in the high altar are particularly stunning. *Daily 6.20am–6.45pm | Piazza del Santo*

CAPPELLA DEGLI SCROVEGNI ★
The rather plain exterior of the 14th century chapel contrasts starkly with the overwhelming interior, painted entirely by Giotto, the trailblazer between medieval and modern artistic styles. Commissioned by the merchant and money lender Enrico Scrovegni, Giotto – Italy's art superstar in the early 14th century – painted vivid, well-preserved scenes from the life of Jesus and Judgement Day. *Daily 9am–7pm | pre-register by phone tel. 04 92 01 00 20 | Corso Garibaldi | www.cappelladegli scrovegni.it |*

GATTAMELATA
In 1453, Donatello created a Renaissance masterpiece with the statue of the Venetian military leader Gattamelata: intelligent moderation in place of martial pose. *In front of the Basilica of St Anthony | Piazza del Santo*

78 statues line the market square of Prato della Valle

and staying in the little fortress town of INSIDER TIP *Glurns* in the stylishly renovated *Grüner Baum (10 rooms | Stadtplatz 7 | tel. 04 73 83 12 06 | www.gasthofgrue nerbaum.it | Moderate)* has a special flair.

PADUA (PADOVA)

(188 C4) *(∅ G3)* **This venerable university town (pop. 209, 000) commissioned Italy's top artists in both the late Middle Ages and the Renaissance.**

MUSEI CIVICI EREMITANI
Interesting archaeological department and priceless art gallery: Bellini, Tiziano, Giorgione, Tiepolo, Giotto and many others. *Tue–Sun 9am–7pm | Piazza Eremitani*

FOOD & DRINK

OSTERIA DAL CAPO
Popular trattoria with delicious local cuisine, always full – so book a table! *Closed Mon noon and Sun | Via degli Obizzi 2 | tel. 0 49 66 31 05 | Budget–Moderate*

LA FINESTRA
Pictures on the wall, framed like windows, reference the name of this pleasant restaurant in the old town which serves imaginative and exquisite southern dishes. *Closed Mon and lunchtime apart from Fri, Sat, Sun | Via dei Tradi 15 | tel. 0 49 65 03 13 | www.ristorantefinestra.it | Moderate*

CAFFÈ PEDROCCHI
For generations *the* elegant coffee house in Padua. *Closed Mon in summer | Via VIII Febbraio 15 | tel. 04 98 78 12 31 | www.caffepedrocchi.it | Moderate*

ENTERTAINMENT

The locals meet for aperitifs around the Palazzo della Ragione on the *Piazza della Frutta* or on the *Piazza delle Erbe;* Padua's nightlife district, the *Ghetto,* adjoins the square to the south.

WHERE TO STAY

AL FAGIANO
Eclectically designed and privately run city hotel not far from the Basilica. *40 rooms | Via Locatelli 45 | tel. 04 98 75 00 73 | www.alfagiano.com | Budget*

VILLA MARGHERITA
Live in noble Venetian style in a country villa by the Brenta Canal in Mira. *19 rooms | Mira Porte | Via Nazionale 416–417 | tel. 04 14 26 58 00 | www.villa-margherita.com | Expensive*

INFORMATION

At the station and in *Vicolo Pedrocchi (behind Caffè Pedrocchi) | tel. 04 98 75 20 77 | www.turismopadova.it.* Ask about the Padova Card, a global ticket.

WHERE TO GO

EUGANEAN HILLS (COLLI EUGANEI)
≈≈ (188 C4) *(ᗰ G3)*
The volcanic hills that suddenly rise up above the flat Po plain are among the most idyllic places to visit in northern Italy: offering vineyards, forests, the *Benedictine abbey of Praglia* (11th century) and renowned thermal spas such as ● *Abano Terme* and *Montegrotto Terme* that offer fango treatments, health and fitness programmes *(www.abanomontegrottosi.it).* The famous poet Francesco Petrarca died in the mountain village of *Arquà Petrarca.* Further sights include the fortified villages *Castelli Carraresi,* such as *Este* with its castle, park and villas: *Museo Nazionale Atestino (daily 8.30am–7.30pm)* is in Villa Mocenigo with interesting exhibits from prehistoric, ancient and Venetian times.

TREVISO (189 D3) *(ᗰ G3)*
The clothes brand Benetton comes from this area as does a particularly popular form of red leaf chicory, the *radicchio di Treviso.* This tranquil, prosperous town (pop. 83,000) has an idyllic river frontage, medieval *palazzi,* a *cathedral* of Roman origin with an altarpiece by Titian, the richly decorated Gothic church *San*

Nicolò, the *Museo Civico (Tue–Sun 9am–12.30pm and 2.30–6pm)* in the former cloister complex of Santa Caterina, with its notable painting collection (Bellini, Lotto, Titian) and a fish market right in the centre on a small island. Also worth a visit is the charming little town of **INSIDER TIP** *Asolo* 30 km/18 miles to the north-west.

VICENZA ★ (188 C3) (*ɱ G3*)

Even if the 16th century's most famous architect to the Venetian aristocracy, Andrea Palladio, actually came from Padua, Vicenza is still "his" town (pop. 112,000). The masterpiece is the *basilica* set within three squares (today an exhibition space), originally Gothic and then surrounded with two-storey stone buttresses by Palladio. Even the exemplary *Teatro Olimpico (Tue–Sun 9am–5pm)* is a design by Palladio, which Vicenzo Scamozzi completed; what is astounding in this particular case is the sense of visual depth achieved with his clever perspective backdrop.

You can obtain information about the visiting times and tours of the numerous splendid villas that once belonged to the Venetian aristocracy in the vicinity of Treviso and Vicenza: *Piazza Matteotti 12 | tel. 04 44 32 08 54 | also MP3 guides | App for smartphones at www.visitpalladio.com | www.vicenzae.org.* The most well-known is *Villa La Rotonda (Tue–Sun 10am–noon and 3pm–6pm, you can only tour the grounds, mid March–early Nov Wed and Sat also possible to go inside | www.villalarotondu.it) 4 km/2.5 miles* from Vicenza, Palladio's most exquisite and original work.

TRENTO

(188 B2) (*ɱ F2*) **The fresh mountain air pervades even the narrowest streets of the city (pop. 117,000).**

From 1027 to 1803, Trento was an influential episcopal principality. It was in *Castello del Buonconsiglio (Tue–Sun 10am–5pm)* that from 1545 to 1563 the council met to devise strategies to fight the Reformation. The castle grounds include the ★ *Torre Aquila (reserve entrance at the desk | www.buonconsiglio.it)* with fascinating frescoes (15th century) that superbly depict work (done by the farmers) and play (enjoyed by the aristocracy) in the form of a calendar, e. g. **INSIDER TIP** the first snowball fight in art history! In the mod-

THE "OMBRA"

The Venetians have always enjoyed drinking their wines at the market, at festivals and on the piazza. Out in the open, before the age of fridges, people used to look for a place in the shade both for the wine, and for themselves. Thus, the equivalent of "let's go for a drink" went from *andemo a bever all'ombra* (let's have a drink in the shade) to *andemo a bever un'ombra* (literally "let's drink the shade"). People still drink *ombra*, the little glass of cold white wine at a bar or – in Venice – in a bacaro served with seafood and ham snacks, the *cicchetti*, e.g. in *Cantina del Vino già Schiavi (closed Sun | Fondamenta Nani | Dorsoduro 992 | tel. 04 15 23 00 34 / Budget).*

ern science museum *MUSE (Tue–Fri 10am–6pm, Sat/Sun 10am–7pm | Corso del Lavoro e della Scienza 3 | www.muse. it)* you can witness the formation of the dolomites.

and old roads are full of castles and palaces – some in good condition, others romantic ruins – that provide the stage for annual summer cultural events. Europe's largest castle building towers majestically

An annual calendar depicted in 15th century frescoes: Torre Aqiola in Trento's Castello Buonconsiglio

On the impressive cathedral square with its medieval pillar basilica and beautifully painted old town houses is the town's enticing *Scrigno del Duomo* restaurant *(daily | Piazza del Duomo 29 | tel. 04 61 22 00 30 | www.scrignodeldu omo.com | Budget–Expensive)*, part top-class restaurant, part wine bar. The *MART* museum *(Tue–Thu and Sat/Sun 10am–6pm, Fri 10am–9pm | www.mart. trento.it)* in nearby *Rovereto i*s a must for aficionados of modern art.

WHERE TO GO

TRENTINO (188 B–C2) *(ⓜ F–G2)*
Like South Tyrol, the Tridentine mountain sides, valley entrances, rocky outcrops

over the Etschtal valley between Rovereto and Trento – *Castel Beseno*, once the military vanguard of the diocese. Not far from the Comano spa resort is one of the most beautiful Tridentine fortified residences, *Castello di Stenico* much of which has been restored *(guided tours Tue–Sun 9.30am–5pm, end Nov–beginning March only Sat/Sun)*.
In the north-west of Trento, you have a bird's eye view of the mountains from the 2125 m/6972 ft ⚡ *Paganella*: in the west you can see the Brenta Dolomites and the glaciers Adamello-La Presanella and Cevedale, nestled between which are famous ski resorts such as *Madonna di Campiglio*. There you can find the comfortable ⓦ *Hermitage,* an eco-friendly

hotel *(25 rooms | Via Castelletto Inferiore 69 | tel. 04 65 44 15 58 | www.biohotel hermitage.it | Expensive)* with a spa area and excellent restaurant *(Expensive)*, which mainly uses organic ingredients. In the north-east, the Dolomites dominate Trentino, approached by a gradual progression of valleys: first, the sunny, vine-growing Cembratal/Val di Cembra, followed by the Fleimstal/Val di Fiemme, in whose main town, *Cavalese* the *Palazzo della Magnifica Comunità* (16th century) bears witness to the fact that in 1110 the farmers wrested independence from the Bishop of Trento and set up the first autonomous community in Italy. The alpine Val di Fassa links up with the *Great Dolomite Road.* Enjoy the high altitude setting of the ● *I Suoni delle Dolomiti (www.isuonidelledolomiti.it),* summer music concerts held in mountain locations, e.g. cello solos or klezmer music in the Fassatal/Val di Fassa at the *Micheluzzi* mountain lodge or in the Feimstal on the *Pampeago meadows* – free of charge. A renowned ski resort is *San Martino di Castrozza* set against the backdrop of the ⛷ Pala Dolomites with the formidable *Cimone della Pala* (3186 m/10,450 ft).

In addition to the lakes *Lago di Caldonazzo* and *Lago di Levico,* the north bank of Lake Garda, very popular with surfers, is part of Trentino. *www.visittrentino.it*

TRIESTE

(189 E3) (∅ H–J3) Streets lined with houses that once belonged to rich merchants (some of which are now museums) and the impressive 19th century palazzi on the Piazza dell'Unità d'Italia by the old harbour all remind visitors that Trieste (pop. 204,000) was once one of the most important Adriatic ports of the Austro-Hungarian Empire.

Admire the remains of the ancient Roman city of Aquileia

Above the old town, the ☼ San Giusto hill offers magnificent views of the town and sea; also here are San Giusto Basilica and the castle. Typical restaurants include the **INSIDER TIP** buffets, e.g. L'Approdo (closed Sun | Via Carducci 34 | Budget) or Da Pepi (closed Sun | Via Cassa di Risparmio 3 | Budget) and the old coffee houses, e.g. Caffè San Marco (Via Battisti 18), Tommaseo (Piazza Tommaseo) and the **INSIDER TIP** Pasticceria Pirona (Largo Barriera Vecchia 12), often frequented by James Joyce. The six tastefully appointed rooms of the Residenza le 6A (Via Santa Caterina 7 | tel. 04 06 72 67 15 | www.residenzale6a.it | Budget–Moderate) located in the central pedestrian zone provide the perfect starting point for a stroll round the town. Information: Piazza dell'Unità d'Italia 4 | tel. 04 03 47 83 12 | www.turismo fvg.it

WHERE TO GO

AQUILEIA ★
(189 E3) (*Ø H3*)

During the time of the Romans and early Christianity, Aquileia (45 km/28 miles to the north-west) was a powerful town on the upper Adria, as is visible from the Roman ruins and the wonderful Romanesque basilica (April–Sept daily 9am–7pm, March and Oct 9am–6pm, Nov–feb 10am–4pm | www.aquileia.net) with its well-preserved mosaic floor.

CIVIDALE DEL FRIULI
(189 E2) (*Ø H2*)

This charming little medieval town (pop. 11,000) in Friuli, picturesquely situated on the Natisone River, has retained fascinating traces of the ancient Lombards. They are exhibited in the Tempietto Longobardo, the basilica, and in the archaeological and the Christian museum.

TRIESTINE RIVIERA ★ ☼
(189 E3) (*Ø H3*)

The coastal road from Trieste to Duino between the Adriatic and karst hinterland is regarded as one of the most scenic routes in Italy. One destination for a daytrip is to the karst rock formations (where care is needed because much of the ground is hollowed out) to visit the giant caves ● Grotta Gigante (Tue–Sun 10am–4pm, April–Sept until 6pm, July/August also Mon) in ☼ Villa Opicina, which you can get to from Trieste by funicular. The brightly lit ☼ Castello di Miramare (April/May and Sept daily 8am–6pm, June–Aug 8am–7pm, March and Oct 8am–5pm, Nov/Dec 8am–3pm, Jan/Feb 8am–4pm) in the wonderful park high above the sea, built for Archduke Maximilian of Austria in 1860, is one of the main sights, as is the much older ☼ Castel Duino in its spectacular location on the cliff (April–Sept Wed–Mon 9.30am–5.30pm, Oct and 2nd half of March Wed–Mon, Nov–mid March Sat/Sun 9.30am–4pm), which you can also reach via the famous ● Rilke Path that starts at the tourist information at the turn-off from the Trieste coastal road to Sistiana Mare and continues to the castle village of Duino.

UDINE (189 E2) (*Ø H2*)

Udine (pop. 100,000) was the capital of the Friuli Venezia Giulia region until 1956 and still is in the hearts of many in the region. Like the star-shaped fortified town of Palmanova 20 km/12.5 miles to the south, Udine also bears the seal of Venice because it served as a stronghold against the Huns, Hungary and the Turks for the maritime republic in the 16th and 17th century. There is an interesting collection of paintings in the castle and Tiepolo's art in the cathedral worth seeing. There are plenty of beautiful squares such as the Piazza della Libertà and Piazza Matteotti to wander round.

VENICE (VENEZIA)

(189 D4) *(ⓜ G3)* **The city (pop. 60,000) on the water – one of the world's most beautiful and iconic places – draws 14 million visitors a year. For a more detailed description refer to the MARCO POLO "Venice" guide.**

SIGHTSEEING

CANAL GRANDE ★

The main canal passes through the city like a mirror-inverted letter S, passing exquisite palace façades, whose Gothic, Renaissance and Baroque architecture give Venice its distinctive filigreed Oriental flair. You pass the *Rialto Bridge* from 1592 with its daily market directly after the first loop in the canal. When the boat reaches the *Piazzetta San Marco*, visitors alight on the forecourt of the *Palazzo Ducale (daily 8.30am–5.30pm, April–Oct until 7pm)*, the former residence of the doges, which is full of magnificent artworks.

COLLEZIONE PEGGY GUGGENHEIM

The American collected the works of her friends Picasso, Matisse, Klee, Giacometti and many others. *Wed–Mon 10am–6pm | in Palazzo Venier dei Leoni | Dorsoduro 701 | www.guggenheim-venice.it*

GALLERIA DELL'ACCADEMIA

All of the great Venetian masters (14th–18th century) are represented here: Bellini, Canaletto, Carpaccio, Titian, Veronese and many more. *Tue–Sun 8.15am–7.15pm, Mon 8.15am–2pm | Campo della Carità Dorsoduro*

PIAZZA SAN MARCO

The city's magnificent "drawing room" with the historic municipal buildings of *Procuratie Vecchie* and *Procuratie Nuove*, the beautiful old cafés and of course the sumptuous, oriental style *Basilica di San Marco (Mon–Sat 9.45am–5pm, Sun 2pm–5pm | Sun admission free)* with its rich cathedral treasury. From the 97 m/318 ft ☽ *tower (Nov–Easter daily 9.30am–3.45pm, Easter–June and Oct 9am–7pm, July–Sept 9am–9pm)* there are stunning views of Venice.

REDENTORE

Andrea Palladio built this magnificent temple-styled basilica on the island of Giudecca opposite Piazza San Marco.

FOOD & DRINK

L'ORTO DEI MORI

Fresh Mediterranean cuisine. In the summer, it is wonderful to sit on the Campo dei Mori; reserve in advance. *Closed Tue | Fondamenta dei Mori | Cannaregio 3386 | tel. 04 15 24 36 77 | www.osteriaortodeimori. com | Moderate*

LA ZUCCA

Wide variety of vegetable dishes; small and popular – arrive early! *Closed Sun | Campo San Giacomo dell'Orio | Santa Croce 1762 | tel. 04 15 24 15 70 | www.la zucca.it | Budget–Moderate*

SHOPPING

Two classic souvenirs come from the islands in the lagoon: blown glass from Murano and lace from Burano, available in many shops or directly on the islands, e.g. in Murano you can buy beautiful vases and glass pearl jewellery from *Ferrevetro (Campo Santo Stefano 7)* and in Burano fine lace from *La Merlettaia (Calle San Mauro 298)*.

At the end of the Canal Grande opposite the Piazza San Marco: Palladio's San Giorgio Maggiore

WHERE TO STAY

CA' DOGARESSA

Small stylish guest house in the old ghetto, good value for money. *9 rooms | Fondamenta di Cannaregio | Cannaregio 1018 | tel. 04 12 75 94 41 | www.cadoga ressa.com | Budget–Expensive*

CA' MARIA ADELE

Expensive but very chic, with oriental style roof terrace, near the Guggenheim museum. *12 rooms | Rio Terrà dei Catecumeni | Dorsoduro 111 | tel. 04 15 20 50 78 | www.camariaadele.it | Expensive*

INFORMATION

Piazza San Marco/Calle Ascensione | San Marco | tel. 04 15 29 87 11 | www.turismo venezia.it

WHERE TO GO

LIDO DI VENEZIA ● (189 D4) *(𝄞 G3)*
Anyone wishing to combine a beach holiday with a visit to Venice should choose the Lido: either in the glamorous luxury hotels or in the charming *Villa Stella (12 rooms | Via San Gallo 111 | tel. 04 15 26 07 45 | www.villastella.com | Budget–Moderate)* with its beautiful garden.

PO DELTA ● (189 D4) *(𝄞 G4)*
The delta landscape of Italy's largest river extends 60 km/37 miles from the Adige estuary below *Chioggia* (well worth seeing, a mini version of Venice with one of Italy's most important fish markets) down to the picturesque *Comacchio,* where the lagoon landscape of Ferrara begins. Most of the former marshland has been drained, although you will still come across some protected wetland. The dykes are ideal for cycling and riding, and there are boat trips on the waterways.

VERONA

(188 B3–4) (*F3*) **Romeo and Juliet, the classic love tragedy, and an evening at the opera in the huge Roman arena (22,000 seats) in the town centre are what one associates with Verona (pop. 259,000), once an important Roman settlement situated where the Adige flows down from the Alps into the North Italian lowlands.**

CASA DI GIULIETTA

Pilgrims of love have added a significant shine to the breasts of the bronze Juliet standing in the courtyard of the house she was supposedly born in. *Tue–Sun 8.30am–7.30pm, Mon 1.30pm–7.30pm | Via Cappello 23*

MUSEO D'ARTE CASTELVECCHIO

Exhibits masterpieces such as the "Madonna of the Quail" by Pisanello or the equestrian statue of Cangrande I

Baroque and Renaissance palazzi: magnificent setting for bars and trattorias on the Piazza Erbe

SIGHTSEEING

ARENA

Towering above Piazza Bra and its many cafés in the town centre is the Roman Empire's largest gladiator arena (1st century), today the summer venue for the opera festival. *Tue–Sun 8.30am–7.30pm, Mon 1.30pm–7.30pm, opera season 8.30am–4.30pm | www.arena.it*

from the 13th century, famous for his mysterious smile. *Tue–Sun 8.30am–7.30pm, Mon 1.30pm–7.30pm | Corso Castelvecchio 2*

PIAZZA ERBE

Towards evening, the in-crowd fills the restaurants under the arcades of this wonderful market square lined with Renaissance and Baroque palazzi.

PIAZZA DEI SIGNORI

Palazzo del Comune with its Romanesque courtyard, Gothic staircase and ᘒ *Torre dei Lamberti* (84 m/276 ft, lift) as well as the early Renaissance *Loggia del Consiglio* keep the Dante statue company in this square.

SAN ZENO MAGGIORE ★

The entrance portal of this wonderful Romanesque basilica is deemed to be one of the most beautiful bronze works of the 12th century. 48 finely sculpted panels vividly portray stories from the Bible. Inside, the altarpiece by Mantegna depicting the Madonna surrounded by saints deserves special attention. The bones of San Zeno, Verona's patron saint, lie in the almost mystical columned crypt, and there is an impressive cloister in the abbey attached to the basilica. *Piazza San Zeno*

FOOD & DRINK

AL CRISTO

Imaginative crossover cuisine and modern styling in old surroundings. *Closed Mon | Piazzetta Pescheria 6 | tel. 045 59 42 87 | www.ristorantealcristo.it | Moderate–Expensive*

SOTTORIVA 23 OSTREGHETERIA

Lively osteria in a popular entertainment area; snacks, cooked meals; meeting place for aperitifs, cultural events. Open until 2am! *Daily | Via Sottoriva 23 | tel. 045 80 00 99 04 | Budget*

WHERE TO STAY

AURORA

Fantastic location near Piazza Erbe, well-kept and welcoming. *19 rooms | Piazzetta XIV Novembre 2 | tel. 045 59 47 17 | hotel aurora.biz | Moderate*

AGRITURISMO SAN MATTIA ᘒ ⊛

A rural oasis in the north of Verona with olive groves, wine, fruit trees, excellent view of the town, good food and environmentally conscious energy. *10 rooms, 5 apartments | Via San Giuliana 2 | tel. 045 913 79 7 | www.agriturismosanmattia.it | Budget*

IL SOGNO DI GIULIETTA ᘒ

The gorgeously charming rooms with a view of Julia's balcony invite you to daydream. *16 rooms | Via Cappello 23 | tel. 045 800 99 32 | www.sognodigiulietta.it | Expensive*

INFORMATION

Via degli Alpini 9 (Piazza Bra) | tel. 045 806 86 80 | www.tourism.verona.it

LOW BUDGET

In South Tyrol's Eisacktal, you do not have to pay an entrance fee at the large leisure pool (except on Sundays and public holidays), the museums or on public transport if you have a Brixen Card. *www.brixencard.info*

Tips for the expensive Venice trip: inexpensive accommodation is available on the mainland, e.g. in Mestre or in Padua (frequent train connections). Look out for tourist travel cards for museums, churches and ferries *(vaporetti)*. In several places you can take a gondola across the Canal Grande for just for 70 cents.

In Verona, it is worth buying a tourist card *(Verona-Card)* for the museums, but also for the churches, because like those in Venice, you have to pay to go inside. *www.veronacard.it*

PO VALLEY AND LAKES

The imposing Alps provide a natural border in the north, and their foothills with the beautiful Italian Lakes slope down to Italy's only large plain, the Padania, which stretches from Turin to the Adriatic Sea and is traversed by the Po, Italy's longest and most majestic river.

This fertile plain is also home to most of Italy's industry. In the south, the foothills of the Apennines border the Padania. Where the mountains meet the plains, the excellent road network and abundance of water facilitated the development of vibrant cities – autonomous regions during the Middle Ages and then the courts of ambitious dynasties such as Piacenza, Parma, Reggio Emilia, Modena and Bologna – along the ancient Roman road Via Emilia.

BOLOGNA

(188 C5) (*m F4*) Bologna (population 384,000) boasts 37 km/23 miles of vault arcades, Europe's oldest university (1088), the famous *tortellini* and *tortelloni* pasta filled with ricotta and spinach or meat, and of course the sprawling and spirited old town with its distinct red-brown façades.

SIGHTSEEING

ARCHIGINNASIO
Built in 1562/63, the Renaissance palace is the seat of the old university. The coats of arms of the students and professors adorn the library's reading rooms and the

In Italy's Lake District, the Po Valley (Padania) and Rimini on the Adriatic coast, holidaymakers are always close to the water

courtyard. You can also admire the *Teatro Anatomico,* a medical lecture hall from the 17th century. *Mon–Fri 10am–6pm, Sat 10am–7pm | Via dell'Archiginnasio/Piazza Galvani*

COMPIANTO DEL CRISTO MORTO
Terracotta was the material of art in the Emilia and the "Lamentation over the Dead Christ" group by Renaissance artist Niccolò dell'Arca in the church of Santa Maria della Vita in the old town is its highlight. *Tue and Sun 10am–7pm, Mon and Wed–Sat 10.30am–6.30pm | Via Clavature 10*

INSIDER TIP ▶ MUSEO GIORGIO MORANDI
One of the truly great 20th century painters, a famous son of the town; now it is also possible to visit his *studio apartment (registration: tel. 051 6496611 | Via Fondazza 36).* *Tue/Wed and Fri noon–6pm, Thu and Sat/Sun noon–8pm | Via Don Minzoni 14 | www.mambo-bologna.org/ museomorandi*

SAN PETRONIO

This enormous Gothic church, which dominates the spacious, almost square Piazza Maggiore, was initially only half finished because the Pope halted construction ing church complex interlinking several religious edifices. They all date back to the period between the 5th and 14th century. *Daily 8am–7pm | Piazza Santo Stefano*

Bologna also has a leaning tower: the almost 100 m/328 ft Torre degli Asinelli

when he discovered the church was to be larger than St Peter's Basilica. The central portal is a masterpiece by Jacopo della Quercia (15th century). The sun shines into the gloomy interior through a small hole directly onto a meridian line. The fountain *Fontana del Nettuno* by Giambologna is in the most wonderful Baroque style. Opposite it is the *Sala Borsa,* a magnificent art nouveau hall and popular meeting place with a café, exhibitions as well as the town library. *Piazza Maggiore/Piazza Nettuno*

SANTO STEFANO ★

The triangular shape of the Piazza Santo Stefano points towards this very interest-

TORRI PENDENTI

There is a terrific view from the higher of the two medieval towers – the symbol of Bologna – the ☆ *Torre degli Asinelli* (97.6 m/320 ft), which has 498 steps to climb. *Daily 9am–5pm, summer until 7pm | Piazza di Porta Ravegnana*

FOOD & DRINK

CANTINA BENTIVOGLIO

Wine, beer, pasta as well as cheese, jazz music and lots of people, in short: a real osteria! *Closed noon and Mon | Via Mascarella 4b | tel. 0 51 26 54 16 | Budget–Moderate*

ROSTERIA LUCIANO
Best traditional Bolognese cuisine in the centre; don't be put off by the sophisticated setting! *Closed Wed | Via Nazario Sauro 19 | tel. 0 51 23 12 49 | Moderate*

SHOPPING

Well-known fashion and shoe shops are located in the streets around Piazza Maggiore and *Galleria Cavour* is particularly elegant. Behind Archiginnasio is the food market district. Here, you will also find INSIDER TIP *Ambasciatori (daily 9am–11.30pm | Budget–Moderate)*: bookshop, culinaria and Eataly on three floors. Fri and Sat clothing and footwear market *La Piazzola (www.lapiazzoladibologna.it)* at *Parco Montagnola*.

ENTERTAINMENT

Most of the pubs are in the university district around *Via Zamboni,* while the night-life area is around *Via Mascarella, Via Augusto Righi* and *Via del Pratello.* Friends meet for aperitifs around *Via Clavature,* e.g. the rustic *Osteria del Sole (Viccolo Ranocchi 1b)* and the museum bar *MAMbo (Museo d'Arte Moderna | Via Don Minzoni 14)* is very popular. In the summer, a comprehensive cultural programme entertains visitors in the squares and parks. Good operas in *Teatro Comunale (Largo Respighi 1 | tel. 0 51 52 99 99 | www.comunalebologna.it).*

WHERE TO STAY

Apart from hotels you will find numerous appealing B & B places, e.g. two enchanting rooms in an historic palazzo: *Ca'Fosca due Torri (Via Caprarie 7 | tel. 0 51 26 12 21 | www.cafoscaduetorri.com | Moderate–Expensive)*; eco-architecture, on the other hand, defines the appearance of the three rooms in ✪ *A Casa Mia (Via del Pratello 85 | tel. 05 16 49 29 55 | www. acasamiabologna.it | Budget).*

MARCO POLO HIGHLIGHTS

Years to mature: Modena is the home of the real aceto balsamico

DEL BORGO
In the north-west of the town, appealing comfort at a good price; guarded parking. *23 rooms | Marco Emilio Lepido 195 | tel. 0 51 40 68 78 | www.hoteldelborgo.it | Budget–Moderate*

METROPOLITAN
In the centre, a pleasant, contemporary city hotel with a superb breakfast. *45 rooms | Via dell'Orso 6 | tel. 0 51 22 93 93 | www.hotelmetropolitan.com | Moderate*

INFORMATION

At the *airport* and *Piazza Maggiore 1 | tel. 0 51 23 96 60 | www.bolognawelcome.com, www.emiliaromagnaturismo.it*

WHERE TO GO

FAENZA (188 C6) *(ഗ G5)*
From Bologna to the beaches on the Adriatic coast, you pass through Faenza (pop. 54,000), a traditional centre for ceramic tiles with ateliers and the *Museo delle Ceramiche (April–Sept Tue–Sun* 10am–7pm, Oct–March Tue–Fri 10am–1.30pm, Sat/Sun 10am–5.30pm | Viale Baccarini 19 | www.micfaenza.org)*. Have a meal or a good wine on the central Piazza della Libertà in the *Enoteca Astorre (closed Mon | Piazza della Libertà 16a | tel. 05 46 68 14 07 | www.enotecaastorre. it | Moderate)*; in the summer, people sit outside on the square.

FERRARA ★ (188 C5) *(ഗ G4)*
The family seat of the House of Este during the 14th–16th century and the most stunning Renaissance town in northern Italy (pop. 138,000), Ferrara lies nestled behind green ramparts in the flat landscape of the Po Delta, with its miles of orchards. To the right of the Romanesque Gothic *cathedral* with its gold interior, you will find 15th century shops and artisans' studios, the *Loggia dei Merciai*. To the south-east of the cathedral is the lively, former ghetto district. Also worth a visit is the *Palazzo Schifanoia,* a Renaissance palace that was once the summer residence of the Este, the *Castello Estense* which is surrounded by a moat and the famous *Palazzo dei*

Diamanti (1492–1567), nowadays the venue for excellent art exhibitions.

Try the *cappellacci con la zucca* (pasta filled with pumpkin) in the trattorias. Ferrara is characterized by beautiful hotels in old palazzi, e. g. *Duchessa Isabella (25 rooms | Via Palestro 70 | tel. 05 32 19 14 293 | www. duchessaisabellaferrara.it | Expensive)* and its charming B & B accommodation, such as *Il Bagattino (6 rooms | Corso Porta Reno 24 | tel. 05 32 24 18 87 | www.ilbagat tino.it | Budget)*.

MODENA (188 B5) (*🗺 F4*)

The legendary Maserati and Ferrari are produced here. Historic cars are exhibited at the INSIDER TIP *Panini Motor Museum (by appointment only, March–July and Sept/Oct Mon–Fri 9am–12.30pm and 2.30pm–6pm, Sat 9am–12.30pm | Via Corletto Sud 320 | www.paninimotormu seum.it)* and in the *Ferrari museum (daily 9.30am–6pm, April–Oct until 7pm | Via Dino Ferrari 43 | museomaranelloferrari. com)* in nearby *Maranello*. Art lovers will appreciate the cathedral ★ *Duomo di Modena*, a masterpiece of Romanesque architecture and sculpture, as well as the impressive cemetery by architect Aldo Rossi in the Madonnina district, a rare INSIDER TIP example of contemporary cemetery architecture. Connoisseurs know Modena for its *aceto balsamico tradizionale* and the celebrated gourmet *Osteria Francescana (closed Sun/Mon | Via Stella 22 | tel. 0 59 22 39 12 | www. osteriafrancescana.it | Expensive)* in the old town.

MILAN (MILANO)

(187 D–E3) (*🗺 D–E3*) **City of fashion, design, finance, advertising, business,**

WHERE TO START?
Piazza del Duomo: From here, streets fan out to the sights: to the north through the Galleria Vittorio Emanuele II to the Scala, to the north-west via Via Dante to the Castello Sforzesco (where you will find the tourist information office). Corso Magenta leads to the "Last Supper" by Leonardo da Vinci. Several car parks are in the vicinity; the Metro line M3 *(station: Duomo)* stops directly underneath the square.

capital of Lombardy, and despite its mere 1.3 million inhabitants, probably the only Italian city with a cosmopolitan city character.

For a more detailed description refer to the MARCO POLO "Milan" guide.

SIGHTSEEING

BASILICA DI SANT'AMBROGIO

St Ambrose, the patron saint of Milan, rests in this impressive early Christian basilica. The famous Renaissance builder Bramante renovated the monastery complex in 1492. *Mon–Sat 10am–noon and 2.30pm–6pm, Sun 3pm–5pm | Piazza Sant'Ambrogio*

CATHEDRAL

The Duomo di Milano, the *Santa Maria Nascente* cathedral *(daily 8am–7pm)*, with its light marble cladding and innumerable turrets, statues and cornices, towers up like a powerful filigree structure against the backdrop of the large piazza. From the 🔍 *roof terrace (daily 9am–7pm)* you have a great panoramic view of the city, the Po Valley in the south and the Alps in the north. *Piazza Duomo*

GALLERIA VITTORIO EMANUELE II ●
From the Piazza Duomo you enter the most beautiful domed shopping arcade in Italy. Completed in 1877 it is known as Milan's "drawing room". Take time for an aperitif in the traditional bar *Camparino in Galleria.*

MUSEO DEL NOVECENTO
An impressive collection of 20th century Italian art in the monumental Palazzo dell'Arengario: groups of work by great masters such as Giorgio de Chirico, Giorgio Morandi, Lucio Fontana, the Arte Povera of the 1970s, contemporary video art. *Mon 2.30pm–7.30pm, Tue, Wed, Fri, Sun 9.30am–7.30pm, Thu, Sat 9.30am–10.30pm | Piazza Duomo | www.museodelnovecento.org*

NAVIGLI
Of the many canals that used to pass through Milan, just three remain: Naviglio Grande, Naviglio Pavese and Darsena; once the workers' and small trade district, now a popular artists' haunt crammed with bars and restaurants – and a wonderful place to wander round on a summer evening. There is an antique and flea market on every last Sunday of the month.

PARCO SEMPIONE AND CASTELLO SFORZESCO
Milan's green lung with museums and cafés as well as the huge castle complex *Castello Sforzesco (Tue–Sun 9am–5.30 pm | Piazza Castello 1 | www.milanocastello.it),* which besides a collection of paintings and art from classical antiquity in the INSIDERTIP *Museo Pietà Rondanini* also exhibits the last, unfinished sculpture of Michelangelo. The park also houses the *Triennale Design Museum (Tue–Sun 10.30am–8.30pm | Viale Alemagna 6 | www.triennaledesignmuseum.it),* a must for design fans with exhibitions, collections of design artefacts, café and events.

PINACOTECA DI BRERA
The richest of the many art collections in Milan exhibits some of Italy's most important works, e.g. the "Cristo morto" by Andrea Mantegna and Raphael's "Lo Sposalizio" (The Marriage of the Virgin). The towering ginkgo in the INSIDERTIP *Botanical Garden* next door was planted by the founder Maria Theresa in the 18th century. *Tue–Sun 8.30am–7.15pm | Via Brera 28 | www.brera.beniculturali.it*

SANTA MARIA DELLE GRAZIE
In the dining room of the Dominican monastery belonging to this beautiful Renaissance church, you will find one of the most valuable art works in the world: ★ *The Last Supper,* painted in 1497 by Leonardo da Vinci on an end wall. The one-point perspective and the emotional presentation of the facial expressions and gestures of the disciples made the fresco a sensation even during the artist's lifetime. *Tue–Sun 8.15am–7pm, pre-booking necessary online or via tel. 02 92 80 03 60 | Piazza Santa Maria delle Grazie | www.cenacolovinciano.net*

FOOD & DRINK

JOIA
Vegetarian cuisine can also serve culinary delights. *Closed Sat noon and Sun | Via Panfilo Castaldi 18 | tel. 02 29 52 21 24 | www.joia.it | Expensive*

BOTTIGLIERA DA PINO
A traditional and very popular trattoria that serves delicious local dishes, near San Babila. *Closed in the evenings and on Sun | Via Cerva 14 | tel. 02 76 00 05 32 | Budget*

TRUSSARDI ALLA SCALA
Fashion-cum-lifestyle brands: Armani has the sushi restaurant *Nobu* in the Armani Palazzo *(Via Pisoni/Via Manzoni 31),* and

Trussardi now has a restaurant, opposite the Scala – elegant atmosphere and excellent innovative cuisine guaranteed *(closed Sat lunchtime and Sun | Piazza della Scala 5 | tel. 02 80 68 82 01 | www.trussardiallascala.com | Expensive)*.

ther. Two superb department stores: *Excelsior (Galleria del Corso 4)* and *La Rinascente (Via Santa Radegonda 3)* with a ☀ **INSIDER TIP** terrace with a café and restaurant that offers a breathtaking view of the cathedral.

A square for sinners and saints alike: the cathedral next to the Galleria Vittorio Emanuele II shopping mall

SHOPPING

In *Quadrilatero della Moda*, the sophisticated, outrageously expensive fashion brands are around *Via Monte Napoleone, Via Sant'Andrea, Via Gesù, Via Borgospesso* and *Via della Spiga*. You can buy the same brands a season later at the *stocchisti* at lower prices, e.g. in **INSIDER TIP** *Il Salvagente (Via Fratelli Bronzetti 16 | www.salvagentemilano.it)*. Lifestyle at its best is seen in Milan's first concept store *Dieci Corso Como (Corso Como 10)*. You should not miss the window displays in Italy's most gorgeous gourmet shop *Peck* in *Via Spadari 9* ei-

ENTERTAINMENT

THEATRE
Milan's legendary opera house *La Scala (Via Filodrammatici 2 | tel. 02 72 00 37 44 | www.teatroallascala.org)* enjoys a worldwide reputation. Modern theatres include *Piccolo Teatro Strehler (Largo Greppi | www.piccoloteatro.org)* and its two branches *Teatro Grassi (Via Rovello 2)* and *Teatro Studio (Via Rivoli 6)*.

MEETING PLACES & LOUNGE BARS
The nightlife districts are Brera, Corso Sempione and Navigli; in the summer restaurants open in the Lambro and

Sempione parks; exclusive aperitif and cocktail meeting places are e.g. at the castle *Serendepico (Piazza Castello 1)*, the trendy *Roialto (Viale Vittorio Veneto 28)* or the *Martini Bar (Corso Venezia 15)* near the Dolce & Gabbana store.

WHERE TO STAY

HOTEL BERNA
Large, appealing and comfortable hotel with an excellent breakfast and central location. *116 rooms | Via Napo Torriani 18 | tel. 0 29 47 53 48 21 | www.hotelberna. com | Moderate–Expensive*

BRERA APARTMENTS
Seven well-equipped and stylish apartments of different sizes in the pretty Brera district. *Via San Fermo 1 | tel. 02 36 55 62 84 | www.brerapartments.com | Moderate–Expensive*

RESIDENCE ZUMBINI ROOMS
In the south of the city, convenient, light and modern with garden, cafeteria and parking facilities. *50 rooms | Via Zumbini 6 | tel. 02 36 55 66 04 | www.zumbinirooms. com | Budget*

INFORMATION

Piazza Castello 1 | tel. 02 77 40 43 43 | www.turismo.milano.it. You can also obtain the "Milanomese" here, a monthly magazine (in English) with all the cultural events.

WHERE TO GO

BERGAMO (187 E2) (*ⓜ E3*)
Enthroned above the busy new town (pop. 129,000), at 370 m/1214 ft, is the old town ☀ Bergamo Alta which you can also reach by funicular. Its centre, the *Piazza Vecchia,* presents a superb backdrop: the *Palazzo della Ragione,* the town hall built in 1198, is next to the *cathedral,* begun in the Lombard period, behind which is the Romanesque *Basilica Santa Maria Maggiore*. Adjacent to them is the *Cappella Colleoni* with its magnificent marble façade dating back to the

APERITIF BARS IN MILAN

Meeting with friends at the bar after work to wind down is a way of life in this busy and vibrant town. After all it was here that the legendary Campari was invented in the mid 19th century. The happy hour *aperitivo* continues to be popular in Milan and elsewhere in the north of Italy. It gets going at 7pm, when bars put out refined titbits, exotic salads, pasta, fruit and vegetable snacks. People do not drink heavily: imaginatively decorated, not very alcoholic drinks made of fruit, mint, sparkling white wines. Or the Milan classic *Zucca* made of rhubarb extract, ice and soda. It is very trendy to meet in the sophisticated bars of the chic hotels, for example in *hclub* in the *Sheraton Diana Majestic (Viale Piave 42 | www.sheratondianamajestic.it)*, near the cathedral in *Straf (Via San Raffaele 3 | www.straf.it)*, in the luxurious *Bulgari Hotel (Via Privata Fratelli Gabba 7b | www.bulgarihotels.com)* or you can try the Garden Bar of the *Enterprise (Corso Sempione 91 | www.enterprise hotel.com)*, with a DJ every Thursday.

Lombard Early Renaissance and Tiepolo's famous dome frescoes, and on the right is the *baptistry*.

Try tasty dishes, delicious cheese and a good glass of wine beneath a high loggia in the old town at *Donizetti (daily | Via Gombito 17a | tel. 0 35 24 26 61 | www. donizetti.it | Budget–Moderate)*. In the surrounding area of the Bergamo Alps is the *Lago d'Iseo*, which in the south adjoins the well-known wine district of Franciacorta and in the north the *Valcamonica (www.invallecamonica.it)*. It was in this valley, e.g. in the archaeological parks *Naquane* and *Ceto* in *Capo di Ponte,* that 300,000 INSIDER TIP rock drawings were discovered, the work of an Alpine tribe that lived in the area over 8000 years ago.

BRESCIA (187 E3) (*ℳ E3*)

This modern industrial town (pop. 190,000) with the highest number of immigrants in Italy has a surprising elegant old town full of cafés and fine shops. It also has an impressive square with the "old" cathedral – the medieval *Rotonda (Duomo Vecchio)* – and the "new" Baroque *cathedral* as well as the *Piazza della Vittoria* with the Caffè Impero and the well-preserved art deco Hotel Vittoria. There is also a rich museum complex in the old *Santa Giulia cloister,* dating back to the Lombard period *(Mid June–Sept Tue–Sun 10.30am–7pm, Oct–mid June 9.30am–5.30pm | Via dei Musei 81b)*.

PAVIA (187 D–E3) (*ℳ D3*)

The *San Michele* church has an impressive rustic façade of light sandstone and dates back to the time when Pavia (pop. 87,000) was the seat of the Lombards (6th–8th century). Another interesting religious building is the Lombard Romanesque church *San Pietro in Ciel d'Oro* with its artistic masonry work.

#cincin: your tweet hashtag for Milan's cool cocktail bars

Close by is the impressive *Castello Visconteo,* now a *museum (Feb–June and Sept–Nov Tue–Sun 10am–5.50pm, July/Aug and Dec/Jan 9am–1.30pm | www.museicivici.pavia.it)*. The river Ticino (Tessin) is spanned by a covered bridge.

The main attraction in the surrounding area is 10 km/6 miles to the north, the ★ *Certosa di Pavia (daily 8.30am–noon and 2.30pm–5pm, April–sept until 6pm | www.certosatourism.it)*, a remarkable 15th century example of architecture and art produced during the Lombard Renaissance. The Visconti princes lie entombed in the church, and also of interest are the cloisters and cells used by the monks.

The headland at Punta San Vigilio; an exclusive spot on the east banks of Lake Garda

VIGEVANO (187 D3) (*D3*)

The little town (pop. 66,000) has one of the loveliest squares in Italy, the ★ *Piazza Ducale,* designed by the stars of the Italian High Renaissance, Donato Bramante and Leonardo da Vinci: *arcades* in the early Renaissance style, a 16th century *cathedral,* a *Castello Visconteo* and inviting cafés. Retaining its traditional craft, the town still plies the shoe trade. In the castle's old stables, there is the very interesting shoe museum *Museo della Calzatura (Tue–Fri 2pm–5.30pm, Sat/Sun 10am–6pm).*

ITALY'S LAKE DISTRICT

On the south side of the Alps, lakes cut their way fjord-like through the steep, thickly forested slopes descending down to the plain at the edge of the mountains.

The climate is becoming mild, the vegetation abundant and Mediterranean. Magnificent villas on expansive grounds and charming little old towns on the waterside bear witness to the fact that life has always been good here. The ancient Roman poet Vergil first lavished praise on Lake Como where many years later Franz Liszt would retreat with his mistress and today is the residence of many Russian millionaires. Italian business magnates like to relax at Lago Maggiore. For more detailed information, refer to the MARCO POLO guide "Lake Garda".

LAKE COMO (LAGO DI COMO) ●
(187 E2) (*D–E2*)

A significant urban centre is the ancient town of *Como* (pop. 83,000) on the farthest south-west tip with its elegant art nouveau architecture and a medieval centre with magnificent churches in the

Lombard Romanesque style. Como is also famous for its silk industry.

From the lake, serpentine streets wind up into the mountains and offer magnificent views, e.g. from ☙ *Monte Bisbino* (1325 m/4347 ft) above Cernobbio. From Sala Comacina or from the neighbouring town of Ossuccio, you come to the picturesque islet in the lake, the *Isola Comacina.* There are ferry connections between the various places, the most beautiful being *Varenna* on the eastern shore with the hotel *Villa Cipressi (33 rooms | Via IV Novembre 18 | tel. 03 41 83 01 13 | Expensive)* in the botanical garden directly on the lake and the enchanting *Bellagio* with its winding staircase lanes at the intersection of the Y-shaped lake. Sumptuous villas testify to the long tradition of noble residences on this beautiful lake, a good example being the 15th century *Villa d'Este (www.villadeste.com)* in *Cernobbio,* now one of the most luxurious hotels in Europe, or the Baroque *Villa Carlotta (www.villacarlotta.it)* in *Tremezzo* with its wonderful park. *www.lakecomo.it*

LAKE GARDA (LAGO DI GARDA)
(188 B3) (*Ø F3*)

Italy's largest lake (140 miles², 51 km/32 miles long and up to 346 m/1135 ft deep) marks where the south begins for northerners. Here, the Mediterranean climate is ideal for the cultivation of citrus fruit and olives. The 2218 m/7277 ft ☙ *Monte Baldo* on the eastern shore produces some of the most varied plant life in Europe. A ☙ *panorama cable car* goes up the mountain from Malcesine. The mountain roads along the upper lake offer spectacular views of the landscape as does the ☙ *Gardesana Occidentale,* the coastal road on the western shore between Gargnano and Limone.

The exclusive *Riva del Garda* (pop. 13,000)

dominates the north tip of the lake exuding both central European and Mediterranean flair, with the winding streets of the old town and elegant hotels – for example the modern *Feeling Hotel Luise (67 rooms | Viale Rovereto 9 | tel. 04 64 55 08 58 | www.hotelluise.com | Moderate–Expensive)* with a swimming pool and innovative cuisine – as well as the windsurfing paradise *Torbole (www.gardasurf.com).*

On the eastern shore, the castles attest to the rule of the Veronese della Scala family in the 13th and 14th centuries. Of these, the most impressive is ☙ *Castillo Malcesine,* perched on a rocky outcrop overlooking the lake. A particularly beautiful spot to bathe is the small headland *Punta San Vigilio* with a beach in an olive grove setting. Concealed in a courtyard in *Bardolino* – the namesake of the thriving red wine produced in this area – is the ancient Carolingian church (9th century) *San Zeno (Via San Zeno).*

The Lombardy shore extends along the south-west part of the lake: on an islet off the tip of the *Sirmione* penisula (pop. 4000) is the formidable ☙ *Castillo Scaligero* and the picturesque old centre of Sirmione, the most-visited sight on the lake. In Sirmione, there are well-known thermal springs – the *Centro Benessere Termale Aquaria (www.termedisirmione.com)* is an oasis of wellbeing –, magnificent luxury hotels and first-class restaurants. At the end of the peninsula lie the imposing ruins of a Roman villa, the *Grotte di Catullo (May–mid Oct Tue–Fri 8.30am–7.30pm, Sat/Sun 9.30am–6.30pm, mid Oct–April Tue–Fri 8.30am–5pm, Sat/Sun 8.30am–2pm).* For those wanting to party there are the discotheques in Desenzano, Lonato and Bardolino.

The *Vittoriale degli Italiani* on a hilltop north-east of *Gardone Riviera* is well worth a visit (*daily 9am–5pm, April–Oct* until 8pm | www.vittoriale.it), a beautifully located estate, which was the home of the controversial and eccentric poet Gabriele D'Annunzio from 1921 to 1938. Another quite different poet, André Heller, gave his name to the *botanical gardens* (March–Oct daily 9am–7pm | www.hel lergarden.com). In the little lakeside town of *Salò* nearby, you can stay in pretty and stylish surroundings, and eat well in *Hotel Benaco* (13 rooms | Lungolago Zanardelli 44 | tel. 0 36 52 03 08 | www.benacohotel. com | *Moderate*) on the beautiful, pedestrian promenade. The popular tourist town of *Limone* in the north-west is a reminder of the lemon orchards that once flourished here in the lake's mild climate.

LAGO MAGGIORE (187 D2) *(ꕉ D2)*

Cannobio, the first little town on the Italian side on the western shore has a charming old centre overlooking the lake, in which you will find the charming hotel *Casa Arizzoli* (11 rooms | Via Giovanola 92 | tel. 0 32 37 20 01 | www.hotelcasaarizzoli. com | *Budget–Moderate*). The imposing *Mottarone* (1491 m/4892 ft) rises above Stresa, on the ꕉ summit there's the lovely *Giardino Botanico*. There are spectacular villas and belle époque style hotels set in gorgeous parks as well as the waterfront promenade in the glamorous main town of *Stresa* (pop. 5000). The promenade looks over to the three enchanting Borromean Islands, the most notable of which is the Baroque *Isola Bella* with its palazzo and refined terraced gardens. A lush botanical garden thrives on the *Isola Madre*. The long, narrow *Isola dei Pescatori* is still the preserve of the local fishermen to this day. A wonderful B & B is the ꕉ *Villa La Camana* (3 rooms | Via per Gignese 10 | tel. 0 32 33 15 53 | www.villalacamana.it | *Budget–Moderate*) with a park and magnificent lake view near the village of *Vedasco*. Palaces, gardens and a beautiful promenade await visitors in *Pallanza*, a district of *Verbania*, which with 30,000 inhabitants is the largest town on the lake. Visitors flock to the *Villa Taranto* to see the beautiful gardens *(mid March–Sept daily 8.30am–6.30pm, Oct 9am–4pm | www.villataranto.it)*.

You will find the largest sandy beach opposite on the east bank, the *Lido di Monvalle*. Also located on a rocky outcrop on the eastern shore is the ꕉ *Rocca Borromeo di Angera* (March–Oct daily 9am–5.30pm), a 13th century fort housing a very interesting doll museum. *www. illagomaggiore.com*

LAKE ORTA (LAGO D'ORTA)
(187 D2) *(ꕉ D 2–3)*

The small, contemplative Piedmontese Lago d ' Orta is nestled at the base of dark green forested slopes dotted with picturesque villages. *Orta San Giulio* (pop. 1000), the main town, has some lovely churches, Baroque villas and a Renaissance town hall with a painted façade. There is a gorgeous view of the little island of San Giulio from the ꕉ piazza.

Above the town is the pilgrimage site **INSIDER TIP** *Sacro Monte*, which also has a Baroque puppet theatre. In Omegna on the northern side of the lake, you can buy quality brand kitchen utensils from the *Alessi factory outlet (Mon–Fri 9.30am–6.30pm, Sat 10am–6.30pm | Via Privata Alessi 6 | Crusinallo di Omegna | www. alessi.it)*.

PARMA

(187 F4) *(ꕉ E4)* **This affluent town (pop. 180,000) lies along the old Roman road Via Aemilia in the midst of fertile agricultural land. It is the main base of Barilla, Europe's largest pasta manufacturer, as well as a musical Mecca: Arturo**

Toscanini and above all Italy's most famous opera composer Giuseppe Verdi (born in the small farming village of Busseto not far from Parma) have made the place popular with music lovers with fan clubs and a festival.

SIGHTSEEING

CATHEDRAL AND BAPTISTRY

In 1530, local master Correggio decorated the dome of this Romanesque basilica that has a Gothic campanile (bell tower). Benedetto Antelami, one of the most important sculptors of the Romanesque period, did the sculptures and reliefs in the gracefully structured ★ baptistry. *Cathedral daily 10am–6.30pm, baptistry March–Oct daily 10am–6.30pm, Nov–Feb Mon–Fri 10am–4.30pm, Sat/Sun 10am–5pm | Piazza del Duomo*

PALAZZO DELLA PILOTTA

The palace houses the *Pinacoteca Galleria Nazionale* with works by Bellini and Correggio and the famous *Teatro Farnese* from 1618 which, with 4500 seats, was once the largest theatre in the world. *Tue–Sun 8.30am–1.45pm | Piazza Pilotta*

SAN GIOVANNI EVANGELISTA

The monastery with the beautiful cloister also contains the original *Antica Spezieria (Tue–Sun 8.30am–2pm)*, a pharmacy set up by the Benedictine monks in 1201. *Mon–Wed and Fri/Sat 9am–noon and 3pm–5pm | Piazzale San Giovanni*

FOOD & DRINK

ENOTECA FONTANA

Centrally located, Fontana's popular Parma ham and cheese specialities are served with a nice glass of wine. *Closed Sun/Mon | Via Farini 24 | tel. 05 2128 60 37 | Budget*

About the life of Christ: dome frescoes in the baptistry in Parma

PARIZZI

Once a butcher, today the town's best state-of-the-art restaurant. Also has 13 suites. *Closed Mon | Via Repubblica 71 | tel. 05 21 28 59 52 | www.ristoranteparizzi.it | Moderate–Expensive*

A delicatessen should be on your list of places to visit: delicate, spicy Parma ham, cured ham *culatello, coppa* (pork neck ham) and the fresh, authentic parmesan cheese Parmigiano-Reggiano.

ENTERTAINMENT

Musical Parma offers a rich programme of operas (naturally a lot of which is Verdi) and concerts: in *Teatro Regio (www.teatroregioparma.org),* in the concert hall *Auditorium Paganini (www.fondazionetoscanini.it)* and in the *Casa della Musica (www.lacasadellamusica.it).*

LOW BUDGET

menù pausa pranzo: with this magic phrase, many – also up-market – restaurants in the busy city centres of northern Italy offer an affordable tasty midday meal.

spiaggia gratis: given the endless rows of sun chairs on the Adriatic beaches, it is important to be aware that you are legally entitled to walk through any beach establishment to the free strip of sand next to the sea and lie down on your own towel.

WHERE TO STAY

TORINO

Friendly, quite stylish B & B in the old town, with parking facilities. *39 rooms | Borgo Mazza 7 | tel. 05 21 28 10 46 | www.hotel-torino.it | Moderate*

INFORMATION

Piazza Garibaldi 1 | tel. 05 21 21 88 89 | turismo.comune.parma.it

WHERE TO GO

CREMONA (187 E–F3) (*Ø E3*)

The town (pop. 71,000) that is home to the world's best violin makers upholds the legacy of Antonio Stradivari (with workshops, *Stradivari Museum, violin museum*). Cremona's heart is the wonderful medieval ● *Piazza del Comune,* lined with cafés, the *town hall* and the *cathedral*, with its beautiful stonework, Flemish tapestries and frescoes, the octagonal baptistry and the brick *Torrazzo,* Italy's highest bell tower (111 m/364 ft). Close by in the cosy, Slow Food *Osteria La Sosta (closed Sun evening and Mon | Via Sicardo 9 | tel. 03 72 45 66 56 | www.osterialasostra.it | Budget–Moderate),* you can order Cremona's typical *mostarda,* fruit preserve spiced with mustard that is served with meat and cheese.

MANTUA (MANTOVA)

(187 F3) (*Ø F3–4*)

Mantua (pop. 62,000), once the ancestral seat of the ambitious dukes of Gonzaga (1328–1708), is partially encircled by the Mincio River. You can explore the resulting lake landscape and prolific bird life on INSIDER TIP guided boat trips *(departure from Ponte San Giorgio).* Wander through the town's three central squares: the Piazza Mantegna where you

Mantua's Piazza Erbe transforms into one enormous al fresco restaurant in summer

will find the *Sant'Andrea* church (early Renaissance and Baroque elements), then the Piazza della Erbe, with the Romanesque round church *Rotonda di San Lorenzo*, and restaurants where in the summer you can eat al fresco in a wonderfully romantic setting surrounded by lanterns. Finally, the Baroque styled cathedral is on Piazza Sordello together with the *bishop's palace* and the imposing ★ *Palazzo Ducale,* behind which is *Castello di San Giorgio*. This castle guards some unique art treasures, including in particular the *Camera degli Sposi*, a bridal chamber with wonderful frescoes by Andrea Mantegna from 1474 *(Tue–Sun 8.15am–7.15pm, pre-booking via tel. 04 12 41 18 97 or www.ducalemantova.org)*. It is nice to stay in the centre of the beautiful old town, e.g. in the quiet, spacious B & B *Casa Casari (3 rooms | Via Isabella d'Este 20 | tel. 34 09 62 33 65 | www. casacasari.com | Budget)*. On the south-

ern outskirts of the town is the summer residence of the Gonzaga, the *Palazzo del Tè (Tue–Sun 9am–6pm, Mon 1pm–6pm | www.palazzote.it)*.

Enjoy Mantuan specialities such as pike with green sauce or pasta filled with pumpkin in the popular *Osteria da Bice la Gallina Felice (closed Mon | Via Carbonati 4–6 | tel. 03 76 28 83 68 | Budget–Moderate)*.

Also worth a visit is the little Renaissance town 35 km/22 miles south-west **INSIDER TIP** *Sabbioneta (www.iatsabbio neta.org)* founded by Vespasian Gonzaga. Another excursion tip: the pilgrimage church 8 km/5 miles west of *Curtatone* **INSIDER TIP** *Santa Maria delle Grazie* with impressive votive figures and the inviting *Locanda delle Grazie (closed Wed | Via San Pio X 2 | tel. 03 76 34 80 38 | Budget–Moderate)* with Mantuan specialities such as risotto, filled pasta, and roast donkey.

ROMAGNA COAST

(189 D 5–6) *(ℳ G4–5)* **Romagna's coastal area fluctuates between two extremes, from Ravenna – a pinnacle of man's artistic creation – to Rimini and the other Adriatic resorts – where summer fun is at its wildest.**

In the undulating interior (wonderful hiking areas) there are small picturesque hamlets in which you can often get a far better meal than provided to the masses along the coast.

A puzzle from the Byzantine era: mosaic in the Galla Placidia mausoleum

PIACENZA (187 E3) *(ℳ E4)*

This amiable old provincial town (pop. 102,000) is scenically situated between the Po Valley and the northern foothills of the Apennines. A 16th century fortified wall running parallel to wide alleys encircles the well-preserved medieval centre with the *Piazza dei Cavalli,* which is adorned with two magnificent Baroque horses. The highlight on the piazza is the imposing *Palazzo Gotico* from 1280. Regional specialities are served at the restaurant *Vecchia Piacenza (closed Sun | Via San Bernardo 1 | tel. 05 23 30 54 62 | ristorantevecchiapia cenza.it | Expensive)* in the centre.

COMACCHIO ★ (189 D5) *(ℳ G4)*

A little lagoon town (pop. 21,000) with colourful fishermen's houses and palazzi spread across 13 islands in the delta region of the Po and other smaller rivers. The *Trepponti* bridge (17th century) is an ingenious design; its five wide sweeping staircases enable people to cross four canals. Eel fishing and processing are a traditional activity in Comacchio. You can explore the extensive wetland in the south of Comacchio with its old fishing cottages, reed-bed islands and flamingo colonies by boat *(March–Oct several times a day from Stazione di Pesca Foce | www.vallidicomacchio.info).* A trip over the Comacchio causeway to Anita d'Argenta demonstrates the efforts undertaken since the time of the Etruscans to reclaim the marshlands of the Po Delta. INSIDER TIP Boat trips through the delta start e.g. from *Gorino* and *Porto Garibaldi.*

20 km/18 miles north is the grandiose *Abbazia di Pomposa,* a 7th century Benedictine monastery. The basilica (8th/9th century) reflecting Ravenna's style is adorned with a wonderful floor mosaic and frescoes from the 14th century.

RAVENNA ⭐ (189 D5) (*ⓜ G 4–5*)

Ravenna (pop. 158,000) used to be located by the sea and like Venice was a lagoon city; then the sea receded, today a 10 km/6 miles long canal keeps the two connected. The town has fantastic examples of early Christian culture *(all sights daily 8.30am–7pm, in the winter 9am–5.30pm | ask for combination tickets! | www.turismo.ravenna.it).* From the 5th century, it was the centre of power following the dissolution of the Roman Empire. Decorated with blue and gold mosaics, the mausoleum *Mausoleo di Galla Placidia* dates from this period as well as the preciously inlaid *Baptistry of bishop Neon,* which dates back to the Ostrogoth King Theoderic (493–526) the stalwart *Mausoleo di Teodorico,* made of stone ashlar without mortar, in the north-east of Ravenna and the breathtaking sacral building *Sant'Apollinare Nuovo* (around 500).

The 6th–8th century – the town's period as the capital of Byzantine Italy – saw the building of the octagonal basilica *San Vitale* (consecrated in 547) and the basilica *Sant'Apollinare* (5 km/3 miles south in *Classe*), both with exquisite interiors decorated with mosaic. The art of laying mosaic has become a tradition at Ravenna, and workshops and schools have been set up for this purpose.

A restaurant in the centre of Ravenna, where both visitors and locals enjoy eating is *La Gardèla (closed Thu | Via Ponte Marino 3 | tel. 05 44 21 71 47 | Budget).*

RIMINI AND SURROUNDS ●
(189 D5–6) (*ⓜ G–H5*)

During the summer, 650,000 people live in this European beach metropolis with its eclectic choice of sport and entertainment activities – four times its normal population of 146,000. In what was ancient Rome's Ariminum, you can still see the triumphant arch *Arco d'Augusto* from 27 BC; the *Corso Augusto* leads across the well-preserved bridge of Tiberius into the picturesque district of San Giuliano, the former fishing quarter. The palazzi around the *Piazza Cavour* and the *Tempio Malatestiano,* renovated in early Renaissance style by Rimini's ruling Malatesta family all date back to the Middle Ages. Hidden away in one of the old town alleys is the restaurant *Abocar (closed Mon | Via Farini 13–15 | tel. 0 54 12 22 79 | abocarduecucine.it | Moderate)* with its delightful courtyard and contemporary cuisine.

Riccione (pop. 32,000) follows in the south, once a bourgeois resort with villas in beautiful grounds, today a fashion trendsetter with the most sophisticated, outlandish shops, and the wildest discos. *Cattolica* (pop. 17,000) is more suited to families and people with disabilities.

The north of Rimini flows into other beach resorts with endless chains of hotels: for example *Cesenatico,* where a INSIDER TIP▶ picturesque fishing harbour with impressive old vessels awaits you. *Cervia* is more traditional with a down-to-earth harbour district and salt works from which even the Etruscans extracted salt (today a nature reserve). By contrast, *Milano Marittima* is probably the most refined seaside resort with villas surrounded by pines, well-run hotels and very trendy cocktail bars. Popular destinations in the hills inland are hamlets such as Sant'Arcangelo di Romagna, Montegridolfo and the castle villages of San Leo and Verucchio, all with nice trattorias. *www.adriacoast.com*

SAN MARINO (189 D6) (*ⓜ G5*)

Europe's oldest republic (pop. 25,000) was founded in the 9th century and covers only 23.5 miles². The medieval capital, surrounded by walls and castles, is perched on ❋ Monte Titano (749 m/2457 ft), a popular destination for coin and stamp collectors.

CENTRAL ITALY

They are also called the three sisters. They straddle the central Apennine region between the Ligurian-Tyrrhenian coast in the west and the Adriatic in the east, right across Italy's "boot leg".

Together, they exude a feeling of harmonious proportion. They have beautiful towns with distinctly medieval and Renaissance features, such as Florence, Siena, Pisa and Lucca in Tuscany, and Perugia, Gubbio, Assisi, Orvieto, and Todi in Umbria, as well as Urbino and Ascoli Piceno in the Marche. There are a variety of landscapes: the Apuan Alps, which separate Tuscany from Liguria and the Po Valley and provide the white marble from Carrara; then there is the Tyrrhenian coast lined with pine woods, the ash-grey clay hills of *Crete* to the south of Siena and the darkly forested volcanic Monte Amiata on the border to Lazio; away from the coast, the undulating landscape of Umbria with its dense forests is called the green heart of Italy and is increasingly popular with the Tuscany fraction; finally the Marche whose fertile slopes of wine terraces, wheat, maize and flax fields, sunflowers and bright green alfalfa gently descend to the Adriatic coast with its flat sand and pebble beaches. In the cosy trattorias, you can savour the full-bodied wines with an excellent meal. There is a general sense of quality of life, which not only the tourists enjoy, but which the locals also take full advantage of.

Tuscany, Umbria and the Marche: the three regions of central Italy known for their gently rolling hills and opulent towns

FLORENCE (FIRENZE)

(190 B1) *(⚐ F5)* **It is Europe's richest art centre, full of incomparably exquisite architecture, monuments, sculptures and paintings.**

From the 14th century, the powerful Medici family steered the city's political and cultural destiny, which reached its zenith during the Renaissance. It was here in 1256 that Dante was born, the writer whose poetical language was to provide the basis for the Italian language. A good 380,000 people live in the capital of Tuscany and they have to put up with the onslaught of millions of visitors each year. From the raised square, *⚜ Piazzale Michelangelo,* on the left bank of the Arno, there is a fantastic view of the whole town, including the river banks, the palaces, the towering cathedral dome. MARCO POLO covers this city in detail in its "Florence" guide.

SIGHTSEEING

CATHEDRAL AND BAPTISTRY ★

Artistic highlights of the octagonal-shaped baptistry (consecrated in 1059) are the

From the Bardini garden this Florence panorama unfolds

portals; the south portal is by Andrea Pisano, the north and east portals by Lorenzo Ghiberti. Construction of the cathedral, the fourth largest Christian church, began in 1296; the powerful dome did not follow until 1420–1434. It was built by Filippo Brunelleschi, who art historians regard as a pioneer of the Renaissance style. And no less than Giotto designed the steeple. *Baptistry, cathedral, dome, campanile and museum have varying opening times, look up the up-to-the-minute opening times at www.ilgrandemuseodelduomo.it | Piazza Duomo*

GALLERIA DEGLI UFFIZI

This vast building complex houses one of the most important art collections in the world, with masterpieces by 13th to 18th century European artists – a must for all art lovers. The museum is being extended and rearranged. Online pre-booking is advisable. *Tue–Sun 8.15am–6.50pm | Piazzale degli Uffizi | www.uffizi.com*

GUCCI MUSEO

The world famous fashion brand Gucci, which opened its doors in Florence in 1921, has its own style museum, right on the Piazza della Signoria in the Palazzo della Mercanzia. The adjoining *café (daily 9am–11pm | Budget–Moderate)* serves good and relatively inexpensive meals. *Sat–Thu 10am–8pm, Fri 10am–11pm | www.guccimuseo.com*

MUSEO NAZIONALE DEL BARGELLO

Renaissance sculptures of the finest quality, with famous works by Donatello, Michelangelo, Giambologna and many others. *Daily 8.15am–1.50pm; closed 1st, 3rd, 5th Mon and 2nd and 4th Sun in the month | Via del Proconsolo 4*

PALAZZO PITTI/GIARDINO DI BOBOLI

The enormous palace which belonged to the Pitti merchant family (15th century) and later to the Grand Dukes of Tuscany on the left bank of the Arno now accommodates a number of museums. You can relax afterwards in the Baroque park *Giardino di Boboli (daily 8.15am–dusk; closed first and last Mon of the month)*. The ticket also includes the park museums as well as the wonderful INSIDER TIP *Giardino Bardini (Tue–Sun 10am–7pm | entrance Via dei Bardi and Costa San Giorgio | www.bardinipeyron.it)* nearby. Enjoy the view of the town from the ☀ loggia of the park café!

PIAZZA DELLA SIGNORIA

This square has been the urban centre for over 700 years – the municipal authorities still meet in the Gothic *Palazzo Vecchio*. World famous sculptures adorn the square, such as Michelangelo's David (a copy; the original is in the *Galleria dell'Accademia* museum | *Tue–Sun 8.15am–6.50pm)*, the group of sculptures (also copies) by Giambologna and Cellini under the *Loggia dei Lanzi,* the *Fontana del Nettuno* by Bartolomeo Ammanati (1576), and cafés to relax.

PONTE VECCHIO ☀

Italy's most famous bridge with numerous goldsmiths' ateliers (since the 16th century) provides a connection between the royal residences of Palazzo Vecchio and Palazzo Pitti.

SAN LORENZO

The private church of the powerful Medici clan contains the family tombs, *Cappelle Medicee,* by Michelangelo in the Sacrestia Nuova. *Mon–Sat 10am–5pm, March–Oct also Sun 1.30pm–5.30pm | entrance Piazza Madonna degli Aldobrandini | www.operamedicea laurenziana.org*

SAN MARCO

At the beginning of the 15th century, a monk resided in the Dominican monastery who was also a fantastic artist: Fra Angelico. His cell frescoes and panels draw thousands of visitors. *Mon–Fri 8.15am–1.50pm, Sat/Sun 8.15am–4.50pm; closed 1st, 3rd, 5th Sun, 2nd, 4th Mon in the month | Piazza San Marco 3*

FOOD & DRINK

IL CIBREO

A real emporium of Tuscan cuisine: in the top-class restaurant *Cibreo (Expensive)*, in the rustic trattoria *Cibreino (Budget–Moderate)*, in the *Caffè. All closed Mon | Via del Verrocchio 8r/Via dei Macci 122r | tel. 05 52 34 11 00 | www.edizioniteatrodel salecibreofirenze.it*

OSTERIA PEPÒ

Comfortable trattoria near the well-stocked market hall Mercato Generale with delicious home cooking, vegetable soups and good meat. *Daily | Via Rosina 4/6r | tel. 0 55 28 32 59 | www.pepo.it | Budget*

INSIDER TIP SANTINO

A small bistro bar with excellent gourmet snacks and organic wines, ideal place for a snack and attached to the popular *Il Santo Bevitore* restaurant next door, located on the left bank of the Arno. *Closed Mon lunchtime | Via Santo Spirito 60 | tel. 05 52 30 28 20 | www.ilsantobevitore.com | Budget*

SHOPPING

The big fashion names are located in *Via Tornabuoni, Via della Vigna Nuova* and in *Borgo Ognissanti.* The clothes and leatherware market *Mercato San Lorenzo* is cheaper *(Mon–Fri 7am–2pm,* *mid Sept–mid June also Sat 7am–5pm)* around its namesake basilica. A gift tip: you can obtain rose water, violet powder etc. in the historical INSIDER TIP *Officina Profumo-Farmaceutica (Via della Scala 16 | www.smnovella.it)* at the Santa Maria Novella church. The leading *La Rinascente* department store is on the Piazza della Repubblica: a highlight is the ☙ terrace café on the roof up close to the cathedral dome. Traditional handcraftsmanship can be found in the *Oltrarno* district on the left side of the Arno.

ENTERTAINMENT

The *Piazza Santo Spirito,* the "Rive Gauche" of Florence is popular with the bohemian crowd while the bars in the *San Niccolò* district are more fashionable. On the right bank of the Arno is the *Santa Croce* district populated by students and young tourists. More glamour can be found in the bars of the elegant hotels, e.g. the *Fusion Bar* in *Gallery Art Hotel (Vicolo dell'Oro 5)*. The monthly magazine *Firenze Spettacolo (www.firenzespettacolo.it)* provides information about what is going on.

WHERE TO STAY

HOTEL AZZI – LOCANDA DEGLI ARTISTI

Small hotel with flair, near the station. *20 rooms | Via Faenza 56/88r | tel. 0 55 21 38 06 | www.hotelazzi.com | Budget–Moderate*

HOTEL BURCHIANTI

Beautifully decorated rooms in an old palazzo, nice service and central location. *11 rooms | Via del Giglio 8 | tel. 0 55 21 27 96 | www.hotelburchianti.it | Moderate–Expensive*

INFORMATION

On the station forecourt, at the airport, at Piazza San Giovanni 1 and Via Cavour 1r | tel. 0 55 29 08 32 | www.firenzeturismo.it

WHERE TO GO

AREZZO (190 C1) *(⌂ G6)*

Of Etruscan origin (pop. 100,000, 75 km/47 miles south-east of Florence), Arezzo was under Roman rule from the 3rd century BC, later becoming a medieval city republic. Today, visitors flock to see the frescoes by Piero della Francesca in the main chancel of the impressive *Basilica San Francesco (April–Oct Mon–Fri 9am–7pm, Sat 9am–6pm, Sun 1pm–6pm, Nov–March Mon–Fri 9am–6pm, Sat 9am–5.30pm, Sun 1pm–5.30pm, pre-booking tel. 05 75 35 27 27 or www.pierodellafran esca-ticketoffice.it)*, the Romanesque *Pieve di Santa Maria* on the central Corso Italia and the renowned *antiques market* on the first weekend in the month on the Piazza Grande with loggias designed by Giorgio Vasari. For an overnight stay, try the elegantly appointed *Hotel Vogue (26 rooms | Via Guido Monaco 54 | tel. 0 57 52 43 61 | www.voguehotel.it | Moderate–Expensive)* in the centre.

CASENTINO (190 C1) *(⌂ G5)*

In the north of Arezzo, hidden away in the mountain world of Casentino are some lovely *monasteries,* such as the one belonging to the Camaldolese in *Camaldoli,* still inhabited by monks today and the 13th century *La Verna* or the *Benedictine abbey Vallombrosa.* Spend the night like a king at the **INSIDER TIP** *Castello di Valenzano (9 rooms | Valenzano 97 district | tel. 05 75 48 72 94 | www.castello divalenzano.it | Budget)* in *Subbiano.* In the east of Arezzo, you come to the village of *Monterchi* with the famous fresco "Madonna del Parto" by Piero della Francesca.

Catching the last evening sun at the Piazza Grande in Arezzo

VAL DI CHIANA (190 C2) (*M G6*)

The Chiana Valley runs across the south of Arezzo, the breeding grounds of the white Chianina cattle used for Italy's *bistecca alla fiorentina*. Medieval fortress towns sit perched on the edge of the hills overlooking this plain, a prime example being picturesque ✂ *Cortona,* once an important Etruscan settlement. In *Chiusi,* the *Museo Archeologico* (daily 9am–8pm) is well worth a visit. The proprietor of *La Zaira (closed Mon | Via Arunte 12 | tel. 0 57 82 02 60 | www.zaira.it | Moderate)* is also happy to show guests round the wine cellar in the ancient Etruscan vaults.

CHIANTI (190 B1–2) (*M F5–6*)

South of Florence, this – for connoisseurs – legendary highland area rich in forests and vineyards extends down to Siena, encompassing pretty villages such as *Greve* with its arcade-lined piazza (● *farmer's market* on Saturday with lots of organic products). From the garden of the B & B ✂ *Ancora del Chianti (8 rooms | Via Collegalle 12 | tel. 0 55 85 40 44 | www.ancoradelchianti.it | Budget)* in an enchanting farmhouse, you have a wonderful view of the landscape. Castle-like vineyards dominate the hilltops, in which the vintners press the red Chianti. Many of the vineyards also offer accommodation, e.g. in *Castello di San Polo (9 apartments, 7 holiday homes | tel. 05 77 74 60 45 | www.san-polo.de | Moderate)* in *Gaiole in Chianti.*

LUCCA ★ (190 A1) (*M E5*)

Lucca (pop. 91,000) deserves its epithet "Italy's largest open air museum". Its 16th century fortified walls encircle the old town, which is brimming with treasures, such as the *San Martino* cathedral (6th/13th century) containing the enchanting marble tomb of Ilaria del Carretto by Jacopo della Quercia (1408), or the oval

Vineyard near Gaiole: many of the vineyards in Chianti are understandably called castello

Piazza del Mercato with the medieval houses lining a Roman amphitheatre. Standing in the shade of the trees on 🌿 *Torre Guinigi,* you can look across to *Garfagnana,* a beautiful place for day trips and walks in the north of Lucca. One highlight: the INSIDER TIP camellia blossoms in spring in the gardens of the old villas.

MEDICI VILLAS (188 B1) (*F5*)

There are some magnificent Medici villas between Florence and Pistoia, including the *Villa Medicea La Ferdinanda* in Artimino in Carmignano and the *Villa Medicea Ambra* in Poggio a Caiano. *Visiting times vary; enquire with the tourist office in Florence*

PISTOIA (188 B6) (*F5*)

Stop off in Pistoia (pop. 90,000), Italy's capital of culture in 2017, on the way to Lucca). In the bustling old town, you can visit the *cathedral* and the *Chiesa*

Sant'Andrea, two of Tuscany's most impressive Romanesque Gothic buildings. Inviting restaurants and shops line the *Piazza degli Ortaggi* and the *Piazza della Scala*. A further highlight is the *Marino Marini museum* in the monastery *(April–Sept Tue–Sat 10am–6pm, Sun 2.30pm–7.30pm, Oct–March Tue–Sat 10am–5pm, Sun 2.30pm–7.30pm | Corso Silvano Fedi 30 | www.fondazionemarinomarini.it).* A native Pistoian, Marini was a leading 20th century sculptor and the museum exhibits both his modern work and pieces inspired by antiquity.

THE MARCHE

Many popular seaside resorts cluster along this predominantly flat coast, which has been heavily developd by the beach tourism industry.

Further inland, many of the ancient towns, villages and abbeys – with their more tranquil and simple way of life – offer excellent panoramic views of the hill landscape down to the sea.

ADRIATIC RESORTS
(191 D–E 1–2) (*H5–6*)

The lively *Gabicce Mare* is one of the most popular resorts in the Marche (boasting the largest number of discos), *Senigallia* with a most impressive marketplace as well as highly acclaimed seafood restaurants or down in the south *San Benedetto del Tronto* with marina and palm-fringed promenade. Many places have two distinct sections: a little medieval town on the hilltop and a modern beach district, e.g. *Civitanova Marche, Cupra Marittima* and *Grottammare.*
A venerable little harbour town directly by the sea is *Fano,* which has a picturesque old town, Roman architecture, a fortress

and palazzi. From here, the route continues to *Cartoceto,* 18 km/11 miles inland, famous for its excellent olive oil and for one of the best restaurants in Italy (with seven guest rooms): *Symposium | daily | Via Mombaroccese | tel. 0721 89 83 20 | www.symposium4stagioni.it | Expensive*

ANCONA (191 E1) (*ⓂⓂ H6*)

The most important seaport (pop. 106,000) in the centre of the Adriatic is the capital of the Marche and an important port for the ferries travelling to Greece. The harbour (which still has an impressive Napoleonic military hospital) and the centre of the town offer some beautiful squares with churches and palazzi and the shopping mile *Corso Mazzini.* In AD 115 the *Arco di Traiano* was built at the farthest point of the harbour in honour of Emperor Trajan. Rising in the background is ☆ *Monte Guasco,* with the town's landmark, the magnificent Romanesque Gothic *San Ciriaco* cathedral.

ASCOLI PICENO ★ (191 E2–3) (*ⓂⓂ H6*)

This picturesque little town (pop. 56,000), encircled by rivers, is set against the mighty mountain backdrop of Monti Sibillini, today a national park and popular hiking destination south of the Marche.

Spanning one of the rivers is the beautifully preserved Roman *Ponte di Solestà.* Sit in the venerable *Caffè Meletti* on the ● *Piazza del Popolo* – with its mirror-smooth travertine flagstones, surrounded by Renaissance façades – and admire the lovely Gothic *San Francesco* church. The *Palazzo Comunale (daily 10am–7pm)* has an art gallery that is well worth a visit.

CINGOLI AND FABRIANO (191 D2) (*ⓂⓂ H6*)

Owing to its epithet "Balcony of the Marche", the ancient little town of *Cingoli* (pop. 10,000) deserves a mention. Indeed, it is true that the loveliest view of the undulating landscape is from the ☆ *Belvedere* behind the San Francesco church. The charming *Fabriano* (pop. 30,000) is famous for the production of high-quality paper; you can admire it (and also make it yourself if you wish) in the *Museo della Carta (June–Oct Tue–Sun 10am–1pm and 2.30pm–7.30pm, Nov–March 9am–1pm and 2.30pm–6.30pm, April/May 9.30am–1.30pm and 2.30pm–6.30pm | Largo Spacca | www.museodellacarta.com),* and buy it in *Bartolini (Via Largo Bartolo di Sassoferrato 7).* Stylish accom-

BORGHI BELLI – BEAUTIFUL VILLAGES

The *Borghi più belli d'Italia (www.borghitalia.it/?lang=en)* is an association that has set itself the task of identifying the most picturesque villages in Italy, and its search has been particularly successful in central Italy. The list includes, for example, *Barga,* the little old town in the Garfagnana woods, the peaceful spa village of *San Casciano* dei Bagni in the south of Tuscany; in the Marche the intact castle village of ☆ *Gradara* with its wonderful panorama and *Offida* with its magical torchlight procession during the carnival; in Umbria *Vallo di Nera*, where you can try fresh trout from the Nera River, and on the other side of the Tiber Valley *Lugnano* in Teverina nestled amongst the olive groves.

modation is available in the manor house of an estate in the nearby village *Moscano: Le Gocce di Camarzano (6 rooms| tel. 3 36 64 90 28 | www.goccedicamarzano.com | Budget)*.

the Marche, the ideal accompaniment to *brodetto,* the local fish soup. The sightseeing programme offers the Renaissance palace *Palazzo della Signoria* and the pictures of the leading

An aperitif-inviting square: the atmospheric Piazza del Popolo in Fermo

FERMO (191 E2) (*⑪ H6*)

Only 7 km/4 miles away from the coast, the town (pop. 38,000) offers a spacious piazza, stately palazzi, an impressive cathedral, prized churches, and above all the INSIDER TIP *piscine romane*, Roman pools built to conserve and purify the town's water. After wandering around the 30 subterranean basins, you can enjoy a good glass of wine with a selection of excellent pecorino cheeses from the Marche on the central *Piazza del Popolo* in the *Enoteca Bar a Vino (closed Tue lunchtime and Mon | tel. 07 34 22 80 67 | Budget–Moderate)*.

JESI (191 D1) (*⑪ H6*)

This is where the Verdicchio grape grows, the dry, slightly bitter white wine from

Marche painter Lorenzo Lotto (16th century) in *Palazzo Pinetti*. The fantastic ☇ dripstone caves *Grotte di Frasassi* further inland are absolutely spectacular.

LORETO (191 E1) (*⑪ H6*)

The imposing Gothic church *Santuario della Santa Casa* in this fortified medieval hill town (pop. 11,000) is one of Italy's most important pilgrimage sites, as is clear from the rich collection of votive pictures and objects. It was here in 1295 that angels are said to have carried the house of Mary of Nazareth. That is why the Madonna di Loreto is the patron saint of pilots. Over the centuries, leading artists have contributed to the church and its interior.

Impressive Adriatic: Monte Conero's steep cliffs in Sirolo

place in a Neoclassical *pallone (ball game) arena* built in 1829. To the north of Macerata are the ruins of a massive *amphitheatre,* the remains of the old Roman settlement *Helvetica Ricina.* In the countryside towards the south, you can visit the impressive Romanesque church *San Claudio al Chienti* as well as the Cistercian abbey *Chiaravalle di Fiastra.*

PESARO (191 D1) *(ᗰ H5)*
Second largest centre of the Marche (pop. 90,000) offering both urban and beach life. Pesaro is the birth place of the opera composer Gioacchino Rossini with a museum in the house he was born in and a renowned Rossini summer festival.

INSIDER TIP ▶ RIVIERA DEL CONERO (191 E1) *(ᗰ H6)*
To the south of Ancona, the Apennines push out into the sea; the 572 m/1877 ft, green, maquis-covered *Monte Conero* crowns the headland with its steep cliffs and wonderful bays, some only accessible by boat. Exclusive hotels, charming little country resorts, a golf course, sailing, surfing and scuba diving facilities, good restaurants and ecological awareness combine to create a first-rate coastal region *(www.rivieradelconero.info).* The European eco label has been awarded to the ⓢ *Country House Acanto* in *Sirolo (9 rooms | Via Ancarano 18 | tel. 07 19 33 11 95 | www.acantocountryhouse.it | Budget–Moderate).*

MACERATA (191 E2) *(ᗰ H6)*
Every year, fans of melodrama flock to this town (pop. 44,000) with its southern flair and impressive and largely intact Renaissance centre for the renowned Macerata opera festival *(mid July–mid Aug | www.sferisterio.it).* It takes

URBINO ★ ☀ (191 D1) *(ᗰ G5)*
The most beautiful view of the exceptional urban masterpiece, Urbino (pop. 16,000), is from the west, from the garden of *Fortezza Albornoz* fortress. During the rule of the Renaissance Duke Federigo da Montefeltro, artists of the calibre of Raphael ("The Mute") and

Piero della Francesca ("The Flagellation of Christ") worked here – and you can admire their oeuvre in the *Galleria Nazionale delle Marche* in *Palazzo Ducale (Mon 8.30am–2pm, Tue–Sun 8.30am–7.15pm)*. The ducal palace houses the dukes' study completely decorated with precious inlay work. Urbino is now a lively student town.

PERUGIA

(190 C2) (*ⁿ* G6) **Umbria's capital (pop. 164,000) the green heart of Italy has managed to protect its urban medieval and Renaissance layout, yet still remain vibrant.**

Perugia was one of the first towns in Italy to pedestrianise the centre in order to stop the escalating volume of traffic. Escalators and lifts provide a connection to the car parks below the town. There is a great deal of activity around the squares, narrow alleys leading to palazzi, churches and businesses, all bustling with students. The prestigious university for foreigners, Università per gli Stranieri, offers regional and cultural studies as well as Italian courses.

FOR BOOKWORMS AND FILM BUFFS

Detective stories – A whole series of Italian detective novelists open up trails for you in Italy. Valerio Varesi and cult author Carlo Lucarelli investigate in the northern region of Emilia-Romagna. With the crime novels by Marco Vichi and Nino Filastro, you learn about Tuscany and Florence, with Giannico Carofiglio you chase round Bari and Apulia, and then cross the sea to Sicily with Andrea Camilleri and Leonardo Sciascia.

Two Greedy Italians – Antonio Carluccio and Gennaro Contaldo left Italy to live in Britain over 30 years ago, where they became leading authorities on Italian cuisine. In this fascinating book, they return to their native land "to reveal Italian food, as cooked by real Italians".

A Room with a View – The beautiful screen adaptation of E.M. Forster's novel with Helena Bonham Carter, Denholm Elliott and Maggie Smith is a classic and a must-see for romantic couples on their way to Florence.

My Brilliant Friend – The four-volume work known as the Neapolitan Novels by Elena Ferrante is an international best-seller which rightly attracted a great deal of hype on its release. It vividly tells the story of a life-long friendship between two girls growing up in a poor district of Naples during the 1950s.

La Grande Bellezza – This Oscar-nominated homage to Federico Fellini is a 2013 art drama film directed by Paolo Sorrentino depicting a fictive journey through Rome and portraying the decadence of Italy's high society.

Passione – This vivid documentary by John Turturro chronicles the rich Neapolitan musical heritage; a cinematic feast for the eyes and ears.

SIGHTSEEING

CORSO VANNUCCI

The main artery through the centre, a car-free boulevard, strings together some of the town's highlights: the imposing Gothic church of *San Lorenzo* with its beautiful choir stalls and staircase, in front of which is the famous *Fontana Maggiore* fountain by the master craftsmen Giovanni and Nicola Pisano (13th century), and finally the formidable *Palazzo dei Priori,* a magnificent palace from the Italian Gothic period, adorned with Renaissance frescoes from Perugino (Pietro Vannucci), Raphael's teacher. It houses a fabulous collection of paintings *Galleria Nazionale dell'Umbria (Tue–Sun 8.30am–7.30pm, April–Sept also Mon 9.30am–7.30pm).*

ROCCA PAOLINA

The escalators take you down into the picturesque underground labyrinth of alleyways beneath a fortress. *Freely accessible | Piazza Italia/Corso Vannucci*

SAN PIETRO

In the southern part of the town, through the beautiful Renaissance town gate of San Pietro, is the monastery complex from the 9th–10th century with an abbey, cloister and appealing kitchen. *Borgo XX Giugno*

SANT'ANGELO

In the north of the old town, this early 5th century Christian temple stands aloft on a green field. Inside, 16 Roman columns dominate the space. *Porta Sant'Angelo*

FOOD & DRINK

LA BOTTEGA DEL VINO

Good atmosphere and good wine, tasty little dishes and occasional jazz evenings; a great place to meet for an aperitif. *Closed Sun | Via del Sole 1 | tel. 07 55 71 61 81 | www. labottegadelvino.net | Budget*

The Sala dei Notari in Perugias Palazzo dei Priori is embellished with frescoes

LA LUMERA

On the northern edge of the old town, Umbrian Slow Food cuisine with a lot of vegetables and good meat. *Closed Mon | Corso Bersaglieri 22 | tel. 07 55 72 61 81 | www.lalumera.it | Budget–Moderate*

WHERE TO STAY

INSIDER TIP **ETRUSCAN CHOCOHOTEL**

A fitting hotel for this city of Etruscans and chocolate, modern and friendly with a fantastic chocolate shop. *94 rooms | Via Campo di Marte 134 | tel. 07 55 83 73 14 | www.chocohotel.it | Moderate*

B & B LE NAIADI

In the old town, a fresh cheerful atmosphere inside historic walls; well-kept and friendly. *3 rooms | Via Bonazzi 17 | tel. 33 37 41 74 08 | www.beblenaiadi.it | Budget*

INFORMATION

Piazza Matteotti 18 | Loggia dei Lanari | tel. 07 55 73 64 58 | turismo.comune perugia.it

WHERE TO GO

ASSISI (191 D2) *(₥ G6)*

In 1228, two years after the death of the charismatic founder of the order St Francis of Assisi, work started on the large twin church ★ ● *Basilica di San Francesco (www.sanfrancescoassisi.org)*, which is absolutely bursting with magnificent frescoes by some of the best artists: by Simone Martini, Cimabue and his students, especially Giotto, who painted the life story of St Francis on the lower walls of the *Chiesa Superiore (daily 8.30am–6pm, April–Oct until 6.50pm)*. No less richly decorated is the *Chiesa Inferiore (daily 6am–6pm, April–Oct until 6.50pm)*, the lower church with the crypt. Assisi (pop. 27,000) with its churches and cloisters has long been a must for art connoisseurs and the disciples of St Francis. On your visit, do the one hour walk up to the *Eremo delle Carceri* on Monte Subasio. In this scenic location 10 km/6 miles to the east, nestled in green hills behind ancient walls is the beautiful country hotel *Le Silve (21 rooms | Armenzano | tel. 07 58 01 90 00 | www.lesilve.it | Moderate–Expensive)* with swimming pool and restaurant.

Santa Maria degli Angeli (daily 6.15am–12.40pm and 2.30pm–7.20pm) in the west of Assisi is a richly decorated, 16th century basilica; it includes the *Porziuncola* chapel in which Francis of Assisi founded the order, as well as the *Cappella del Transito,* in which the saint later died.

Further opportunities to view impressive frescoes in Umbria can be found on the way from Assisi to Spoleto in the little town of *Spello* with work by Pinturicchio in the Romanesque church *Santa Maria Maggiore* as well as in the lofty ⬆ *Montefalco* with the frescoes by Benozzo Gozzoli in the *Chiesa Museo di San Francesco (April/May and Sept/Oct daily 10.30am–6pm, June/Aug 10.30am–7pm, Nov–March Wed–Sun 10.30am–1pm and 2.30pm–5pm | www.museodimontefalco. it)*, which like those of Giotto in Assisi, also focus on the life of St Francis.

INSIDER TIP **CITTÀ DI CASTELLO**

(190 C1) *(₥ G6)*

In the town on the Tiber (pop. 15,000), it is also possible to get to know the work of one of the most important contemporary artists in Italy: Alberto Burri's material pictures, paintings and sculptures in two permanent exhibitions in the centre in *Palazzo Albizzini (June–Sept Tue–Fri 10am–1pm and 2.30pm–6.30pm, Sat/Sun 10.30am–1pm and 3pm–6.30pm, Oct–May Tue–Fri 9am–12.30pm and 2.30pm–6pm, Sat/Sun 10am–1pm and 3pm–6pm | www.*

fondazioneburri.org) and on the edge of the town in the former tobacco drying plant *Ex Seccatoio Tabacchi (same times)*. The *Pinacoteca* is also worth a visit *(April–Oct Tue–Sun 10am–1pm and 2.30pm–6.30pm, Nov March 10am–1pm and 3pm–6pm)* in *Palazzo Vitelli* as well as the beautiful woven fabrics in the workshop store *Tela Umbra (Tue–Sat 9am–1pm and 3.30pm–7.30pm | Via Sant'Antonio 3)*.

In *Montone,* 20 km/12.5 miles out in the middle of the countryside, the dream retreat *Torre di Moravola (7 suites | tel. 0759 46 09 65 | www.moravola.com | Expensive)* in a renovated medieval watchtower is a very successful example of how old and new can be brought together in design.

LOW BUDGET

DERUTA (190 C2) *(ﾑ G6)*
Ceramics, ceramics and more ceramics, and that since 1290: there is one workshop, one factory after another! A *ceramic museum (April–June Wed–Sun 10.30am–1pm and 3pm–6pm, July–Sept 10am–1pm and 3pm–6pm, March and Oct 10.30am–1pm and 2.30pm–5pm, Nov–Feb 10.30am–1pm and 2.30pm–4.30pm)* with a splendid majolica collection is in the *Palazzo Comunale.*

GUBBIO ☆ (191 D2) *(ﾑ G6)*
This enchanting town (pop. 32,000) ascends in broad storeys up the slope of Monte Ingino and overlooks a fertile plain. Founded in pre-Roman times, it was rebuilt during the Middle Ages in hard limestone, thus explaining its excellent condition. In the *Palazzo dei Consoli (core time daily 10am–1pm and 3pm–5.30pm),* built by the confident citizens of Gubbio in the 14th century, a museum houses the Eugubinian tablets, seven bronze plates with Latin and Etruscan texts recording the ancient Umbrian language. There is also an imposing ducal palace (with renowned exhibitions of contemporary art), churches, palazzi, a Roman theatre and a large loggia complex: all good reasons to stay overnight, for example in the well-established *Grotta dell'Angelo (18 rooms | Via Gioia 47 | tel. 0759 2717 47 | www.grottadellangelo.it | Budget)* with a pleasant restaurant.

NORCIA (191 D3) *(ﾑ H7)*
St Benedict came from this picturesque little town (pop. 5000), founder of the

fraternities of Norcia. The beautiful Piazza San Benedetto and the Gothic church that was almost completely destroyed in the heavy earthquake in October 2016 were both named after him. The Norcini are famous for their skill in breeding pigs and for producing ham and salami. In the autumn they supplement their cuisine with black truffles, which they serve with the famous Castelluccio lentils from the nearby Monti Sibillini. They are tastefully prepared in the *Locanda de' Senari (6 rooms | Via della Bufera | Castelluccio | tel. 07 43 82 12 05 | www.agriturismosenari. it | Budget)*, one of the many local *agriturismo* establishments.

ORVIETO (190 C3) (*M G7*)

Set on a plateau of a tuff rock rising up from the Praglia Valley, this old town (pop. 21,000) is clearly visible from a distance. The Etruscans established a rich centre here 2500 years ago. In the rock cliffs below the town an intricate labyrinth of tunnels opens up forming an exciting **INSIDER TIP** underworld *(guided descent several times daily | meeting point Piazza Duomo 23 | www.orvietounderground.it)*. Owing to a lack of space on the hilltop, Orvieto has continued its growth in the valley. This has enabled the beauty of the old town to be preserved, in particular the 14th century ★ *Duomo Santa Maria* cathedral with a façade that is an elegant mixture of French and Italian Gothic that is second to none in Italy; the interior has radiant frescoes by Luca Signorelli.

SOLOMEO (190 C2) (*M G6*)

Many bon vivants live in Umbria's valleys. One of them is Brunello Cucinelli *(www. brunellocucinelli.it)*, who manufactures elegant cashmere clothing, a shrewd businessman and, at the same time, a humanist idealist. He started his factory

in the deserted medieval village of Solomeo halfway between Perugia and Lago Trasimeno: in the wonderfully restored rooms, some of which are adorned with frescoes. You can buy the soft cash-

The Gothic façade of Orvieto's cathedral is very elegant

mere pullovers with a 40 per cent discount in the *Cuccinelli Outlet* on the Piazza Alberto Dalla Chiesa 6.

SPOLETO (191 D3) (*M G7*)

The town was a Roman settlement, seat of the Lombards and later of the papal governors. The most important sight is the *cathedral* (12th century) with Romanesque and Renaissance elements as well as frescoes. Spoleto (pop. 38,000) is famous for its renowned theatre and music festival *dei Due Mondi* in July *(www.festival dispoleto.com).* Classy accommodation directly next to the cathedral: the ancient *Palazzo Dragoni (14 rooms | Via del*

Stefano church with its crypt of mummies as well as the spectacular waterfalls *Cascate delle Marmore (www.marmore falls.it)* south of Terni. The water from

Siena's Piazza del Campo slopes down to the town hall with its narrow Torre del Mangia

Duomo 13 | tel. 07 43 22 22 20 | www.pa lazzodragoni.it | Moderate). It is well worth making a trip to ⚜️ *Monteluco* for the breathtaking panoramic view of Umbria.

TODI (190 C3) *(📖 G7)*
This medieval town (pop. 17,000) overlooks the wonderfully winding Tiber. A broad, much photographed staircase leads to the piazza – widely regarded as one of Italy's particularly stunning squares.

VALNERINA (191 D3) *(📖 G7)*
Experience Umbrian nature at its best in the wild, secluded Nera Valley, where you will discover the solitary old abbey *San Pietro in Valle,* now a charming hotel, and *Ferentillo* with its castle ruins and Santo

Velino, dammed further up the valley in order to produce energy, is released several times a day for the waterfall (only on Sundays in the winter).

SIENA

(190 B2) *(📖 F6)* This town (pop. 54,000) is a medieval jewel, its golden age lasted until the 16th century, clearly evident from the palazzi, churches and art collections.

An unswervingly confident focus on conservation has since been an integral part of Siena's lifestyle, thus ensuring that the town has remained intact. For a more detailed description refer to the MARCO POLO "Tuscany" guide.

SIGHTSEEING

DUOMO SANTA MARIA DELL'ASSUNTA

This magnificent example of Italian Gothic architecture was started in the mid 12th century and displays skilful marble inlay work, graffito technique on the floor, as well as many masterpieces by painters and sculptors. Pinturicchio painted the frescoes in the famous, early Renaissance cathedral library *Libreria Piccolomini (Duomo and Libreria March–Oct Mon–Sat 10.30am–7.30pm, Sun 1.30pm–6pm, Nov–Feb Mon–Sat 10.30am–5.30pm, Sun 1.30pm–5.30pm | www.operaduomo.siena.it).* The Gothic baptistry *San Giovanni* has a hexagonal-shaped baptismal font with bas-reliefs by Donatello, Ghiberti and Jacopo della Quercia (1427–1430). Next to the cathedral is the ancient *Spital Santa Maria della Scala (Mon and Wed–Fri 10.30am–4.30pm, Sat/Sun 10.30am–6.30pm | www.santamariadellascala.com)* with its vividly painted scenes in the pilgrim hall, old prayer chapels and the new and interesting Etruscan collection. *Piazza del Duomo*

MUSEO CIVICO

Highlights of the exhibition in the Palazzo Pubblico include the Sala del Mappamondo with frescoes by Simone Martini as well as Sala della Pace with frescoes by Ambrogio Lorenzetti depicting the "Effects of Good Government on Town and Country". *Daily 10am–6pm, in summer until 7pm | Piazza del Campo*

MUSEO DELL'OPERA METROPOLITANA

Exhibits include masterpieces by Giovanni Pisano, Ambrogio Lorenzetti and Jacopo della Quercia; the main attraction is the altarpiece panel "Maestà" by Duccio di Buoninsegna. *March–Oct Mon–Sat 10.30am–7pm, Sun 1.30pm–6pm, Nov–Feb Mon–Sat 10.30am–5.30pm, Sun 1.30pm–5.30pm | Piazza del Duomo*

PIAZZA DEL CAMPO ★

Many people regard the Piazza del Campo as one of the most beautiful squares in the world. It lies at the intersection of the town's three hills, on which a sea of ochre-coloured houses is sprread out. The town hall, *Palazzo Pubblico,* from the 13th/14th century is on the straight side of the square. Its ⁂ *Torre del Mangia (daily 10am–4pm, March–mid Oct until 7pm)* affords a magnificent view over the town. On 2 July and 16 August, the Piazza del Campo provides the stages for the famous Palio, a hair-raising horse race between Siena's different districts.

PINACOTECA NAZIONALE

One of Tuscany's most important galleries is in the Gothic Palazzo Buonsignori. *Sun, Mon 9am–1pm, Tue–Sat 8.15am–7.15pm | Via San Pietro 29 | pinacotecanazionale.siena.it*

FOOD & DRINK

COMPAGNIA DEI VINATTIERI

Fantastic wine cellar, which also serves hungry guests fine Tuscan specialities, occasional live jazz, and a good atmosphere. *Daily | Via delle Terme 79 | tel. 05 77 23 65 68 | www.vinattieri.net | Moderate*

WHERE TO STAY

BERNINI

A simple and affordable hotel, very centrally located in the old town: yes, something like that is available even in touristy Siena. With ⁂ terrace. *10 rooms | Via della Sapienza 15 | tel. 05 77 28 90 47 | www.albergobernini.com | Budget*

PALAZZO FANI MIGNANELLI

In the old town, pretty rooms of various sizes in an old palazzo. *11 rooms |*

Via Banchi di Sopra 15 | tel. 05 77 28 35 66 | www.residenzadepoca.it | Budget–Expensive

Piazza Duomo 1 | tel. 05 77 28 05 51 | www.terresiena.it

WHERE TO GO

LE CRETE AND THE SOUTH
(190 B2) *(ω F–G6)*

Ash-grey hills of clay soil, slopes suddenly torn by deep ravines, ridges dramatically furrowed by erosion – it is with this landscape, called the *Crete,* that the region south-east of Siena begins its journey to the Benedictine abbey *Monte Oliveto Maggiore.* Further south, on a hill, is the medieval *Montalcino,* home of the excellent wine Brunello di Montalcino. You can choose from a selection of this wine at the lovely *Caffè Fiaschetteria Italiana* on the *Piazza del Popolo.* 10 km/6 miles to the south, the monks still sing Gregorian masses in the atmospheric surroundings of the *Sant'Antimo* abbey dating from the Carolingian period.

Travelling east, the route takes you to the enchanting little Renaissance town of *Pienza,* which is also full of atmosphere in the evening. The eight stylish rooms of the hotel *Arca di Pienza (Via San Gregorio 19 | tel. 05 78 74 94 26 | www.arcadipienza.it | Budget)* offer a hospitable welcome. Nearby, on a solitary clay mountain, is the fortified *Monticchiello,* the annual stage for **INSIDER TIP** one of Italy's most interesting theatre events: at the end of July or beginning of August the villagers enact a play they write themselves *(www.teatropovero.it).*

Montepulciano (pop. 14,000), place of origin of the Vino Nobile di Montepulciano and the venue of interesting cultural events, presents a wonderful setting with its steep, narrow streets and a beautifully arranged square with medieval palaces. Resplendent at the foot of the hill is the 16th century pilgrimage church *Madonna di San Biagio.* With so many good trattorias, it is difficult to decide where to go. One tip is the cosy and popular *Osteria Acquacheta (closed Tue | Via del Teatro 22 | tel. 05 78 71 70 86 | www.acquacheta.eu | Budget–Moderate)* with

ART GARDENS IN TUSCANY

Tuscany's glorious landscape seems to inspire the aesthetic senses of artists and art connoisseurs. The artist Niki de Saint Phalle is a case in point with her sculpture garden *Giardino dei Tarocchi* in Maremma. This also applies to the Swiss artist Daniel Spoerri and many of his colleagues for whom the South Tuscan countryside provides the ideal setting for their works, which can be viewed in

Giardino di Daniel Spoerri in Seggiano *(Easter–June Tue–Sun, July–mid Sept daily 11am–8pm, mid Sept–Oct Tue–sun 11am–7pm, Nov–Easter by appointment | www.danielspoerri.org).* How well contemporary art fits in this arcadia is also visible in *Parco delle Sculture del Chianti (Easter–Oct daily 10am–sunset, Nov–March by appointment | www.chiantisculpturepark.it)* in Pievasciata near Castellina in Chianti.

The pilgrimage church Madonna di San Biagio in the hills of Montepulciano

tasty soups, succulent meat and, naturally, excellent wine.

MASSA MARITTIMA (190 B2) (*M F6*)

The town (pop. 10,000) on a hill belonging to the metalliferous Colline Metallifere is famous for its beautiful Romanesque Gothic *Cattedrale di San Cerbone.* Mining for ore, silver and copper has been the basis of the town's livelihood since the Middle Ages. The *Museo della Miniera (guided tours April–Oct Tue–Sun 10am–1pm and 3pm–6pm, Nov–March 10am–noon and 3pm–4.30pm | Via Corridoni)* in a former mine provides information on this subject.

MONTE AMIATA (190 B2) (*M F6*)

The two crests of the densely forested volcano, which is 1738 m/5702 ft high, dominate the landscape in the south of Tuscany and are a popular hiking area. Old villages and castles such as Arcidosso, Santa Fiora, Castell'Azzara, Piancastagnaio and Abbadia San Salvatore are dotted around the summits.

SAN GALGANO (190 B1) (*M F6*)

The romantic ruins of this 13th century Cistercian abbey, one of the first examples of Gothic sacral architecture in Tuscany, provide the spectacular stage for concerts during the summer. A small Romanesque church, with beautiful interior masonry and frescoes by Ambrogio Lorenzetti, forms part of the complex.

SAN GIMIGNANO ★ (190 B1) (*M F6*)

Today, just 15 of the once 72 medieval towers remain and keep lookout over the little town (pop. 8000) – and you can visit *La Torre Grossa,* the highest tower. Apart from enjoying the atmosphere in the pretty squares and alleys, you should also visit the *cathedral* and the *Sant'Agostino* abbey church with frescoes by the famous Benozzo Gozzoli (15th century). It is best to find a place to stay in the gorgeous surrounding countryside, e.g. 15 km/9 miles to the north-west in *Montaione* one of almost 100 holiday flats in twelve former farmhouses on the wine-growing estate *Castellare di Tonda*

Resort & Spa (Via Cerroni | tel. 05 71 69 77 06 | www.castellareditonda. com | *Moderate–Expensive*), where you can also book cooking classes.

VOLTERRA (190 D1–2) (*∅ F0*)

The town (pop. 11,000) preserves rich traces of the great cultural eras of the past 3000 years – seen for instance in the remains of the city walls and the *Arco Etrusco* – and has one of the best museums in Italy about Etruscan culture, *Museo Guarnacci (mid March–Oct daily 9am–7pm, Nov–mid March 10am–4.30pm)*. The archaeological sites also include an ancient Roman theatre. Medieval streets and buildings still lend the town a distinctive character. Turning and polishing alabaster is a traditional craft in Volterra, and there are plenty of shops and ateliers for you to browse round.

TUSCAN COAST

ETRUSCAN RIVIERA
(190 A1–2) (*∅ E6*)

The Etruscan Riviera begins in the south of Livorno, taking its name from the many former settlements found there. A highlight is ⚜ *Populonia*, which has an Etruscan necropolis overlooking the **INSIDER TIP** Golfo di Baratti. Camping sites are dotted along the coast in the shade of the pines. In between you will discover coastal towns, such as the elegant *Castiglioncello*. Towards Vada, the cliff beaches of Catiglioncello join up with the light sandy beaches **INSIDER TIP** *spiagge bianche* of *Rosignano Solvay*.

LIVORNO (190 A1) (*∅ E5*)

If you wish to get away from the tourist hotspots and enjoy the hustle and bustle of harbour life, you should visit Livorno (pop. 160,000) and enjoy the typical Livornese fish soup *cacciucco*, for example in the rustic *Osteria La Barrocciaia (closed Sun lunchtime and Mon | Piazza Cavallotti 13 | tel. 05 86 88 26 37 | Budget)* in the market square or in the small seafood restaurant *Osteria del Mare (closed Thu | Borgo dei Cappuccini 5 | tel. 05 86 88 10 27 | Moderate)* near the harbour.

MAREMMA (190 B3) (*∅ F6–7*)

Apart from the hilly hinterland of Grosseto, Maremma also boasts some lovely, transformed coastal areas, formerly malaria-infested swamps and grazing land for wild horses and cattle. The *Parco Regionale della Maremma*, a nature reserve south of Grosseto with the estuary area around the river Ombrone, the mountain range Monti dell'Uccellina and its coast, sometimes rocky, sometimes with long unspoilt sandy beaches (only accessible on foot), retains its primordial nature. Interesting excursions are available from *Alberese* in the centre of the park.

Punta Ala has become an expensive tourist resort. Looming up from the sea on the southern horizon is *Monte Argentario* (635 m/2083 ft), with pretty harbour towns such as *Porto Santo Stefano,* the fine *Port'Ercole* and the little lagoon town of *Orbetello.*

To the east of the largely modern provincial capital of *Grosseto,* you reach the tuff stone mountains of south Tuscany with their ruggedly romantic little towns built high up on rock plateaus such as ⚜ *Pitigliano, Sorano* or *Sovana* with interesting Etruscan rock tombs. The spa resort of *Saturnia* is here. You can enjoy its hot sulphurous water in the exclusive spa hotel *(Terme di Saturnia | 128 rooms | tel. 05 64 60 01 11 | www.termedisaturnia. it | Expensive)* or ● free of charge under the **INSIDER TIP** hot waterfalls, the

Cascata del Molino (3 km/1.8 miles towards Montemerano).

Near *Capalbio*, where Italy's smart set likes to meet, is the dream INSIDER TIP ▶ *Giardino dei Tarocchi (April–mid Oct daily 2.30pm–7.30pm, Nov–March 1st Sat in the month 9am–1pm | www.ilgiardinodeita rocchi.it)* with Niki de Saint Phalle's colourful and exuberant sculptures inspired by the tarot symbols.

PISA (190 A1) (*Ⅲ E5*)

Hardly any other monument in Pisa (pop. 88,000) is as famous as the *Leaning Tower (current opening times and tickets via www.opapisa.it | no children under 8)*. Its tilt started quite soon after its construction in 1173 on the shifting sands of a former estuary. It stands on the ★ ⊥⊿⊢ *Campo dei Miracoli* (Field of Miracles), as do the magnificent Romanesque *cathedral,* the *baptistry* and the *Camposanto,* a cemetery full of precious sculptures and frescoes from the town's golden age. Good food and a lively atmosphere are available in the *Osteria dei Cavalieri (closed Sat lunchtime and Sun | Via San Frediano 16 | tel. 0 50 58 08 58 | www.osteriacavalieri.pisa.it | Budget– Moderate).*

VERSILIA (188 A6) (*Ⅲ E5*)

Versilia denotes the fashionable upper region of the Tuscan coast from Liguria to Viareggio: 25 km/15.5 miles of fine sandy beaches, shady pines, holiday resorts, villas and hotels, and in the background the steep ★ ⊥⊿⊢ *Apuan Alps.* For hundreds of years, people have been quarrying enormous blocks of marble from the mountain. You can visit the marble quarries *(cave)* and workshops of *Carrara* and in the especially pretty *Pietrasanta*. Elegant bathing resorts on the Versilia coast are *Forte dei Marmi* and *Viareggio.*

The angels are not too sure either. Is the tower going to topple over or not?

ROME AND THE APENNINES

Since the completion of the motorway to L'Aquila in Abruzzo, the inhabitants of Rome have discovered new destinations: they now visit the large Abruzzo National Park and its wildlife, the rugged mountains full of attractive villages, or they go skiing on the Gran Sasso, which at 2912 m/9554 ft is the highest summit of the Apennines.

Located further south, Molise nonetheless belongs to this part of Italy, both geographically and culturally. It shares the Adriatic coast's wide beaches and coastal towns with Abruzzo. The centre includes Rome, the city swathed in history and myths, and the green melancholic Lazio: together with Rome the ancient heartland of the Roman Empire, which embraces the historic towns of Tarchna (today Tarquinia) and Caisra (today Cerveteri) home of the Etruscans, the mysterious, highly advanced civilisation that inhabited central Italy before the Romans.

L'AQUILA

(191 E3) *(ⅅ H7)* ⛷ The route to this pretty medieval university town (pop. 70,000), which leads from Rome or the Adriatic coast via Teramo, passes through an impressive mountain panorama; the imposing Gran Sasso massif looks down on L'Aquila, the capital of Abruzzo.

In 1240, Count Conrad IV of Hohenstaufen set up an outpost here against Papal Rome. In the ensuing period, the town

Bears and wolves in Abruzzo, the Adriatic and Apennines, the vibrant capital and the ancient civilisation of the Etruscans

nonetheless came under the influence of the Papal State, and this is still visible today in the many churches. The ruins of Roman theatres in *Amiternum* 9 km/5.5 miles to the north-west and the *Santa Maria ad Cryptas* church in Fossa, 10 km/6 miles to the south-east – whose precious medieval frescoes were damaged during the severe earthquake in 2009 – bear witness to the earlier settlements here and their cultural creativity.

During the earthquake, more than 300 people were killed and more than 65,000 lost their homes. The beautiful old town of L'Aquila is still secured by barriers and supports in many places. Many of the houses are vacant and have not yet been repaired. That does not mean that you should avoid the town, however. On the contrary, the Aquilans regard interested visitors as heralds of the new beginning; thankfully the ornate façades of their churches were largely spared from damage. Colourful new buildings have been constructed on the outskirts of the town.

SIGHTSEEING

FONTANA DELLE 99 CANNELLE

The "Fountain of 99 Spouts", constructed in 1272, is a huge fountain with 99 stone masks that spout water. They recount the story of L'Aquila's foundation, according to which the town originally con-

SAN BERNARDINO DI SIENA

The highlight of this richly decorated church is the beautiful Renaissance façade by Cola d'Amatrice. *Via di San Bernardino*

SANTA MARIA DI COLLEMAGGIO ⭐

This sacral building is regarded as one of the most splendid examples of Roman-

Harvesting saffron in L'Aquila is hard physical work

sisted of 99 castles, each one of which had a church, a square and a fountain. *Piazza San Vito*

MUSEO NAZIONALE D'ABRUZZO

Located in a park, the *Castello* is a powerful fortress built in the Spanish style of the 16th century. Until the severe damage it suffered during the earthquake, it housed an extensive art collection with works by Abruzzo artists spanning from the Middle Ages to the present. At the moment, the provisional museum is location in a former abattoir opposite the Fontana delle 99 Cannelle.

esque architecture in Abruzzo, due to its grandiose façade with three Romanesque Gothic rosette windows and three Romanesque portals. Whilst the façade can already be admired in its full splendour again, work in the interior was just short of completion at the time of going to press. *Piazza di Collemaggio*

FOOD & DRINK

LOCANDA AQUILANA DA LINCOSTA

This trattoria in the old town serves specialities from Abruzzo such as homemade *spaghetti alla chitarra* with ricotta and saffron. B&B rooms also available. *Closed*

Sun evening | Via Antonelli 6 | tel. 08 62 20 43 58 | dalincosta.it | Moderate

SHOPPING

An ideal souvenir is the famous soft *torrone* made of nougat and honey from *Fratelli Nurzia – Fabbrica del Torrone dal 1835 (Piazza Duomo 74 | www.torronenurzia.it).* You can also buy the highly acclaimed L'Aquila saffron called *zafferano di Navelli* from the local grocery stores.

WHERE TO STAY

LA COMPAGNIA DEL VIAGGIATORE
Well-managed modern guesthouse with good restaurant and small pool located out in the countryside 6 km/3.5 miles to the north-west. *33 rooms | Cansatessa district | SS80 | tel. 08 62 31 36 27 | www.compagniadelviaggiatore.it |* Budget

INFORMATION

Container kiosk at the car park of the rugby stadium Acquasanta in the east of the town | tel. 08 62 41 08 08 | www.abruzzoturismo.it

WHERE TO GO

ATRI (191 E3) *(🕮 J7)*
The small medieval town (pop. 11,000) on the ridge of a hill 12 km/7.5 miles from the Adriatic has a very interesting Romanesque Gothic cathedral *Santa Maria Assunta* (13th century) with prized frescoes. It is also popular for its liquorice specialities and the impressive eroded rock formations on the way to Teramo, called *calanchi, balze* or *bolge*.

BOMINACO (192 E4) *(🕮 H7)*
The sleepy hilltop village about 25 km/15.5 miles south-east of L'Aquila has two art highlights: firstly, the Biblical scenes from the 13th/14th century still in good

MARCO POLO HIGHLIGHTS

★ Santa Maria di Collemaggio in L'Aquila
Abruzzo's most beautiful Romanesque building with an impressive façade → p. 108

★ Parco Nazionale d'Abruzzo, Lazio e Molise
Wolves and walks → p. 111

★ San Clemente Abbey in Casauria
Masterful Romanesque stonework → p. 112

★ Forum Romanum
The ancient world empire was governed from here → p. 113

★ Vatican museums
One of the largest museum complexes in the world → p. 115

★ Tivoli
Roman villas of the Emperor Hadrian, theatre, temple, spas and the most beautiful park in Italy before the gates of Rome → p. 120

★ Tarquinia
Etruscan site with necropolis and museum → p. 121

★ Sistine Chapel in the Vatican
The famous depiction of the Book of Genesis by Michelangelo → p. 116

condition displayed in the frescoes that richly adorn the *San Pellegrino* church and, secondly, the *Santa Maria Assunta* built in the most beautiful Romanesque style.

CHIETI ⊠ (191 F3) (*Ⓜ J7*)

Built on the summit of a hill, the provincial town (pop. 52,000) merits a visit in particular for its historic centre and the view it affords of the Maiella massif and the sea. There is a vibrant town centre with shops and cafés on and around the *Corso Marrucino,* as well as the remains of three Roman temples, an amphitheatre, spa, a Gothic Baroque *cathedral* and Abruzzo's leading *archaeological museum (Tue–Sat 9am–8pm, Sun 2pm–8pm | Villa Frigerj | Via Villa Comunale 2)* with pre-historic and Roman exhibits, such as the famous "Warrior of Capestrano".

In nearby *Guardiagrele,* a well-stocked handicraft market in the first half of August sells wrought-iron work, copper items and jewellery *(Mostra dell'Artigianato Artistico Abruzzese | www.artigianatoa bruzzese.it)*. *Villa Maiella* is a good place to stay, and its first-rate Abruzzo cuisine is especially recommendable *(14 rooms | closed Sun evening and Mon | Via Sette Dolori 30 | tel. 08 71 80 93 19 | www.villa maiella.it | Moderate)*.

GRAN SASSO D'ITALIA
(191 E3) (*Ⓜ H–J7*)

The "great rock of Italy" includes the highest peak of the Apennines, the *Monte Corno* (2912 m/9554 ft), tunnelled through by the 10 km/6 miles long motorway from L'Aquila to Teramo. Those who want to enjoy some wonderful landscapes should opt for the ⊠ scenic route (SS 80) on the north-west side of the massif. From here, the road runs to the coast and goes past the commanding Romanesque abbeys of *San Clemente al Vomano* and *Santa Maria di Propezzano.* Extending on the south side of the Gran Sasso is the impressive landscape of the *Campo Imperatore* plateau. In *Assergi,* you will find the *Park Office (Via del Convento 1 | tel. 0 86 26 05 21 | www. gransassolagapark.it)*, which provides information about walking and skiing, flora and fauna. In the picturesque mountain village of INSIDER TIP *Santo Stefano di Sessanio,* some 29 guest rooms are available throughout the village, organised by *Sextantio (tel. 08 62 89 91 12 | www. sextantio.it | Moderate–Expensive)*, a so-called *albergo diffuso,* a new method for revitalising the old mountain villages, in rustic style, but very elegantly done – which is reflected in the prices. The six nice holiday flats in the centre of the village offer a more inexpensive alternative, *Residenza la Torre (tel. 34 75 38 74 51 | www.residen za-latorre.it | Budget)*.

The Navelli plain in the south, famous for cultivating saffron, extends between the stupendous mountains of Abruzzo – providing a magnificent backdrop for the picturesque village of *Navelli.* You can stay in the hospitable *Abruzzo Segreto* B & B *(4 rooms | Via San Girolamo 3 | tel. 08 62 95 94 47 | www.abruzzo-segreto.it | Budget)*.

MOLISE (191 F5) (*Ⓜ J8*)

Off the beaten track, a visit to the Molise, the second smallest region in Italy, takes you through pastoral landscapes, with traces of prehistoric and ancient settlements. The region's capital *Campobasso* (pop. 50,000) has an old town full of little alleyways, an imposing castle, and an INSIDER TIP enchanting procession with the local children on Corpus Christi, as well as a number of very good restaurants, e.g. *Miseria e Nobiltà (closed Sun | Via Sant'Antonio Abate 16 | tel. 0 87 49 42 68 | Budget–Moderate)*.

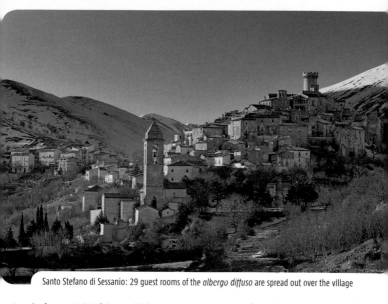

Santo Stefano di Sessanio: 29 guest rooms of the *albergo diffuso* are spread out over the village

Isernia (pop. 18,000) is world famous among palaeontologists. It was here that they found the oldest traces of early human life in Europe; the remains of hunting trophies and fireplaces are at least 730,000 years old (*Museo Paleolitico Nazionale* | *Tue–Sun 9am–7pm* | *La Pineta district*).

PARCO NAZIONALE D'ABRUZZO, LAZIO E MOLISE ⭐
(191 E4) (*ⓜ H–J 7–8*)

This approximately 232 miles² nature park is one of the most famous in Italy – thanks to its wild, unspoilt landscape and its unique wildlife, which includes wolves and the small brown bears from Abruzzo. There are 150 trails on which visitors can explore this austere landscape; four visitor centres with exhibitions and game reserves.

The focal point in the park is *Pescasseroli*, which is also a winter ski resort. In addition to the campsites and mountain chalets, you will also find hotels, e.g. *Il Bucaneve* (*15 rooms* | *Viale Colli dell'Oro* | *tel.*

08 63 91 00 98 | *www.hotelbucaneve.net* | *Budget–Moderate*). You can savour traditional Abruzzo cuisine at the *Ristorante Plistia* (*Via Principe di Napoli 28* | *closed Mon* | *tel. 08 63 91 07 32* | *www.albergo ristoranteplistia.it* | *Moderate*). Information: *Via Principe di Napoli* | *tel. 08 63 91 04 61* | *www.abruzzoturismo.it*, *www.parcoabruzzo.it*

PESCARA (191 F3) (*ⓜ J7*)

This large urban centre (pop. 121,000) on Abruzzo's flat Adriatic coast offers a contrast to the mountains: there is no old town worth mentioning, but instead shopping, beaches, innumerable hotels, beautiful beach promenades and seafood restaurants. Pescara's dried cod specialities (*baccalà*) are particularly good in *Taverna 58* (*closed Fri lunch, Sat lunch and Sun* | *Corso Manthone 46* | *tel. 0 85 69 07 24* | *www.taverna58.it* | *Budget–Moderate*); an excellent gourmet address directly on the sea is *Café les*

Take to the Tiber and see Rome from the water on a tour starting here at Ponte Sant'Angelo

Paillotes (closed Sun, Mon | Piazza Le Laudi 2 | tel. 08 56 18 09 | www.lespail lotes.it | Moderate–Expensive). Outside the town, the best beaches in the north are *Silvi Marina,* in the south *Lido Riccio* and *Lido dei Saraceni.*

SULMONA (191 E4) (*∅ J7*)

The impressive Maiella mountain range rises above this delightful little town (pop. 24,000), popular for its tradition of *confetti,* glazed almonds. In addition to the many churches, picturesque streets and squares, it is the elegant Gothic and Renaissance 15th century palace and church complex *Santissima Annunziata* that deserves special attention.

You can eat extraordinarily well in the traditional family restaurant INSIDER TIP *Taverna de Li Caldora (closed Mon lunchtime | Piazza Umberto I | tel. 0 86 44 11 39 | Moderate)* in the pretty village of ☙ *Pacentro* 8 km/5 miles to the east. A scenically impressive trip leads through the ☙ *Gola del Sagittario* gorge to the

very charming mountain village of *Scanno.* For those wishing to spend a bit longer in this magnificent setting, a good choice of accommodation is the organic farm 🌐 *Le Prata (5 rooms | Le Prata | tel. 08 64 57 83 03 | www.agriturismoleprata.it | Budget)*. On the way from Sulmona to the coast, you will see in a garden the splendid Romanesque abbey ⭐ *San Clemente in Casauria (Mon–Sat 8am–2pm | www. sanclementeacasauria.beniculturali.it)*.

TERMOLI (192 B2) (*∅ K8*)

The picturesque medieval town of Termoli (pop. 34,000) juts out into the sea on the narrow spur of the Molise. There is always a lot of activity in the fishing harbour. It is from here that the ferries depart for *Isole Tremiti,* a popular group of islands just off Apulia's Gargano promontory. The coast up towards Pescara between Vasto and Ortona is called INSIDER TIP *Costa dei Trabucchi,* taking its name from the wooden fishing structures suspended above the water, which are a ubiquitous sight here.

ROME (ROMA)

MAP INSIDE BACK COVER
(190 C4) (∭ G8) **Rome's appeal is in its unique mix of ancient past, dynamic present and a mild climate that allows much of life to be al fresco.**

In the centre of this metropolis (pop. 3 million) awe-inspiring ruins bear testimony to the city's time as the pulsating heart of the Roman Empire, while magnificent churches and palazzi from the medieval, Renaissance and Baroque periods provide equally clear evidence of its role as a centre of Christianity. Enthroned above it all is the ostentatiously monumental *Vittoriano* "altar of the fatherland", offering a breathtaking panorama from the ☀ *Terrazza delle Quadrighe*, where a glass elevator will take you.

A fresh wind is blowing through the city: museums for contemporary art (MACRO and MAXXI), first-class concerts, exhibitions and film festivals are regular features in the lively cultural scene, and besides well-established, traditional trattorias and local bars, there are sophisticated restaurants and trendy lounge bars, and in addition to the classically elegant boutiques, there are also stores of a younger style. Walk through the fashionable areas such as the serene Trastevere and vibrant Testaccio or to the elegant Piazza del Popolo. It is not that surprising to see crowds at Rome's magnificent Baroque fountain Fontana di Trevi. It is believed that anyone who throws a coin in here will return to Rome again one day. MARCO POLO's "Rome" guide provides a more detailed description of the city.

SIGHTSEEING

ARA PACIS AUGUSTAE *(U C2) (∭ d3)*
Ancient meets modern: American architect Richard Meier designed a modern cover building over this magnificent piece of sculptural art, the carved altar to peace in honour of Augustus (9 BC), also the venue for art exhibitions. *Daily 9.30am–7.30pm | Lungotevere in Augusta | www.arapacis.it*

BOAT TRIPS
Cruises through Rome on the Tiber run from April–Oct, leaving several times a day from the Sant'Angelo bridge *(U B3) (∭ c4)* and on the Tiber island *(U C–D5) (∭ d–e7)*.*www.battellidiroma.it*

FORUM ROMANUM ★
(U E4–5) (∭ f–g 6–8)
The Roman Empire was once governed from here. Today, it is an impressive park of ruins: the remains of once magnificent residences on the Palatine, of temples, markets and triumphal arches. Each emperor built his own forum. *Daily 8.30am– 1 hour before sunset | entrances Via San Gregorio and Largo della Salaria Vecchia | archeoroma.beniculturali.it*

WHERE TO START?
Piazza del Popolo **(U C–D1)** *(∭ e2)*: From here, it is possible to explore the centre on foot (Metro A, Flaminio). You can work your way south along the Via del Corso. If you decide to take the car to Rome, you should look for a guarded car park near your hotel accommodation: *www.myparking.eu/parcheggio_ roma.php*. From the main station, Stazione Termini, there are connections with the underground Metro A and Metro B as well as numerous city buses *(ticket 1.50 euros, single day ticket 7 euros)*.

CAPITOLINE MUSEUMS
(MUSEI CAPITOLINI) (U D4) (🚇 f6)

In addition to the Roman copies of Greek and Hellenic statues, the palaces on the wonderful Campidoglio Square also exhibit the legendary Capitoline she-wolf from 6 BC. Fascinating: the exhibition of ancient sculptures from the Capitoline museums INSIDER TIP in the dramatic setting of a disused power station (*Centrale Montemartini | Tue–Sun 9am–7pm (O) (🚇 0) | Via Ostiense 106 | www.centralemontemartini.org). Daily 9.30am–7.30pm | Piazza del Campidoglio | www.museicapitolini.org*

CHURCHES ●

Among the many outstanding churches that are to be found in Rome, the capital of Christianity, are the four patriarchal basilicas: *San Giovanni in Laterano ((O) (🚇 j8) | Piazza San Giovanni),* the oldest early Christian papal cathedral (4th century) and Catholic mother church, richly decorated with marble, gold and statues, then of course the largest Christian church there is: *St Peter's Basilica ((U A3) (🚇 a4) | Piazza San Pietro)* built over the grave of St Peter; the third is *San Paolo fuori le Mura ((O) (🚇 0) | Via Ostiense)* built over the burial place of St Paul; its splendid interior is subdivided into five naves and also includes a particularly beautiful cloister; the fourth is dedicated to the Virgin Mary: *Santa Maria Maggiore ((U F4) (🚇 h5) | Piazza Santa Maria Maggiore)* is also of early Christian origin, and is famous for its fantastic apse mosaic.

COLOSSEUM (COLOSSEO)
(U E–F5) (🚇 g7)

This gigantic amphitheatre could hold about 70,000 people. At its inauguration in AD 80, Emperor Titus ordered 100 days of non-stop, bloodthirsty games. An extensive restoration was finished in 2016, financed by the Italian shoe company Tod's. *Daily 8.30am–1 hour before sunset, Easter–Aug until 7.15pm | Piazza del Colosseo*

MAXXI (O) (🚇 0)

The audacious and stylishly dynamic building by architect Zaha Hadid for collections of modern art, architecture and photography in the midst of tenement buildings in the north of the Flaminio residential area represents 21st century Rome. *Tue–Fri and Sun 11am–7pm, Sat 11am–10pm | Via Guido Reni 4a | www.fondazionemaxxi.it*

MUSEO NAZIONALE ROMANO

The most comprehensive collection of art from Roman antiquity distributed between four different exhibition sites: *Palazzo Massimo ((U F3) (🚇 h5) | Largo di Villa Peretti 1), Palazzo Altemps ((U C3) (🚇 d5) | Piazza Sant'Apollinare 46), Crypta Balbi ((U D4) (🚇 e6) | Via delle Botteghe Oscure 31), Terme di Diocleziano ((U F2–3) (🚇 h4) | Viale De Nicola 79);* the collection includes the excavations of the grandiose imperial villa *Domus Aurea ((U F5) (🚇 h7) | Sat/Sun 9.15am–3.45pm by phone booking, tel. 06 39 96 77 00)* near the Colosseum. *Terme di Diocleziano Tue–Sun 9am–7.30pm, all others Tue–Sun 9am–7.45pm | archeoroma.beniculturali.it*

PANTHEON (U D3) (🚇 e5)

This temple to the gods dating back to 27 BC is the only ancient domed structure still in existence; many Italian kings and the artist Raphael are interred within the impressive interior. In the evening, the square is a popular meeting place. *Mon–Sat 9am–7.30pm, Sun 9am–6pm | Piazza della Rotonda*

ST PETER'S BASILICA
(SAN PIETRO) (U A3) (🚇 a4)

You enter the most important sanctuary of Catholicism via the harmonious square,

Missed an audience with the Pope? A service at St Peter's Basilica is also special

created by Rome's master of the Baroque style, Gianlorenzo Bernini, in 1667. Bramante, Carlo Maderna and Michelangelo worked on the gigantic cathedral, the *Basilica di San Pietro,* which can hold 60,000 people. From its ☀️ dome (admission fee), you have a splendid view. Inside are the relics of St Peter and St Paul and among the many artworks Michelangelo's "Pietà". *April– sept daily 7am–7pm, Oct–March 7am– 6.30pm | Piazza San Pietro*

SQUARES

The *Campo de' Fiori* (U C4) *(🗺 d6)*, "field of flowers" – during the Middle Ages it was a cattle pasture and a place of execution – today it is one of the most beautiful Roman fruit, vegetable and flower markets; if you want a quick snack, go to number 22 and try the delicious *pizza bianca* from the *Forno Campo de Fiori* bakery *(www.fornocampodeifiori.com).* The elongated *Piazza Navona* (U C3) *(🗺 d5)* boasts the magnificent Baroque

fountain of the four rivers by Bernini and flower-laden balconies, street artists and street cafés. A broad, stage-like staircase the *Scalinata Trinità dei Monti,* the Spanish Steps, at the ☀️ *Piazza di Spagna* (U D2) *(🗺 f 3–4)* provides a popular place to sit for tired tourists and young people.

TRASTEVERE (U B–C 5–6) *(🗺 c–d 7–8)*

Once known mainly for its narrow, winding streets and traditional-folksy character, Trastevere has now become the in-place to live for members of the cultural scene and well-to-do foreigners, and its creative shops, bars, cafés and trattorias make it a popular nightlife area.

VATICAN MUSEUMS ⭐
(U A2) *(🗺 a3–4)*

With 14 museums, the Vatican City has one of the largest museum complexes in the world; an immeasurable abundance of masterpieces from antiquity and leading artists such as Giotto, da Vinci,

Caravaggio, Raphael and many others. The highlight has to be the ★ *Sistine Chapel (Cappella Sistina)* with Michelangelo's paintings based on the Book of Genesis (1508–1512) on the ceiling of the large chapel, still used by Catholic popes today. INSIDER**TIP** A tip when visiting the chapel: arrive early in the morning when it opens and hurry there through the museums. That will give you half an hour almost on your own – soon afterwards it will be teeming with people. It is generally worth reserving a ticket *(biglietteriamusei.vatican.va)*, in order to avoid having to queue. *Mon–Sat 9am–6pm, last Sun of the month (no admission fee) 9am–2pm | main entrance Viale Vaticano | mv.vatican.va*

VIA APPIA ANTICA AND CATACOMBS
● *(0) (∭ 0)*

In the lovely archaeological park on the south-east border of Rome, you can easily imagine how the most important road towards the south of the Roman Empire and the Adria must have looked; the site encompasses the subterranean burial chambers, the *Calixtus (March–Jan Thu–Tue 9am–noon and 2pm–5pm), Sebastian (Jan–Nov Mon–Sat 10am–5pm | www.catacombe.org)* and the large *Domitilla* catacombs *(Wed–Mon 9am–noon and 2pm–5pm | www.domitilla.info)*. *www.parcoappiantica.it*

VILLA BORGHESE
(U E–F1) (∭ f–g 1–2)

While wandering through this hilly, popular public park, you will come to the *Galleria Nazionale dell'Arte Moderna,* which is well worth seeing and has the INSIDER**TIP** inviting terrace café *Caffè delle Arti (closed Mon evening | www.caffedelleartiroma.it),* the Etruscan museum *Villa Giulia,* the cinema centre *Casa del Cinema* and the *Museo di Galleria Borghese (Tue–Sun 8.30am–7.30pm by appointment, tel. 0 63 28 10 or www.tosc.it | www.galleriaborghese.it)* with the famous marble sculptures by Gian Lorenzo Bernini. A highlight in all senses is the ↘↗ *Belvedere Pincio* overlooking the Piazza del Popolo.

LOW BUDGET

With the *Roma Pass (48 or 72 hours 28/38.50 euros)* you can visit a lot of sights free of charge or at a discounted price; what is more you can use the Metro and bus for free *(www.romapass.it)*.

Arrosticcini is the name given to lamb – grilled on skewers until it is nice and crispy – cheap and delicious; in Abruzzo, you will find them in many *macellerie and rosticcerie.*

FOOD & DRINK

RISTORANTE AD HOC *(U C2) (∭ e3)*
Fine-dining restaurant with seasonal produce, truffle specialities and an exclusive wine cellar. Near the Piazza del Popolo. *Daily | Via di Ripetta 43 | tel. 0 63 23 30 40 | www.ristoranteadhoc.com | Expensive*

CAFÉS

Historic figures such as Byron, Goethe, Keats and Wagner have had coffee in the *Antico Caffè Greco* on the elegant *Via Condotti 86 (U D2) (∭ f4)*; Rome's most famous ice cream parlour is the *Gelateria Giolitti (U D3) (∭ e5)* in the *Via Uffici del Vicario 40;* a classic favourite until late at night is the art nouveau *Caffè della Pace* (U C3) (*d5*) in the *Via della Pace 3.*

CASA COPPELLE (U C3) (*d–e5*)

A cheerfully elegant trattoria not far from the Piazza Navona with local homemade pasta dishes and excellent meat. *Daily | Piazza delle Coppelle 49 | tel. 06 68 89 17 07 | www.casacoppelle.it | Moderate–Expensive*

IL MARGUTTA RISTO-ARTE ❷
(U D2) (*e3*)

Vegetarian-vegan lunch buffet, imaginative vegetable dishes, organic bar and art events in the tranquil artists' street not far from the hubbub of Via del Corso. *Daily | Via Margutta 118 | tel. 06 32 65 05 77 | www.ilmargutta.bio | Budget–Moderate*

NECCI DEL 1924 (O) (*0*)

Café, trattoria with modern inspired Roman cuisine, meeting place for aperitifs in the popular Pigneto district behind the station. *Daily | Via Fanfulla da Lodi 68 | tel. 06 97 60 15 52 | www.necci1924.com | Moderate*

SHOPPING

The best fashion designers have their top-quality shops on and around the *Via Condotti* (U D2) (*e–f4*); *Via del Corso* (U D2–3) (*e–f 3–5*) offers more variety. There is a flea market at the *Porta Portese* (U C6) (*d8–9*) in Trastevere on Sundays.

ENTERTAINMENT

Superb aperitifs and cocktails are served in the garden bar *Stravinskij* in the luxury hotel *De Russie* ((U D1) (*e3*) | *Via del Babuino 9*). An ever-popular choice among the hip places to meet for drinks in

Trastevere: *Freni e Frizioni* ((U C5) (*d7*) | *Via del Politeama 4–6*); alternative bar crowd in *Monte Testaccio* (O) (*0*). Good range of concerts in the *Auditorium* ((O) (*0*) | *www.auditorium. com*). A highlight for jazz musicians

Cult address: Giolitti, a regular haunt of politicians from the Parliament building nearby

and jazz lovers: *Casa del Jazz* ((O) (*0*) | *Viale di Porta Ardeatina 55 | www.casajazz. it*). Rich cultural programme *Estate Romana* during the summer *(www.estate -romana.it).*

WHERE TO STAY

For B & B rooms, see *www.bedandbreak fastroma.com,* apartments *www.trianon borgopio.it* and *www.palazzo-olivia.it*

FONTANA DI TREVI (U D3) (*m̄ f5*)
Charming hotel opposite the Trevi fountain. *25 rooms | Piazza di Trevi 96 | tel. 06 67 86113 | www.hotelfontana-trevi. com | Expensive*

MEDITERRANEO (U F3) (*m̄ h5*)
Not far from the main station a comfortable hotel in 1930s style with original art deco furniture and a beautiful ❄ roof terrace. *251 rooms | Via Cavour 15 | tel. 06 4 88 40 51 | www.romehotelmediterraneo. it | Moderate–Expensive*

HOTEL SELENE (U F3) (*m̄ h5*)
Centrally located near the main train station, this hotel offers tastefully decorated rooms. *40 rooms | Via del Viminale 10 | tel. 06 4 82 44 60 | www.hotelseleneroma.it | Moderate*

ST PETER GUEST HOUSE
(U A2) (*m̄ a–b3*)
Elegant B&B close to St Peter's Basilica in the popular Prati neighbourhood. *6 rooms | Via Ottaviano 98 | tel. 33 55 64 37 42 | www.stpeterguesthouse. com | Budget–Moderate*

INFORMATION

Numerous information points in the city (first and foremost the *Visitor Center* in *Via Fori Imperiali),* at the airports and at the station Stazione Termini. *Tel. 06 06 08 | www.turismoroma.it, www. roma-antiqua.de, www.romaculta.it, www. romaepiu.it*

WHERE TO GO

ABBEY OF MONTECASSINO
(191 E5) (*m̄ H8*)
Founded by St Benedict of Norcia in AD 529, this abbey in Cassino is the oldest Benedictine monastery complex; it was bombed in 1944 but has since been beautifully restored.

INSIDER TIP ▶ BRACCIANO AND CERVETERI (190 C4) (*m̄ G7*)
A beautiful ❄ panoramic route leads around the crater lake, Lago di Bracciano, north-west of Rome, through picturesque villages to the little town of *Bracciano* (pop. 19,000) and its Renaissance castle *Castello Orsini-Odescalchi.* One of the most interesting Etruscan necropolises, the *Necropoli della Banditaccia (Tue–Sun 8.30am–1 hour before sunset),* is in nearby *Cerveteri:* the 400 opened burial tombs (including burial chambers you can walk into) with stone decorations (and many more unopened in the ground), are a Unesco World Heritage Site and an absolute sensation; you can admire some of the artistic burial objects in the *museum* in *Rocca Ruspoli (Tue–Sun 8.30am–7pm | Piazza Santa Maria 1).*

CASTELLI ROMANI (191 D4) (*m̄ G8*)
When the Romans drive south-east of the city for a day's ❄ outing here in the summer, they cool down in the *taverne* with a pleasant white wine, such as Colli Albani, Marino or Frascati, or during their walk by the cool, dark crater lakes *Lago di Albano* and *Lago di Nemi.* In *Ariccia* the piazza designed by Gian Lorenzo Bernini is well worth seeing. Every year in the summer, the Pope comes to *Castel Gandolfo* for a summer break. Bernini was also responsible for the very fine work on the church *San Tommaso da Villanova* (1661). *Frascati* was particularly popular with the cardinals and patricians, as is obvious from the magnificent Renaissance and Baroque villas, of which only the park of *Aldobrandini* is open to the public. Pretty villa hotels in the country entice you to stay overnight, for instance at the ❄ *Park Hotel Villa Grazioli (62 rooms | Via Umberto Pavoni 19 | tel. 06 94 54 00 |*

www.villagrazioli.com | Moderate–Expensive) near Grottaferrata with park and a wonderful view of Rome in the distance. Of the numerous restaurants and osterias in Frascati, the traditional Slow Food restaurant *Zarazà* is highly recommended *(closed Sun evening and Mon | Via Regina Margherita 45 | tel. 06 94 22 05 3 | Moderate)* with ❧ a panoramic terrace. The ruins of the ancient town of *Tuscolo* (5 km/3 miles from Frascati) also offer a spectacular view of Rome.

time and Mon | Via Prenestina 27 | tel. 0 77 55 60 49 | www.salvatoretassa.it | Expensive).

OSTIA ANTICA (190 C4) (*⌘ G8*) ●

One of the best preserved ancient Roman ruined cities, once belonging to the trading port at the mouth of the Tiber (building began in the 4th century BC). The huge *Roman Theatre* has space for 2700 spectators and excellent acoustics; in the summer, performances still take place

Summer residence of the Pope: Castel Gandolfo above the crater lake Lago di Albano

CIOCIARIA (191 D4) (*⌘ H8*)

Popular excursion area south-east of Rome with beautiful little towns in the mountains of Monti Ernici, such as *Anagni* with the Palace of the Popes and `INSIDER TIP` medieval frescoes in the *cathedral crypt (Via Leone XIII | www.cattedraledianagni.it)*, *Alatri*, *Ferentino* or the spa *Fiuggi* with a magnificent hotel, the *Grand Hotel Palazzo della Fonte (153 rooms | Via dei Villini 7 | tel. 07 75 50 81 | www.palazzodellafonte.it | Expensive)*, and in the excellent restaurant *Le Colline Ciociare (closed Sun evening, Tue lunch-*

there. Ostia Antica is easy to reach from Rome on the Roma–Lido train (26 min), which runs from the town station Stazione Ostiense and takes you directly to the terminus at Ostia Lido.

PALESTRINA ❧ (191 D4) (*⌘ H8*)

From the ancient Etruscan Praeneste, there is a fantastic view across to the Alban Mountains and Monti Lepini in the south. The archaeological museum, *Museo Nazionale Archeologico Prenestino* is very interesting *(daily 9am–8pm | Piazza della Cortina).*

PARCO NAZIONALE DEL CIRCEO
(191 D5) (*𝄞 H8*)

This national park starts just below Latina and stretches to the promontory of ☘ Monte Circeo (541 m/1775 ft). *San Felice Circeo* harbours the ruins of a Roman *Acropolis,* at the tip of the promontory is the *grotto of the sorceress Circe* who lent her name to the area and along the coast there are large lakes with an abundance of fish and birdlife. Long unspoilt sandy beaches roll up to *Sabaudia;* from San Felice Circeo in the south towards Terracina, they have been extensively developed for tourists. Elt is worth visiting the island of *Ponza* with its picturesque port by taking for example the speedboat from Terracina which takes less than an hour.

SPERLONGA (191 E5) (*𝄞 H8*)

The INSIDER TIP old town of this most beautiful place on the Lazio coast perches picturesquely in typical white Mediterranean style on a hilltop overlooking the sea. Below it are beautiful and exclusive beaches as well as a museum with precious finds from ancient Roman villas and caves.

TIVOLI ★ (191 D4) (*𝄞 G8*)

The huge complex of ruins of *Villa Adriana (daily 9am–1.5 hour before sunset | www.villaadriana.beniculturali.it)* 30 km/18.5 miles east of Rome was once the splendid country residence of Emperor Hadrian (AD 117–138) and includes palaces, temples, spas, libraries and theatre. Also in Tivoli is the *Villa d'Este,* a Renaissance palace *(Tue–Sun 8.30am–1 hour before sunset | www.villadestetivoli.info)* with the most beautiful park in Italy.

VITERBO

(190 C3) (*𝄞 G7*) **The town (pop. 67,000) steeped in Etruscan history has an enclosed medieval centre with palaces churches and squares.**

Three squares, the *Piazza del Plebiscito,* the *Palazzo dei Priori* (15th century with an attractive courtyard, fountain and frescoes) and the *Palazzo del Podestà* (13th century with 15th century tower) form the heart of the old town. Even more impressive is the *Piazza San Lorenzo*

TERRAZZE ROMANE

Terrazza romana, the Roman roof terrace is the epitome of Roman joie de vivre: celebrating on roof terraces in a mild climate and against the backdrop of the hills, church domes and parks is all part of this lifestyle, something shown in Woody Allen's film "To Rome with Love". Visitors to Rome can also experience it in the rooftop restaurants and bars of many elegant hotels, such as the *St George ((U B4) (𝄞 c5) | Via Giulia 62),* the *Capo d'Africa ((U F5)* *(𝄞 h7) | Via Capo d'Africa 54),* the Exedra *((U F3) (𝄞 h4) | Piazza della Repubblica 47),* the Locarno *((U C1) (𝄞 d3) | Via Penna 22).* There is a wonderful choice of terrace cafés as well: the wine bar *Il Palazzetto* at the top of the Spanish Steps, the *Caffè Capitolino* in the Capitoline museums on Piazza del Campidoglio, the *caffetteria* on the fourth floor of the Castel Sant'Angelo and the *Caffetteria Italia* at the Altare della Patria Vittorio Emanuele.

with the *San Lorenzo* cathedral and the *Palazzo Papale* with its wonderful pillared loggia. The *Museo Archeologico* exhibits Etruscan treasures *(Tue–Sun 8.30am–7.30pm | Piazza della Rocca)* in *Rocca Albornoz* fortress.

You can dine on home-made pasta with porcini and deep-fried pizza in the rustic *Al Vecchio Orologio (closed Mon, Tue | Via Orologio Vecchio 25 | tel. 3 35 33 77 54 | Budget–Moderate)* in the old town. You can also enjoy thermal and spa treatments in the elegant thermal hotel *Niccolò V Terme dei Papi (23 rooms | Strada Bagni 12 | tel. 07613501 | www.termedeipapi.it | Expensive)*. In nearby *Bagnaia,* the Baroque park and villas of *Villa Lante (Tue–Sun 8.30am–2 hours before sunset)* exude enchantment.

WHERE TO GO

LAGO DI BOLSENA (LAKE BOLSENA)
(190 C3) *(ﾉﾉ G7)*

Take a trip (20 km/12.5 miles) to the crater lake Lago di Bolsena: a serene summer resort on crystal-clear water. The wine Est! Est!! Est!!! comes from the medieval *Montefiascone* with its interesting twin church of Romanesque origin *San Flaviano* as well as a lovely castle park. Further on towards Orvieto is the hamlet ⚓ *Civita di Bagnoregio* dizzily perched on a steep tuff cliff, and at risk of landslides – a tourist attraction with cafés, trattorias and wine bars.

The main lakeside town, *Bolsena,* has a charming medieval town centre and is where you will find the *Santa Cristina* church (with its interesting catacombs). *Da Picchietto* serves deliciously prepared fresh fish from the lake *(closed Mon | Via Porta Fiorentina 15 | tel. 07 61 79 91 58 | www.ristorantepicchiettobolsena.com | Moderate)*.

In Tarquinia's museum: tomb frescoes from the Etruscan necropolis

TARQUINIA ⭐ (190 C4) *(ﾉﾉ G7)*

Towers dominate the skyline of this little medieval town and on the main square is the splendid Gothic Palazzo Vitelleschi with the *Museo Nazionale Tarquiniese (Tue–Sun 8.30am–7.30pm)*, which like the *necropolis* (4 km/2.5 miles to the east) is a must for anyone wishing to learn more about the Etruscans and their ancient town of Tarxna, also called Turchuna.

TUSCANIA (190 C3) *(ﾉﾉ G7)*

Even the Etruscans made use of the strategic location on this tuff stone hill. The *Museo Nazionale Etrusco (Tue–Sun 8.30am–7.30pm | Largo Mario Moretti 1)* exhibits numerous terracotta tombs from the Etruscan site of Tusena, which belonged to the city-state of Tarxna (Tarquinia).

SOUTHERN ITALY

The light is blinding, there is a fragrant mix of sea, pines and salt in the air and the midday calm of the weathered little town in white and grey hues highlights the beauty of its stage-like squares – a fitting backdrop for an evening stroll.

Travellers have always been drawn to the south – on a honeymoon to the Gulf of Naples, to the *Costa Divina* "divine coast" of Amalfi and Positano and to Mount Versuvius. Travellers on the grand tour followed the trail of the ancient civilizations to the ruins of the Greek temples and the Greek towns of the Magna Graecia, which once thrived along the southern Italian coast, and to ruined cities like Roman Pompeii. And in Apulia they looked for the medieval cathedrals and castles that revealed the creative combination of the Nordic culture of the Normans and Hohenstaufens and the Byzantine influence of the Orient. These days, Apulia is admired for its splendid cliffs and sandy coast, fertile landscape and rustic *trulli* houses and the white *masserie* – old manor houses that have often been transformed into attractive country hotels – and for its neat, almost Oriental little towns, the good fresh food, in short: To visitors of the 21st century, Apulia is a kind of Tuscany of the south.

The neighbouring region of Basilicata presents a highlight in the form of its spectacular cave town of Matera. Together with rugged Calabria, it shares the secluded mountain region of Pollino, now

Greek temples and cave towns, Oriental flair and secluded beaches: southern Italy is a region of cultural intersection

a nature reserve and and an ideal wilderness area for hikes.

On the partly developed Calabrian coast with its lovely clean sea, stylish resorts have been set up that are now advertised in the catalogues of exclusive travel agents. The most beautiful strip of coast is the Gulf of Maratea. It joins up with the Cilento in the north, an area of physical beauty with wonderful beaches, crystal-clear water, grottoes, and mountains – unspoilt nature at its best – and naturally the fascinating, vibrant Naples.

The MARCO POLO "Naples and the Amalfi Coast" guide offers a more detailed description of the region.

BARI

(193 D4) *(Ⓜ L9)* **Apulia's capital (pop. 327,000) is also called the "Milan of the South": for centuries it has been a trade window to the Orient, and each year in September, it hosts the largest trade fair in the Mediterranean, the Fiera del Levante.**

Santa's house? The bones of St Nicolas rest in the crypt of San Nicola

Bari's white old town with the beautiful old church exudes the air of a Kasbah. Until a few years ago, it was still a bit grim and by no means completely safe, but in recent years a lot has been restored, and the two attractive squares *Piazza Ferrarese* and *Piazza Mercantile* have become a centre of the *baresi* nightlife thanks to the new cafés, bars and nice restaurants.

The elegant hotels as well as vibrant shopping avenues full of people browsing are in the chessboard-styled new town of Bari, which is on the other side of the massive road Corso Vittorio Emanuele. You should however, avoid the proliferating, neglected outskirts at all costs.

SIGHTSEEING

BASILICA SAN NICOLA

This stately Apulian Romanesque church (11th/12th century) in the old town is very impressive. Inside, look out for the ancient episcopal throne, made of marble and borne by tiny, groaning figures. Below the silver altar is a crypt supported by 26 columns holding the reliquary of St Nicholas, Bishop of Myra, patron saint of Bari and highly respected in the Orthodox Church – which is why there are a lot of Russian pilgrims. *Piazza Elia*

CATTEDRALE SAN SABINO

Bari's cathedral, like the Basilica San Nicola, is one of the best examples of Romanesque architecture in Apulia. In the church's archive, there is a precious Exsultet Roll (scroll bearing the Catholic Easter liturgy) from the 11th century. *Piazza Odegitria*

HOHENSTAUFEN CASTLE

This massive castle overlooking the sea was reconstructed by Emperor Frederick II of Hohenstaufen on an earlier Byzantine Norman bastion. Inside, a collection of plaster casts show how artistic the decoration on Apulian church façades can be. *Thu–Tue 8.30am–7.30pm*

FOOD & DRINK

LA CANTINA DI CIANNACIANNE
Popular restaurant in the old town near the Lungomare. Try the small meat balls *bombette!* Good seafood dishes. *Closed Mon in winter | Via Corsioli 3 | tel. 08 05 28 93 82 | www.ciannacianne.com | Moderate*

LOCANDA DI FEDERICO
Orecchiette, Apulian "ear-shaped" pasta, fresh fish on the piazza. *Daily | Piazza Mercantile 63 | tel. 08 05 22 77 05 | www.locandadifederico.com | Moderate*

WHERE TO STAY

HOTEL ADRIA
Renovated, friendly, functional and centrally located, with restaurant. *38 rooms | Via Zuppetta 10 | tel. 08 05 24 66 99 | www.adriahotelbari.com | Moderate*

HOTEL ORIENTE
This stylish palazzo hotel, not far from the equally stylish Teatro Petruzelli, is an appropriate choice for Bari. *75 rooms | Via Cavour 32 | tel. 08 05 25 51 00 | www.orientehotelbari.it | Expensive*

INFORMATION

Piazza del Ferrarese 29 | tel. 08 05 24 22 44 | www.viaggiareinpuglia.it

WHERE TO GO

ALBEROBELLO (193 E4) *(ᘯ M9)*
Home of a unique vernacular architecture: the *trulli*, little circular white dry-stone houses with dark conical roofs. You can see

them dotted around in the triangle between Bari, Taranto and Brindisi, scattered among the olive groves, almond orchards, vegetable fields and grapevines of the garden-like Valle d'Itria. In Alberobello (pop. 10,000), they form a town, even the Sant'Antonio church is built in *trulli* style, which has turned Alberobello into a tourist hotspot. Inhabited until into the late 20th century, some of the buildings have now been transformed into hotels, holiday homes, souvenir shops and pizzerias.

The somewhat rustic **INSIDER TIP** holiday accommodation offered in the *trulli*, which was initially rather damp and spartan, has nonetheless improved tremendously, for instance at *Trulli Holiday Resort (Piazza Antonio Curri 1 | tel. 08 04 32 59 70 | www.trulliholiday.com | Budget–Moderate)* and the *Tipico Resort (Via Brigata Regina 47 | tel. 08 04 32 41 08 | tipicoresort.it | Budget–Moderate)*. A beautiful hotel with a swimming pool and good food (20 km/12 miles to the east in Fasano) is the *Masseria Marzalossa (12 rooms | Contrada Pezze Vicine 69 | tel. 08 04 41 37 80 | www.masseriamarzalossa.com | Expensive)*, a fine example of how elegantly and charmingly Apulia's beautiful manor houses, once at risk of all falling into disrepair, are now being used.

CASTEL DEL MONTE AND CANOSA DI PUGLIA (192 C4) (*M L9*)

From afar, one sees the "crown of Apulia" on the hill, the octagonal ★ *Castel del Monte (April–Sept daily 10.15am–7.30pm, Oct–March 9am–6.30pm | www.casteldelmonte.beniculturali.it)*, built 1240–50, with eight towers, eight interior rooms and an octagonal courtyard. It was one of the architectural projects of Emperor Frederick II of Hohenstaufen, and displays an almost esoteric touch. Once this austere castle was richly adorned with marble and Byzantine mosaics. Plan a culinary treat in the nearby village of *Montegrosso d'Andria* and enjoy the meticulous Apulian Slow Food cuisine in *Trattoria Antichi Sapori (closed Sat evening and Sun | Piazza Sant'Isidoro 10 | tel. 08 83 56 95 29 | antichisapori.pietrozito.it | Budget–Moderate)*.

You can drive to the castle inland via *Canosa di Puglia*, a fine example of Apulia's cultural diversity: the Romanesque *cathedral* ruins, the Byzantine *Basilica San Leucio* and in the Via Cadorna the Roman *Ipogei Lagrasta (March–Oct daily 9am–1pm and 4pm–6pm, Nov–Feb 8am–2pm)*, burial caves dug into the tuff stone and dating back to the 4th century BC.

GARGANO (192 C2–3) (*M K–L8*)

In the centre of Gargano, the ancient *Foresta Umbra*, a protected forest of shady deciduous trees, spreads out over 42 miles² on the massive 1000 m/328 1ft high promontory, the spur of the Italian boot and national park *(www.parks.it/parco.nazionale.gargano)*. The coast in the south-east is steep and rocky with little sandy coves and bizarre rock formations, such as at Pugnochiuso. Picturesque fishing towns such as *Rodi Garganico, Vieste* and *Peschici* turn into teeming holiday spots in the summer.

Near Manfredonia in the south, there are two sanctuaries that are reminders of the ancient town of Sipontum: the Romanesque Oriental church of *Santa Maria di Siponto*, a square construction with a crypt, and 7 km/4 miles further on *San Leonardo di Siponto* with beautiful sculptures on the portals and capitals. In *Manfredonia* itself, the *Museo Archeologico Nazionale del Gargano (daily 8.30am–7.30pm)* in the Hohenstaufen Angevin fortress complex is worth seeing as it contains the mysterious stone stelae of the Daunians, who settled around the Tavoliere – the Apulian corn plain around

Foggia and the Gargano – about 2500 years ago.

Above Manfredonia there is a magnificent ✼ panoramic drive up to *Monte Sant'Angelo* with the cave sanctuary of St Michael (note the wonderful bronze steep cliff surrounded by sandy beaches on the east tip of Gargano – boat trips set off to spectacular *grottoes* such as *Smeralda* and *Campana,* which can only be reached by sea. Soaring up from the edge of the beach is the Gargano land-

As strange as their name: *trulli,* the round structures in and around Alberobello

door from 1076!) and the unusual terrace house architecture in the medieval district of *Junno.* 25 km/15.5 miles north-west in *San Giovanni Rotondo* more than six million pilgrims come to pay homage to a contemporary saint, the faith healer Padre Pio.

Bizarre rocks rise up from the beach of the hotel *Baia delle Zagare (143 rooms | tel. 08 84 55 01 55 | www.hotelbaiadelle zagare.it | Moderate −expensive),* which has a stunning location on terraces between olive trees on the coastal road 17k m/10 miles north-east of Mattinata.

From *Vieste* – which has a picturesque old town and a Hohenstaufen castle on a mark, the *Pizzomunno,* a towering chalk monolith, the "top of the world". Other typical landmarks are the *trabucchi,* the fishing structures which stretch right out into the sea, some of which are now used as restaurants.

Following a scenic coastal route, the boat arrives at *Peschici* high up the farthest side of the promontory, with a pleasing old town and a small harbour, a particularly popular holiday hamlet in Gargano. Spend the night far from the hustle and bustle at the *Agriturismo Torre dei Preti (20 rooms | Valle Croci district | tel. 08 84 96 30 66 | www.torredeipreti.it | Budget)*

A splendid starting point in the Murgia: the small Baroque town of Martina Franca

MARTINA FRANCA (193 E4–5) (*M9*)

The elegant little Baroque town (pop. 49,000) in the centre of the Murgia, at an elevation of 430 m/1410 ft, used to be the family seat of an aristocratic family whose enterprising work triggered a building boom among the middle classes. Whole roads of Baroque façades were the result, e.g. the Via Cavour, with its richly embellished stone and latticework. The blacksmith's trade is still pursued to this day. Every July/August, the famous INSIDER TIP music festival *(www. festivaldellavalleditria.it)* takes place. Rather original accommodation is available in renovated apartments right in the centre: *Villaggio In (24 apartments | Via Arco Grassi 8 | tel. 0 80 70 59 11 | www. villaggioincasesparse.it | Budget– Moderate).*

This is a good base for tours to the ceramic centre of Grottaglie, to Taranto, to see the many *trulli,* to the grotto churches between Massafra, Mottola and Matera, and to the pretty, whitewashed little towns with their Oriental flair such as Cisternino, the popular Ostuni or Ceglie Messapica, which all have a whole range of good restaurants, including the *Al Fornello da Ricci (closed Mon evening and Tue | Contrada Montevicoli | tel. 08 31 37 71 04 | Moderate–Expensive). Polignano a Mare* has a fantastic position on the cliffs overlooking the sea.

GROTTE DI CASTELLANA (193 D4) (*M9*)

In Castellana on the road to Putignano, visitors can stop off in Italy's most beautiful *dripstone caves*, a labyrinth of passages and caves. A highlight is the *Caverna Bianca,* a cavern of alabaster. Daily tours, a short (1 km/0.6 mile) and a long (3 km/1.8 mile) one. *Varying opening times, see website | www.grot tedicastellana.it*

RUVO DI PUGLIA (193 D4) (*L9*)

This friendly little country town 35 km/ 22 miles to the north-west is worth a visit to see the wonderful Romanesque *cathedral* and the *Museo Nazionale Jatta (Mon–Wed, Fri, Sun 8.30am– 1.30pm, Thu and Sat 8.30am–7.30pm | Piazza Bovio 35),* for the beautiful antique vases and the *rython,* INSIDER TIP drinking vessels in the shape of animal heads.

TARANTO (193 E5) (*M9*)

Don't be deterred by the steel foundries of the industrial and harbour town of Taranto (pop. 202,000). If you are looking for traces of Tarras's past, which was one of the richest and most developed trading towns of the Magna Graecia two and a half thousand years ago, visit the *Marta-Museo Archeologico Nazionale (daily 8.30am–7.30pm| Via Cavour 10 | www.museotaranto.org)* with a famous gold collection.

The topographical location of the town is interesting. It extends over two headlands that form a sort of inland sea, the *Mare Piccolo,* with a little island, on which the old town extends. The medieval INSIDER TIP *Castello Aragonese (guided tours daily 9.30am, 11.30am, 2pm, 4pm, 6pm, 8pm, 10.30pm, midnight, 1.30am | Piazza Castello | www.castelloaragonese taranto.com)* and the Romanesque cathedral with Baroque façade are particularly worth visiting.

TRANI (193 D3–4) (*L8*)

This pleasant town (pop. 56,000) has carved out a special reputation among the little coastal towns between Bari and the Gargano spur thanks to its very bright

Norman Romanesque ★ ⚘ *cathedral* with its unusual architecture, precious stone embellishments and the bronze portal as well as its unique position on the coast – once a point of orientation for seafarers. It is the queen among the many beautiful churches in Apulia. Directly on the coast is the *Hohenstaufen castle.* The old town on the *lungomare,* the sea promenade, turns into a vibrant nightlife area each evening, with bars, pubs and restaurants. *www.traniweb.it, www.pugliaimperiale.com*

ISOLE TREMITI (TREMITI ISLANDS) (192 B2) (*K7*)

People refer to them as Italy's most beautiful "tropical islands": first the large flat mountain ridge of *Isola San Domino* covered in pine woods and with a coast full of grottoes, a diver's paradise *(www.merlintremiti.com, www.tremitidiving center.com),* then the uninhabited cliff splinter *Isola Cretaccio,* finally the *Isola San Nicola* with a once fortified *Benedictine abbey* from the 9th century that acquired a Gothic character under the Cistercians. Just under 500 people inhabit the group of islands in the little fishing villages that are now tailored to

PASTA ANTIMAFIA

Do you want to support the fight against the mafia on your trip to Italy? You can do so by buying *Libera Terra* pasta in Coop supermarkets, the organic food chains ⊕ NaturaSi and Alce Nera, and in ⊕ fair trade shops, which can now be found in all of the main towns. Hundreds of acres of land on Sicily have been confiscated from the convicted Mafia bosses and given to

dedicated organic farmers who cultivate wheat, tomatoes, olives, and grapes on the land, and turn them into pasta, tinned tomatoes, oil and wine. The Sicilian example is catching on, so that now new legal farming enterprises are being set up on former mafia land in Campania, Calabria and Apulia. *www.liberaterra.it*

the tourist industry. On some days in the summer, ships from Manfredonia, Vieste, Rodi Garganico, Ortona, Vasto and especially Termoli in Molise bring over 10,000 day trippers to the islands.

BASILICATA

APPENNINO LUCANO
(192–193 C–D5) (*ɱ L9–10*)

From the coast of Metapontos eroded river valleys lead up into the mountain world of Basilicata, through the Valle del Basento to the Lucanian Dolomites. They are named after their bizarre cliff formations. The district also encompasses beautiful woods and two very picturesque mountain towns, *Pietrapertosa* and *Castelmezzano.* Regional organic food is served at the ☻ *Azienda Agrituristica La Grotta dell'Eremita (20 rooms | Contrada Calcescia 1 | tel. 09 71 98 63 14 | www.grot tadelleremita.com | Budget),* where you can spend the night in a hamlet dating to the 14th century.

Near the coastal town of Policoro, you enter the *Val d'Agri* (with Europe's largest onshore oil field) at the beginning of which is the impressive medieval church complex *Santa Maria d'Anglona.* Continuing along the valley, the mountains of the *Parco Nazionale dell'Appennino Lucano (www.parcoap penninolucano.it)*rise to an elevation of 1800 m/5906 ft.

INSIDER TIP MARATEA
(192 C6) (*ɱ K10*)

The 26 km/16 miles long Costa di Maratea on the Golfo di Policastro is one of the most beautiful stretches of coast in southern Italy. The mountains back on to the sea, the sand and pebble bays are great for bathing, and the clean water is a paradise for divers. Pretty coastal and sea-side resorts such as *Acquafredda, Cersuta, Fiumicello San Venere, Castrocucco* provide a contrast to the more elevated old towns such as *Maratea Borgo* and *Maratea Superiore.* The enchanting hotel *Villa Cheta Elite (23 rooms | tel. 09 73 87 81 34 | www.vlllacheta.it | Expensive)* overlooks the beautiful beach of Acquafredda.

MATERA (193 D5) (*ɱ L9*)

Matera (pop. 52,000), chosen as Europe's Capital of Culture for 2019, boasts a Romanesque Norman cathedral (13th century), a *feudal fortress* from 1515 and naturally the main sight, the ★ ● *sassi:* a subterranean cave town with enchanting cave churches cut into the rock beneath the new Matera. Over 20,000 people lived here well into the 1950s, but their living conditions in the dark, unhealthy cave homes were regarded as a national disgrace. New buildings and resettlements were the results; there is now a resurgence of interest (using public funds) because, ironically, the *sassi* are now on Unesco's World Heritage List.

Luxurious hotels with an atmosphere all of their own are now in the cave dwellings, such as the ⤬ INSIDER TIP *Hotel Sant'Angelo (23 rooms | Rione Pianelle | Piazza San Pietro Caveoso | tel. 08 35 31 40 10 | www.hotelsantangelo sassi.it | Expensive),* but also comfortable B & B accommodation *(www.sassi web.it, www.bbsangennarosassi.it | Budget).*

MELFI (192 C4) (*ɱ K9*)

An important northern stronghold in the Basilicata is Melfi (pop. 18,000) on the northern face of Monte Vulture (1327 m/ 4354 ft). Its thick woods are a reminder of the region's original name: Lucania (from *lucus* = wood). A popular destination thanks to the two *Monticchio crater*

Breathtaking Mediterranean coastline: the SS 18 along the Gulf of Policastro near Maratea

lakes with two 12th century *Benedictine monasteries,* one of which is a ruin, the other rebuilt in the 18th century.

Melfi itself, in the 11th century, was the first stronghold of the Normans in southern Italy. Today the castle, which was later remodelled by Friedrick II, houses the *Museo Nazionale Archeologico (Mon 2pm–8pm, Tue–Sun 9am–8pm | Via dei Normanni)* with interesting exhibits about the early history of the Lucanians, the original settlers and the sarcophagus of a Roman woman with wonderful stone reliefs dating back to the second century BC. On the outskirts of Melfi, you will find the *rupestrian churches Madonna della Spinelle, Santa Lucia* and *Santa Margherita* with Byzantine inspired wall paintings from the 13th century. Ask about tours in the *tourist information (Piazza Umberto I 11 | tel. 09 72 23 97 51 | www.prolocomelfi.it).*

Melfi produces a famous red wine, the full-bodied Aglianico, traditionally stored in rock cellars to mature, in villages such as Barile, Rapolla, Rionero in Vulture. It is served along with delicious regional cuisine in the country inn *Cantuccio del Vulture (closed Sun evening, Mon, Tue | Piano delle Nocelle-Rionero | tel. 09 72 73 13 14 | www.cantucciodelvulture.it | Budget)* with seven simple rooms.

20 km/12 miles to the east of Melfi, you reach *Venosa* with its stately *castle* and *cathedral* from the 15th century including the *birthplace* of the Roman poet Horace (born here in 65 BC). Highlights on the north-east outskirts of the town are the archaeological excavations of the Roman *Venusium,* the impressive early Christian abbey *Santissima Trinità* as well as the wildly romantic unfinished ruin church *Incompiuta.* 2 km/1.2 miles further on you reach the early Christian *catacombs,*

which have been accessible for some years now.

METAPONTO (193 D5) (⟁ L9–10)

Today ● Metaponto is a modern town on the Ionian coast, which earns its living from the summer tourists and vegetable cultivation. It was once the famous Greek town of Metapontum in which Pythagoras lived and died (around 510 BC), as evident by the *Tavole Palatine,* the temple dedicated to the Greek goddess Hera, with its remaining 15 Doric columns that loom into view near the main road 106. Among the Greek remains is also the *Parco Archeologico* as well as the *Antiquarium (Mon 2pm–8pm, Tue–Sun 9am–8pm | Via Artistea 21)* with a rich collection of archaeological finds, vases and jewellery.

A second important Greek town was *Heraclea,* 20 km/12 miles to the south of Metaponto. The *Museo Nazionale della Siritide (Wed–Mon 9am–8pm, Tue 2pm–8pm | Via Colombo 8)* in *Policoro* contains the finds from this site and from *Siris,* a third Greek town, as well as the *Parco Archeologico di Herakleia.*

CALABRIA

ASPROMONTE (194 C5) (⟁ K–L12)

The toe of the boot, the most southern point of the Apennine peninsula between the Tyrrhenian and the Ionian Sea, is surrounded by more than 300 km/186 miles of coastline. High mountain ranges traverse the area, in the south the Aspromonte, rugged, impassable end of the Apennines: crags and labyrinthine folds covered in thick vegetation. ☆ INSIDERTIP Traversing the Aspromonte, for example from Bagnara Calabra by the Tyrrhenian Sea to Melito di Porto Salvo on the Ionian Sea offers fantastic views of the landscape. It is here at the top that pilgrims visit the *Santuario Madonna di Polsi,* which has a special feast day at the end of Aug/be-

In southern Italy there is history in nearly every stone – columns, pedestals, sculptures in Metaponto

ginning of Sept. Down below, stretching off towards the north-east is the *Costa dei Gelsomini* with numerous seaside resorts and beaches.

CAPO RIZZUTO (195 D4) *(ᗞ M11)*

The craggy peninsula, a nature reserve, offers a beautiful spectacle: cliffs and rock plateaus roughened by wind and erosion, beaches and bays, the cape *Capo Rizzuto* jutting out into the crystal-clear sea. Equally spectacular is the fortress on the coast ⚲ *Le Castella* in the south and the Greek ruins at *Capo Colonna* in the north. And even the industrial town of *Crotone* (pop. 60,000), founded 2500 years ago as the Greek Kroton, still has a nice old town.

LOCRI (194 C5) *(ᗞ L12)*

On the Ionian coast with its beaches and resorts, near the modern town of Locri (pop. 13,000) towards Bovalino, is the archaeological site of the Greek *Locri Epizephyrii.* It contains remains of an Ionic and Doric temple, a Greco-Roman theatre as well as the holy shrine of Persephone. The *museum (Tue–Sun 9am–8pm)* exhibits, among other things, Persephone votive plaques made of terracotta. You can savour delicious local cuisine in the *Trattoria U Ricriju (closed Sun. | Via Circonvallazione Nord 173 | tel. 38 99 68 72 28 | Budget– Moderate)* in the coastal town of *Siderno,* 5 km/3 miles to the north.

Above Locri is *Gerace* (11 km/7 miles), a medieval hamlet spread out over three terraces, which boasts a wonderful, extensive Romanesque *cathedral;* the columns in the interior and the crypt are remains from ancient Locri. Continuing up into the mountains along the pass, you will reach the other side of the coast on the Tyrrhenian Sea at Gioia Tauro. The ⚲ *Passo del Mercante* (952 m/3117 ft) offers a view of both seas.

INSIDER TIP ▶ MONTE POLLINO

(194 C2) *(ᗞ L10)*

Castrovillari, a small modern town (pop. 22,000) situated in a fertile basin – with a picturesque centre, Aragonese *castle* and the Renaissance church *San Giuliano* – is one of the starting points for excursions to the Pollino massif, southern Italy's highest mountain range (up to 2248 m/ 7375 ft) and national park, which northern Calabria shares with the southern Basilicata. There are river valleys full of verdant vegetation and rough, bare, chalky heights. The symbol of this wild mountain world is the *pino loricato,* a rare pine unique to the area. First-class local cuisine is available at the inn *La Locanda di Alia (14 rooms | closed Sun | Via Ietticelli 55 | tel. 0 98 14 63 70 | www.alia.it | Expensive)*.

Tours leave from *Rotonda* (the park administration: *Via delle Fiette Tricolori 6 | tel. 09 73 66 93 11 | www.parcopollino.it*) and *San Severino Lucano* with nice restaurants. The centre in the north-east of the park is *Terranova del Pollino;* an ideal base for hiking tours is the organic farm ⚙ *La Garavina (Contrada Casa del Conte | tel. 0 97 39 33 95 | www.lagaravina.it | Budget)* with five simple rooms and delicious mountain cuisine using its own organic ingredients. Hiking enthusiasts regard the ⚞ route from coast to coast through the Pollino mountains as a highlight. Information regarding the park and trekking trips can be found on the following websites: *www.guidaparcopollino.it, www.parcopollino.gov.it, www.aptbasilicata.it* and *www.bikebasilicata.it*.

Morano Calabro is a mountain village worth special mention, with picturesque old houses clustered around the ruined castle. The Baroque *Santa Maria Maddalena* church with its colourfully shingled dome roof stands out among the churches.

REGGIO DI CALABRIA
(194 C5) (*Ø K12*)

This ancient Greek town (pop. 186,000) has an elegant palm-lined waterfront promenade, the ● *Lungomare Falcomatà,* named after the mayor who died in 2001 and was responsible for reviving the quality of life in the town known for its ugly urban sprawl and *mafioso* connections: you can sit here and enjoy the sunset and the views of Sicily, which seems almost close enough to touch.

A further reason to come here are the two magnificent bronze figures, the ★ *Bronzi di Riace* (5th century BC), found in the sea

in 1972. They can be admired in the *Museo Archeologico Nazionale (Tue–Sun 9am–7.30pm | Piazza De Nava 26)*.

ROSSANO (195 D3) (*Ø L10–11*)

Located on the eastern slopes of the Sila Greca, once the centre of Byzantine culture, this town (pop. 36,000) guards a very special treasure in the *Museo Diocesano di Arte Sacra (in summer daily 9.30am–1pm and 4.30pm–9pm, in winter Tue–Sat 9.30am–12.30pm and 3pm–6pm, Sun 10am–noon and 4pm–6pm | Via Largo Duomo 5| www.artesacrarossana.it)*. Here, pages of the "Codex Purpureus Rossanensis" are on display, a gospel written and painted by Greek monks on purple-dyed parchment in the 6th century AD.

Rossano is also famous for its liquorice manufacture, e.g. in the little tins from *Amarelli (museum and shop on the main road SS 106 | www.amarelli.it)*. Spend the night at the affordable B&B *La Gatta sul Tetto (3 rooms | Vico Martucci 7 | tel. 32 90 07 93 24 | www.lagattasultetto.it | Budget)*.

SAN DEMETRIO CORONE
(195 D3) (*Ø L10*)

One of two dozen Albanian villages in Calabria. At the end of the 15th century, Albanians fleeing from the Turks ended up in Italy. They settled in southern Italy and Sicily, mostly here in Calabria, east and west of the Sila Greca. Every year in May, a large colourful Albanian festival takes place in the nearby *Santa Sofia d'Epiro*.

SCILLA ⚞ (194 C5) (*Ø K12*)

A highlight on the coast of Calabria is this mythical ("Scylla and Charybdis") fishing village (pop. 5000), picturesquely situated on the coast overlooking the Strait of Messina to Sicily and the Aeolian Islands, also known for its swordfish fleet. The fishing district of *Chianalea* with its winding streets is among the most beautiful villages in Italy.

STILO (195 D5) (*∭ L12*)

In this hamlet (pop. 2600), perched at 400 m/1312 ft on a rocky hillside over-

At *Genius Loci (closed Wed | Largo Vaccari 51 | tel. 34 55 89 64 75 | Moderate)* you can dine with a view of the Santa Maria dell'Isola church. Not far from the vibrant centre of Tropea, you can stay in the charming Mediterranean *Villa Antica*

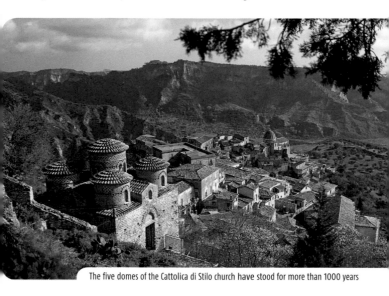

The five domes of the Cattolica di Stilo church have stood for more than 1000 years

looking the Ionian Sea, you will see one of the most important sights in Calabria: the ★ *Cattolica,* a small Byzantine brick church from the 10th century with five domes and a partially preserved mosaic floor.

TROPEA ☀ (194 C4) (*∭ K12*)

Tropea (pop. 6600), with an important *cathedral* in a superb location on a steep cliff above the beach, is one of the most attractive and expensive coastal towns in Calabria. Bizarre rock forms rise from the sea and a fine sandy beach leads into the clean water, for example at ☀ *Capo Vaticano* at the southernmost point.

(28 rooms | Via Pietro Ruffo di Calabria 37 | tel. 09 63 60 32 45 | www.villaanti catropea.it | Moderate).

LECCE AND SALENTO

(193 F5) (*∭ N9–10*) Lecce (pop. 91,000) offers unique scenes of Baroque magnificence from the 16th, 17th and 18th century, a result of the Spanish influence. Yellow tuff stone ornaments adorn Lecce's palazzi, churches and especially the spectacular *cathedral complex*. The most magnificent example of Lecce Baroque is the

Basilica di Santa Croce (daily 9am–noon and 5pm–8pm | Via Umberto I 3) with its richly adorned facade. In the centre, there is a Roman a*mphitheatre* and a *castle* built by Charles V (large market daily).

In recent years, a whole range of INSIDER TIP pretty B&B accommodation has become available in Lecce's atmospheric old town, e.g. *L'Orangerie d'Époque (3 rooms | Viale Lo Re 24 | tel. 08 32 24 41 31 | www.lorangeriedepoque.com | Budget)*. Try the local specialities at the gastronomic shop-cum-bistro *Mamma Elvira (closed Sun | Via Umberto I 19 | tel. 08 32 169 20 11 | www.mammaelvira.com | Budget)*.

Lecce is the urban centre of INSIDER TIP Salento *(www.salentonline.it, www.salento dolcevita.com)*. The flat, almost island-shaped boot heel, with its ancient olive groves and enchanting seaside towns with *masserie* – farmhouses converted into holiday accommodation – and lively music scene, which culminates in the *Pizzica Taranta* festival in the summer on numerous village squares, deserves consideration on any holiday itinerary. Beach life takes place along the Adriatic. In *San Cataldo* and from there down to pretty *Torre dell'Orso* and further south in the direction of Otranto, you will reach the popular sandy beaches of *Alimini* as well as *Baia dei Turchi*.

WHERE TO GO

GALLIPOLI (193 F6) (*Ϭ M10*)
One of the most beautiful towns (pop. 20,000) in southern Italy (certainly the old town full of narrow, winding alleys, whitewashed buildings and Baroque palaces on an ☼ island off the coast in the Ionian Sea). The church *Santa Maria della Purità* is decorated with lovely majolica. The fresh, beautifully prepared fish served at the traditional *Grotta Marinara* restaurant *(closed Tue | Via Battisti 13 | tel. 08 33 26 40 30 | Moderate–Expensive)* in the heart of the old town comes from Gallipoli's famous fish market. There are numerous terrace restaurants on the ☼ promenade around the old town, ideal in the summer to sit and relax. Especially lovely sandy beaches – in summer the youth meet here – stretch south towards Pescoluse and Torre San Giovanni.

GREEK VILLAGES (193 F5–6) (*Ϭ N10*)
There are still villages in Salento where an ancient form of Greek is spoken: Calimera, Sternatia, Soleto, Martignano, Martano, Castrignano de'Greci and Corigliano d'Otranto. It is called *Griko* and more recently cultural associations have been trying to save it from extinction. Every year in August, thousands of young people gather in *Melpignano* for the INSIDER TIP *Notte della Taranta (www.lanottedellataranta.it)*, to dance the traditional rhythmic folk dance of the Salento.

OTRANTO (193 F5) (*Ϭ N10*)
Italy's easternmost town on the peninsula where the Ionian Sea meets the Adriatic is one of country's most attractive holiday resorts. Otranto (pop. 5000) has a picturesque, whitewashed lively old town, clean sea and a variety of places to stay, from simple B&Bs, to holidays on the farm (in the stately, pale grey *masserie)* and luxurious resorts. It also has one of the most important ★ *mosaic artworks* in the world: on the *floor of the cathedral* a 1596 m²/17,200 ft² area displaying images of mythological figures, enigmatic symbolism and Biblical stories. It is a unique example of the mystical union between Christian and Eastern culture that the monk Pantaleone created from 1163–66, using around 10 million mosaics.

One of the most beautiful coastlines in Italy is the ☼ rocky coast south from

Santa Maria Finis Terrae: is this really the 'end of the world'? No, just the heel of Italy's boot

Otranto down to Santa Maria di Leuca, with attractive places, such as the elegant spa town *Santa Cesarea Terme* or the meandering *Castro*. There is a marvellous view of the coast and sea from the ☼ terrace of the country hotel *Masseria Panareo (18 rooms | Litoranea Otranto | tel. 08 36 81 29 99 | www.masseriapanareo.com | Moderate)*, which has a very good restaurant, in Santa Cesarea Terme.

On the ☼ forecourt of the pilgrimage church *Finis Terrae* in *Santa Maria di Leuca* – on the extreme tip of the boot's heel – you really do feel as if you have reached the "end of the world".

NAPLES (NAPOLI)

(191 F6) (*Ø J9*) **Seen from the sea, in the distance, Naples – the most dense-ly populated city in Europe (pop. 1 million) – appears wonderfully promising. Dominating the south is the broad cone of Mount Vesuvius, Italy's second largest active volcano after Mount Etna, which has been dormant for the last 70 years.**

The city has existed for the last 3000 years, initially merged together from three Greek settlements, later becoming Roman and Byzantine; from 1266 to 1860 it was the capital of the kingdom of Naples which encompassed all of southern Italy, as well as the seat of French, Spanish, Habsburg and Bourbon royal families.

In the city's interwoven fabric, you will find legacies of this royal past – elegant public squares, palazzi and gardens – right next to labyrinthine districts of chaotic proportions. Yet the city also boasts a lot of contemporary culture. Contemporary art centres such as *PAN*

WHERE TO START?
Via Benedetto Croce–Via San Biagio dei Librai–Via Vicaria Vecchia: the 3 km/1.8 mile main street cuts through the old town, which is why it is called *Spaccanapoli*. The other axis (**Via Toledo**–Via Pessina) connects the main Piazza del Plebiscito with the archaeological museum. Naples can best be explored by metro. If you arrive by car, use a P&R car park such as *Parking Ferraris (Via Brin Stefano 20) or Italpark (Via Giulio Cesare 50 | www.myparking.it).*

(*Palazzo delle Arti di Napoli)* and *MADRE (Museo d'Arte Contemporanea Donna Regina)* contribute to the cultural variety. During the cultural event *Maggio dei Monumenti* in May, numerous events are being staged.
For a more detailed description of the city, refer to the MARCO POLO "Naples and the Amalfi Coast" guide.

SIGHTSEEING

CAPPELLA SANSEVERO

The small rococo church contains some exceptional sculptures, especially the "Veiled Christ", with its intricate drapery a masterpiece by Giuseppe Sammartino (1753). *Wed–Mon 9.30am–6.30pm | Via de Sanctis 19–21 | www.museosansevero.it*

CASTEL NUOVO

Also called the Maschio Angioino, this castle was the residence of Neapolitan kings from the 13th century; the wonderful Renaissance arch was added in the 15th century. Today, it hosts exhibitions. *Mon–Sat 8.30am–7pm | Piazza Municipio*

CASTEL DELL'OVO

Standing on a small rocky outcrop, this formidable Norman castle has become a symbol of the indestructibility of Naples: Virgil is said to have placed an egg in the wall, prophesying that Naples would continue to exist for as long as the egg remained intact. The castle overlooks the busy fishing harbour of *Porto Santa Lucia* and the *Borgo Marinaro,* popular with night owls, with its trattorias and cafés.

CASTEL SANT'ELMO AND CERTOSA SAN MARTINO

The 1329 fort rises above the eastern rim of the Vomero plateau; in front of it is the Baroque Carthusian cloister of *Certosa*

San Martino (Thu–Tue 8.30am–7.30pm | Largo San Martino 5) home to a beautiful *collection of nativity scenes.* There are magnificent views of the gulf from the ❀ park.

CATACOMBE DI SAN GENNARO

The most impressive subterranean cemetery in southern Italy with early Christian graffiti (2nd century). *Mon–Sat 10am–5pm, Sun 10am–1pm | Tondo di Capodimonte 13 | entrance near the Basilica della Madre del Buon Consiglio www.catacombedinapoli.it*

DUOMO SAN GENNARO

In the repeatedly redesigned French Gothic cathedral of the patron saint of Naples is the San Gennaro (St Januarius) chapel with reliquaries, also a vial of what is thought to be his blood, which liquefies twice a year in September and May during ardent prayers when it is brought out during a special religious ceremony. Enjoy the panoramic view while ❀ **INSIDER TIP** taking a stroll on the cathedral's roof. *Via Duomo*

MUSEO ARCHEOLOGICO NAZIONALE ★

The museum contains one of the largest and most famous archaeological collections in the world, with murals from Pompeii and Herculaneum. Don't forget to go and see the collection of artistic and unambiguous erotica from ancient pleasure houses, exhibited in the *Gabinetto Segreto. Wed–Mon 9am–7.30pm | Piazza Museo*

MUSEO E GALLERIE NAZIONALI DI CAPODIMONTE ★

The magnificent royal palace of Capodimonte, set in a beautiful ❀ park high above the city, houses the art collections

The sleeping giant: Vesuvius always dominates the view of Naples and its Gulf

handed down over the years by the different rulers of Naples and includes works by Simone Martini, Masaccio, Caravaggio, Correggio, Titian, Breughel and many others. The residential chambers include a salon made entirely of porcelain, a work

daily 10am–6pm | www.napolisotterranea. org

PALAZZO REALE

This impressive royal palace (17th century) was the seat of the Bourbon govern-

Napoli Sotterranea: Naples underworld – this time the literal one

by the famous porcelain manufactory of Capodimonte. Also exhibitions of contemporary art. *Thu–Tue 8.30am–7.30 pm | Via di Capodimonte | museocapo dimonte.beniculturali.it*

INSIDER TIP NAPOLI SOTTERRANEA (NAPLES UNDERGROUND) ●

The town is built on tuff stone, into which caves, cisterns and catacombs have been dug. On the *Piazzetta San Gaetano 68* in the old town you can walk down into Naples's underworld, a labyrinth cut into the volcanic rock by the Greeks and Romans. *Guided tours (also in English)*

ment from 1734 to 1860. You can visit the lovely staircase and the magnificently decorated rooms *(Thu–Tue 9am–8pm)*. The palazzo is on the broad restored *Piazza del Plebiscito,* which is framed by the neoclassical church of San Francesco di Paola modelled on the Roman Pantheon.

SAN LORENZO MAGGIORE

One of the most stunning medieval churches in Naples. Remains of the ancient Roman market have been found under the Franciscan monastery. *Daily 9.30am–5.30pm | Piazza San Gaetano | www.sanlorenzomaggiore.na.it*

SANTA CHIARA

The *Convento dei Minori* belongs to the French-Gothic church, famous for its *Chiostro delle Clarisse,* a cloister with majolica tiled porticos. *Mon–Sat 9.30am–5.30pm, Sun 10am–2.30pm | Via Benedetto Croce | www.monasterodisan tachiara.com*

TEATRO SAN CARLO

Temple of melodrama, originally decked out in the Baroque and then restored in neoclassical style after a fire in 1816. One of the most beautiful opera houses in Italy, open to the public. *Via San Carlo 98f | tel. 08 17 97 24 12) | www. teatrosancarlo.it*

RACK RAILWAYS (FUNICOLARI) ⚙

They will take you up to the Vomero, once the appropriately higher ground for the upper classes: *Funicolare Centrale* (*Via Toledo–Piazza Fuga*), *Funicolare di Chiaia* (*Via Parco Margherita–Via Cimarosa*), *Funicolare di Montesanto* (*Piazza Montesanto–Via Morghen*); lovely views during the ride with the *Funicolare di Mergellina* (*Via Mergellina–Via Manzoni*).

FOOD & DRINK

INSIDER TIP ANTICA CAPRI

This small, family-run trattoria in the Spagnoli district is very popular with locals for its authentic Neapolitan cuisine. *Closed Sun evening and Thu | Via Speranzella 110 | tel. 08 10 38 34 86 | www. anticacapri.it | Budget*

DA MICHELE

The restaurant is always full because, as the Neapolitans say themselves, you can eat the best pizzas here, in a convivial atmosphere sitting on wooden benches at marble tables. *Closed Sun | Via Cesare*

Sersale 1–3 | tel. 08 15 53 92 04 | da michele.net | Budget

PASTICCERIA SCATURCHIO

This confectionery in the old town is celebrated for its delicious *sfogliatella* (pastry filled with ricotta) and *babà* rum cake. *Daily | Piazza San Domenico Maggiore 19 | www.scaturchio.it*

SHOPPING

The streets *Via Chiaia, Via dei Mille, Via Roma* are full of exclusive boutiques. The *Spaccanapoli* and their side streets are full of small shops and tradesmen. In the **INSIDER TIP** street of nativity scenes *Via San Gregorio Armeno,* you can watch the artisans at work all year.

ENTERTAINMENT

Besides national, puppet and avant-garde theatre as well as opera, Naples has a lively music scene. A popular meeting point is the snug *Piazza Bellini* with its tree-shaded cafés, such as the *Intra Moenia.* Event programmes and tickets: *Box Office | Galleria Umberto I 16 | tel. 08 15 51 91 88 | Inx.boxofficenapoli.it*

WHERE TO STAY

B & B GRAND TOUR

In the elegant Chiaia district near the promenade guests stay in country-style-rooms, some with a view of the sea. *6 rooms | Via Santa Lucia 76 | tel. 0 81 19 32 44 10 | www.grandtourbb.com | Budget–Moderate*

HOTEL PIAZZA BELLINI

Successful contrasts: ultramodern interior, superb comfort and perfect location in the middle of the old town, good value for money. *48 rooms, 2 apartments | Via*

Santa Maria di Costantinopoli 101 | tel. 0 81 45 17 32 | www.hotelpiazzabellini.com | Budget–Moderate

INFORMATION

Main Station, Via San Carlo 9 and *Piazza Gesù Nuovo | tel. 0 81 40 23 94 | www.regione.campania.it, www.inaples. it.* Naples and the surroundings also offer a visitor's pass that provides discounts and is valid for three or seven days: *Campania Artecard (www.artecard.it).*

WHERE TO GO

AMALFI AND THE SORRENTO PENINSULA (191 F6) *(ØØ J9)*

South of Naples, the rocky ᴺᴸᴱ peninsula of Sorrento juts far out into the sea towards the island of Capri, a powerful partition between the Gulf of Naples and the Gulf of Salerno. Situated on a rocky plateau, high above the coast, *Sorrento* (pop. 17,000) – a lively tourist centre with many traditional luxury hotels – specialises in the craft of wood carving/inlay, which you can admire at the *Museo Correale di Terranova (Tue–Sat 9.30am–6.30pm, Sun 9.30am–1.30pm | Via Correale 5 | www.*

museocorreale.it). In the heart of the old town you can stay at the guesthouse *Casa Sorrentina (5 rooms | Corso Italia 134 | tel. 08 18 78 27 38 | www.casasorrentina.com | Moderate).*

On the Sorrento peninsula there are masses of superb, star-studded gourmet addresses: in *Sant'Agata sui Due Golfi* the *Don Alfonso 1890 (www.donalfonso.com),* in Vico Equense the highly acclaimed *Torre del Saracino (www.torredelsaracino.it)* and in *Nerano-Massa Lubrense* the *Quattro Passi (www.ristorantequattropassi.com).*

On the south side is the "divine" ★ ᴺᴸᴱ *Costiera Amalfitana* with the famous Oriental-looking towns of Positano, Amalfi, Ravello: probably Italy's most beautiful coast with rugged cliffs, precipitous cliffs, terraces of lemon groves, vineyards, almonds and olive trees and everywhere climbing flowers, wild roses, and bougainvillea. Experience breathtaking views on a hike on the ᴺᴸᴱ **INSIDER TIP** *Sentiero degli Dei* ("Path of the Gods") above the Amalfi coast.

The enchanting *Positano* (pop. 4000) is characterised by bright and red-tinted houses with arcade loggias clinging to the cliffs, and the *Santa Maria Assunta* church with majolica dome. From a his-

PIZZA NAPOLETANA

It appeared for the first time in the 18th century as a fast and cheap snack on the streets of Naples: a simple, malleable dough made of flour, yeast, water and salt, seasoned with olive oil, oregano and garlic. Tomatoes mozzarella and basil came later. At the beginning of the 19th century, Naples was already full of pizzerias, but nobody had heard about them in the rest of Italy. They only caught

up in the 20th century and then via America. There pizza had spread like wildfire thanks to the Italian immigrants and it was from there that it began its triumphal march through Europe. Although you can now get it everywhere, the taste of a real *pizza napoletana* (with tomatoes, mozzarella and basil, also known as Pizza Margherita) in Naples remains a special experience.

A cascade of houses clings to the cliffs and the striking majolica dome: Positano on the Amalfi coast

torical point of view, *Amalfi* (pop. 5100), once an influential maritime republic, is more important. The superb architecture seems to cling to the cliffs, such as the *cathedral* with its magnificent steps, colourful mosaic façade and Arabic Norman *campanile*.

Here, it earns the epithet "divine coast" because of its enchanting luxury hotels, but there is also charming and reasonably affordable accommodation, e.g. in Positano ☆ *Palazzo Talamo (11 rooms | Viale Pasitea 117 | tel. 0 89 87 55 62 | www. palazzotalamo.it | Expensive)* or a mile outside of Amalfi *Locanda Costa d'Amalfi (6 rooms, 3 apartments | Via Giovanni Augustoriccio 50 | tel. 08 9 83 19 50 | www.locandacostadamalfi.it | Budget–*

Moderate). A shopping tip is Amalfi's handmade paper: you can buy the traditional paper from shops in Amalfi and Positano and admire its production in the *Museo della Carta (March–Oct daily 10am–6.30pm, Nov–Feb Tue/Wed and Fri–Sun 10am–3.30pm | Via delle Cartiere 24 | www.museodellacarta.it).*

In the mountains above Amalfi, perched on large rock and tucked away in lush vegetation, is the enchanting *Ravello,* famous for its music festival and very modern *auditorium,* Romanesque *cathedral* and precious villas such as the Arabic *Villa Rufolo* (13th century). From the ☆ terrace in the garden of *Villa Cimbrone* (with renovated charming hotel), there is a breathtaking view of the gulf. *www.amalficoast.com*

Wall-spanning fresco revealing what went on behind the walls of the Villa dei Misteri

CASERTA AND CAPUA
(191 F6) (𝑀 J9)

Visit the impressive gardens in Caserta, a Unesco site, with the enormous Baroque castle *Reggia di Caserta (Wed–Mon 8.30am–7.30pm, park 8.30pm–2 hours before sunset)* with 1200 rooms, 1790 windows and 94 steps (construction period of the facade alone 1752–74): the ambitious "Versailles" of Bourbon King Charles III of Naples.

In *Capua* in the *Museo Campano (Tue–Sat 9am–1.30pm, Sun 9am–1pm, Tue, Thu also 3pm–6pm)*, the INSIDER TIP quite unique votive statues (7th–1st century BC) of Mater Matuta, goddess of fertility and maternity, are well worth seeing. The stone mother figures hold swaddled babies in their arms. Equally fascinating is the Roman *amphitheatre* in *Santa Maria Capua Vetere* – the second largest in Italy – with a nearby *Mithraic temple*.

HERCULANEUM (ERCOLANO)
(191 F6) (𝑀 J9)

When Mount Versuvius erupted in AD 79 Pompeii was showered with lava rain and Herculaneum was smothered under hot mud. From Corso Ercolano, you can ascend to the Roman sports arena and enter the still not completely excavated town. *Daily*

9am–5pm, April–Oct until 7.30pm | Corso Resina

PAESTUM AND CILENTO
(194 B1–2) (𝄞 K9–10)

At the southern arc of the Gulf of Salermo – in the harbour town that has recently received a facelift – these wonderfully preserved Doric temples dedicated to Hera and the fertility goddess of Ceres rise into view in the old Greek commercial town of Poseido. The Romans called it ★ *Paestum*. The Arabs destroyed the town; its ruins lay under a thick layer of vegetation until 200 years ago. *Temple site daily 8.45am–1 hour before sunset, museum daily 8.30am–6.45pm, closed on 1st and 3rd Mon in the month | www.infopaestum.it).*

Following the plain of Paestum is INSIDER TIP *Cilento,* a beautiful, unspoilt, accessible coastline with ● sandy beaches, bays and grottoes – e.g. between Pisciotta and Palinuro or between Marina di Camerota and the Golfo di Policastro. Inland, the *Monti Alburni* and the *Monte Cervati* reach heights of almost 2000 m/6562 ft: the national park is a popular holiday destination and offers attractions such as the Baroque cloister *Certosa di San Lorenzo (Wed–Mon 9am–7.30pm | Via Certosa 1)* in *Padula.*

POMPEII (POMPEI) ★
(191 F6) (𝄞 J9)

What makes this town excavated from the hard lava stone *(daily 9am–5pm, April–Oct until 7.30pm | www.pompeiisites.org)* so unique is not its buildings as such but the insight it provides into everyday Roman life. Shops, bars, cobbled streets worn with deep grooves from the wagons of the ancients Romans... The phallic symbols on the entrances were used to ward off evil spirits. Here are also the famous frescoes depicting scenes of the initiation of women into the cult of Dionysus in the *Villa dei Misteri.*

VESUVIUS (VESUVIO) ᴧ⊻
(191 F6) (𝄞 J9)

An absolute must when visiting Naples is a trip to the impressive, still active volcano, Mount Vesuvius (1281 m/4200 ft) in the south-east of the city. A road with hairpin bends leads to a fee-paying car park. From here you can walk across the lava fields to the rim of the crater (20 min) where you can get a glimpse of the abyss. *April–June and Sept daily 9am–5pm, July/Aug 9am–6pm, March and Oct 9am–4pm, Nov–Feb 9am–3pm | www.epnv.it/grancono*

DISCOVERY TOURS

1 ITALY AT A GLANCE

START: ❶ Lake Como
END: ㉚ Bolzano

32 days
Driving time
(without stops)
approx 65–80 hours

Distance:
➡ approx. 4200 km/2610 miles

COSTS: approx. 7000–9000 euros for 2 people (petrol, toll fees, admission costs, food, accommodation)

WHAT TO PACK: sun protection and rainwear, hiking boots, comfortable shoes for city tours, swimwear, daypack, sports gear for windsurfing, diving and snorkelling if needed

IMPORTANT TIPS: We recommend pre-booking online to visit many of the famous sights in Rome, Milan, Verona, Pisa or Florence to avoid queuing; for some sights, tickets *must* be bought online.

Would you like to explore the places that are unique to this region? Then the Discovery Tours are just the thing for you – they include terrific tips for stops worth making, breathtaking places to visit, selected restaurants and typical activities. It's even easier with the Touring App: Download the tour with map and route using the QR Code on pages 2/3 or from the website address in the footer to your smartphone – and you'll always have the perfect orientation even when you're offline.

TOURING APP

→ p. 2/3

Fascinating art heritage cities, long stretches of beaches and impressive mountain scenery: this tour right around Italy's boot explores the vast diversity of the country's cultural heritage and rich landscapes. Starting in the north, your route heads down south to Calabria and along the Ionian and Adriatic coast back to the Alps.

The tour starts **directly after the Swiss border** at ❶ **Lake Como** → p. 76. Take a boat trip on the *lago* to soak in the elegance of the old villas with their splendid gardens and the magnificent alpine scenery. Attractive accommodation

DAY 1–4
❶ Lake Como

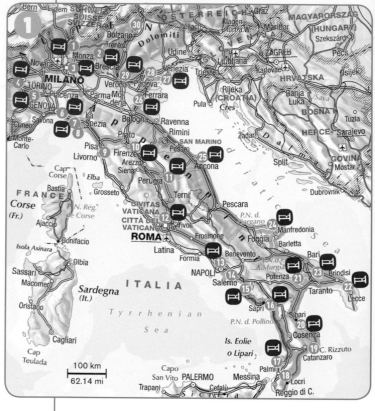

(131 km/81 miles)

②Valcamonica 🌳 🛏

(133 km/83 miles)

③Milan 🎭 🏛 🛍 🛏

DAY 5–10

(144 km/89 miles)

④Turin 🎭 🏰 🍷 🛏

for the night can be found in **Varenna**, for example. **Drive along the east banks of the lake with its wonderful views of the Bergamo Alps, over the Aprica Pass and into the ② Valcamonica Valley → p. 75**, where you can see its famous prehistoric rock art (8000 years old) at **Capo di Ponte**. Schedule two days to explore the art and design of Lombardy's capital **③ Milan → p. 71**. Visit Leonardo da Vinci's mural **"The Last Supper"** in the **Santa Maria delle Grazie church** and stroll through Milan's high-end fashion quarter **Quadrilatero** around the **Via Monte Napoleone**.

Italy's first capital city **④ Turin → p. 46** welcomes tourists with its elegant arcades in its Baroque city centre. No doubt you will be tempted more than once to a cappuccino and mouth-watering *gianduiotti* at one of the city's traditional coffee houses. A relaxing spot for an aperitif is at one of the trattorias of the *murazzi* quays **along the Po riverfront. Head south of Turin to the** ⑤ **Langhe** → p. 49 where you can spend two days meandering through the region's vine-covered hillsides and tasting the regional specialities and wines. If in season, order a dish with local truffles – the smell alone is hypnotizing. **The Italian Riviera, or coast of Liguria, is just an hour's drive from here. In** ⑥ **Genoa** → p. 39 a visit to the noble palaces in the old city centre, the **Palazzi dei Rolli**, reminds you of the city's proud maritime republic past. **The SS 1 coastal road takes you to** ⑦ **Levanto** → p. 43, a good base for two nights, from where you can explore the ⑧ **Cinque Terre** → p. 43 National Park on foot. The coastal path next to fragrant pine forests leads to the pretty village of **Monterosso** with spectacular sea views and a tiny **beach** for hikers to cool down.

Your first stop in Tuscany has to be ⑨ **Pisa** → p. 105 with a climb up its world-famous **Leaning Tower**! Continue on to ⑩ **Florence** → p. 85 where your city tour should also start by ascending some stairs: those of the iconic **Duomo** for amazing views over the medieval cityscape; spend your second day exploring the city below on foot, packed with extraordinary Renaissance art and architecture master-pieces at every turn. Nestled in Umbria's delightful hillside is ⑪ **Assisi** → p. 97 where you can take time out to visit the famous **Basilica**, before heading off the day after to ⑫ **Rome** → p. 113 with its astounding array of sights which you need three days at least to explore. Are your feet ach-ing from all the walking? Then hire a Segway from the agency **Segway Roma** *(tel. 38 03 01 29 13 | www.segway roma.net),* to glide effortlessly around the capital's streets.

The imposing Vesuvius → p. 145 greets you from afar in the buzzing and vibrant city of ⑬ **Naples** → p. 137. Travel around the city on the **Metrò dell'Arte** → p. 133 and hire a rickshaw from **Foxrent Bike** *(Via Partenope 37 | tel. 08 17 64 50 60 | www.foxrent.it)* to ride along the prome-nade at sunset. During your two days in Naples, **the train ride to the excavations at** ⑭ **Pompeii** → p. 145 is a must and transports you back in time to the Roman Empire. And you can't visit Naples without trying the best-flavoured pizza in the whole of Italy. The **coastal roads along the Sorrento Peninsula** offer some of the most spectacular scenery and lead you to another landmark of classical an-

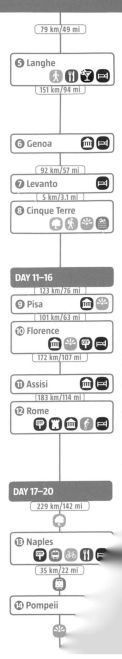

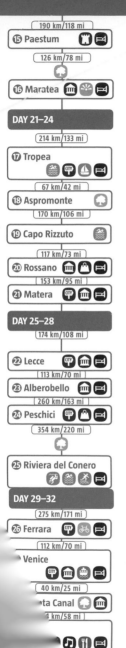

190 km/118 mi

⑮ Paestum

126 km/78 mi

⑯ Maratea

DAY 21–24

214 km/133 mi

⑰ Tropea

67 km/42 mi

⑱ Aspromonte

170 km/106 mi

⑲ Capo Rizzuto

117 km/73 mi

⑳ Rossano

153 km/95 mi

㉑ Matera

DAY 25–28

174 km/108 mi

㉒ Lecce

113 km/70 mi

㉓ Alberobello

260 km/163 mi

㉔ Peschici

354 km/220 mi

㉕ Riviera del Conero

DAY 29–32

275 km/171 mi

㉖ Ferrara

112 km/70 mi

Venice

40 km/25 mi

ta Canal

㉔ km/58 mi

tiquity: the ancient Greek city of ⑮ **Paestum** → p. 145. Try and get there INSIDERTIP early the next morning to avoid the coach loads of tourists and the midday sun. **Head along the unspoilt Cilento coast to** ⑯ **Maratea** → p. 130. From the gigantic **Statue of Christ** you have views along the entire Gulf of Policastro.

Relax on the beach, stroll through the old town and take a boat trip: your checklist of things to do in ⑰ **Tropea** → p. 135, maybe the prettiest of all coastal resorts on Calabria's Tyrrhenian Coast. It is worth spending two days breathing in this town's captivating prettiness. **The SP 1 road leads you through the rugged** ⑱ **Aspromonte** → p. 132 **mountain massif to the Ionian Sea** on the east coast where you can bathe in refreshing waters at the beaches along the ⑲ **Capo Rizzuto** → p. 133. Spend the night in the liquorice-manufacturing town of ⑳ **Rossano** → p. 134 with a museum and shop belonging to **Amarelli**. The next stop is the famous cave city of ㉑ **Matera** → p. 130 with its beguiling churches and hotels carved from the soft volcanic rock.

Your route takes you on to Salento and the Baroque town of ㉒ **Lecce** → p. 135. Its splendid **Basilica di Santa Croce** will surely impress any visitor, whatever their religion or faith. **Traverse through the typical *trulli* landscape to** ㉓ **Alberobello** → p. 125 to spend a night in one of the town's curiously round buildings. **After returning to the coast,** ㉔ **Peschici** → p. 127, located in the picturesque region of **Gargano,** has an enticing **old town centre** with stylish arts and crafts. Now try your hand at diving or surfing at the ㉕ **Riviera del Conero** → p. 94, a particularly beautiful spot along the Adriatic coast **to the south of Ancona.**

The Renaissance gem of ㉖ **Ferrara** → p. 70 is situated on the flat Po plain. Take time out for a short bike ride through Italy's mecca for cyclists. On the upper Adriatic, you will reach the unique lagoon city of ㉗ **Venice** → p. 62. The best view of the majestic palazzi can be had by taking to the water in a vaporetto on the **Canal Grande. Continue along the** ㉘ **Brenta Canal,** where many Venetian aristocratic families built their summer residences, **to Padua and from there on to** ㉙ **Verona** → p. 64. A highlight in summer is to visit a Verdi opera in the city's gigantic Roman **Arena** right in the centre which seats up to 22,000 people. But don't forget to take a picnic; performances can last up to

can find these tours as an app at: go.marco-polo.com/ita

156 km/97 mi

30 Bolzano

four hours. On arrival in the South Tyrol capital of **30 Bolzano → p. 52** you will notice that your tour is coming to an end when you hear German on the streets. Stroll through the Austro-Hungarian looking **old town centre** with its pretty arcades and enjoy an apple strudel or the typical *Schlutzkrapfen* (similar to Ravioli) to finish your tour.

2 PILGRIMAGE TO ROME ALONG THE VIA FRANCIGENA

START: ① Great Saint Bernhard Pass **END: ⑯ Rome**	**6 days** Driving time (without stops) approx. 18–24 hours

Distance:
➡ around 1000 km/620 miles

COSTS: approx. 1400–1800 euros for 2 people (petrol, accommodation, food, admission costs)
WHAT TO PACK: sun screen and rainwear, swimwear

IMPORTANT TIPS: The **①** Great Saint Bernhard Pass is usually open from May to October.
Pre-book concert tickets for **⑦** Parma before starting the tour.

The route of the medieval pilgrims from the Alps to Rome takes you through some of the most beautiful Italian towns and countryside. The Via Francigena *(www.viefrancigene.org),* the old Franconia road, runs from the North of Italy to the country's centre to Rome.

Your route starts at the ① Great Saint Bernhard Pass (2473 m/8144 ft) with its breathtaking alpine landscape and waterfalls, inviting you to take a short walk before setting off on your tour. **Your first stop is in ② Aosta → p. 35,** where you can visit the monastery of **Santi Pietro e Orso** with its unique cloister. **In the afternoon the route continues along the Dora Baltea Valley (SS 26) in front of an impressive alpine mountain backdrop and past the castles → p. 37** of the former feudal lords. Take a break in the small town of **③ Vigevano → p. 76** with its delightful oval **Piazza Ducale,** where you can enjoy the afternoon sun in one of square's inviting cafés. Your day ends in the charming *agriturismo* **④ Cascina Mora** *(8 rooms | Strada Mora 800 | tel. 03 82 52 60 81 | www.cascinamora.it | Budget)* set in the tranquil rice fields on the outskirts of Pavia.

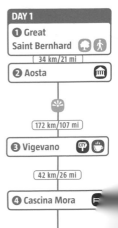

DAY 1

① Great Saint Bernhard

34 km/21 mi

② Aosta

172 km/107 mi

③ Vigevano

42 km/26 mi

④ Cascina Mora

"Medieval Manhattan": two of the 72 towers of San Gimignano

10 km/6 miles to the north of Pavia is the renaissance gem of ⑤ **Certosa di Pavia** → p. 75 with its ornately decorated facade. After your visit, treat yourself to exquisite Lombardi gourmet cuisine at the **Locanda Vecchia Pavia Al Mulino** *(closed Sun evening and Mon | Via al Monumento 5 | tel. 03 82 92 58 94 | www.vecchiapaviaalmulino.it | Expensive)*. Spend the afternoon at the ⑥ **INSIDERTIP** **Labirinto della Masone** *(Wed–Mon 10.30am–7pm | Strada Masone 121 | www.labirintodifrancomariaricci.it)* **near Fontanellato.** The phrase "You have to lose yourself to find yourself" will help you get through Italy's largest garden labyrinth. Finish the day by attending a concert in ⑦ **Parma** → p. 78, a city with a rich musical heritage.

Once you have stocked up on Parma ham at **La Prosciutteria** *(Strada Farini 9c)* head **through the Taro Valley and up into the Apennines.** This beautiful route takes you through picturesque countryside and the ever-changing mountain meadows and woods. **Crossing the Cisa Pass (1093 m/3586 ft)**, you will enter Tuscany. Explore the medieval town of ⑧ **Pontremoli** with its castello, housing the **Museo delle Statue Stele Lunigianesi** *(Tue–Sun 9am–12.30pm and 3pm–5.30pm | www.statuestele.org)* where you can study the enigmatic steles, statue menhirs dating to 1200 BC. Enjoy lunch at the idyllic **Cà del Moro** *(closed Sun evening and Mon | Località Casa Corvi 9 | tel. 01 87 83 05 88 | www.cadelmororesort.it | Expensive)* with its panoramic views. In the afternoon, **continue on the SS 1 against the back-drop of the marble mountains of Carrara to** ⑨ **Pietrasanta**, where you can find out more about the Carrara marble in **MuSA** *(Thu–Sun 6pm–11pm | Via Sant'Agostino 61 | www.musapietrasanta.it)*. In ⑩ **Lucca** → p. 90, spend the night close to the city centre in the modern **Hotel San Marco** *(42 rooms | Via San Marco 368 | tel. 05 83 49 50 10 | www.hotelsanmarcolucca.com | Budget–Moderate)* with a splendid terrace.

After breakfast, borrow one of the hotel's bikes to explore Lucca's delight-

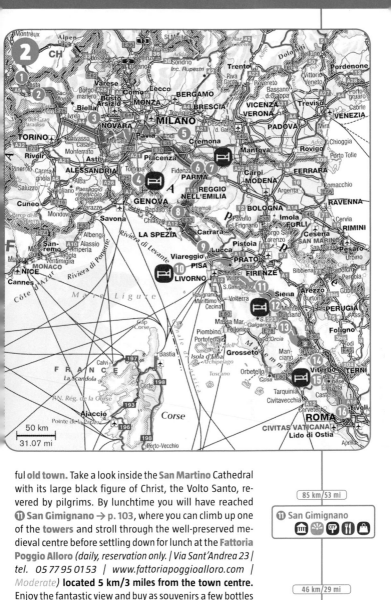

ful **old town.** Take a look inside the **San Martino** Cathedral with its large black figure of Christ, the Volto Santo, revered by pilgrims. By lunchtime you will have reached **⑪ San Gimignano → p. 103**, where you can climb up one of the **towers** and stroll through the well-preserved medieval centre before settling down for lunch at the **Fattoria Poggio Alloro** (daily, reservation only. | Via Sant'Andrea 23 | tel. 05 77 95 01 53 | www.fattoriapoggioalloro.com | Moderate) **located 5 km/3 miles from the town centre.** Enjoy the fantastic view and buy as souvenirs a few bottles of wine and olive oil produced by this family-run business. By late afternoon you will have reached the medieval masterpiece of **⑫ Siena → p. 100**, where you can take

85 km / 53 mi

⑪ **San Gimignano**

46 km / 29 mi

⑫ **Siena**

an evening stroll on one of Italy's prettiest squares, the **Piazza del Campo**.

Countryside roads lined with cypress trees **lead you southwards through the Crete Senesi hillside.** Make sure you reach the Romanesque monastery of ⑬ **Sant'Antimo → p. 102**, by 1pm in time to hear the Gregorian chants of the residing monks. You will arrive at the ⑭ **Lago di Bolsena → p. 121** in the afternoon where you can take a plunge in its crystal-clear waters. It is not far now to your overnight accommodation in ⑮ **Viterbo → p. 120**. Walk through Viterbo's medieval centre the next morning before heading to your final destination of ⑯ **Rome → p. 113 along the SP 1.**

DAY 5–6

┌── 56 km/35 mi ──┐

⑬ Sant'Antimo 🏛 🎵

┌── 73 km/45 mi ──┐

⑭ Lago di Bolsena 🏊

┌── 39 km/24 mi ──┐

⑮ Viterbo 🍴 🏙

┌── 82 km/51 mi ──┐

⑯ Rome

3   CYCLING THROUGH THE DOLOMITES

START: ❶ Toblach **END:** ⓫ Calalzo di Cadore	**2 days** Cycling time (without stops) 5–7 hours
Distance: ➡ 80 km/50 miles	**Level of difficulty:** .ıl easy

COSTS: approx. 140 euros per person (bike hire, accommodation, admission costs, cable car, not including food)

WHAT TO PACK: snacks and drinking bottle for the bike, sun protection and rainwear, swimwear

IMPORTANT TIPS: bike hire at the station in ❶ Toblach: Dolomitislowbike *(Dolomitenstr. 27a | tel. 34 86 63 35 39 | www.dolomitislowbike.com).* Return your bikes in ⓫ Calalzo or, from the end of June to the end of August, return to ❶ Toblach with Bike 'n' Bus *(daily 3.45pm | tel. 04 37 21 72 26 | www.dolomitibus.it)*

On the cycling route most commonly known as "The Great Dolomite Road", you will be exposed to unique rugged rocky mountain scenery which contrasts spectacularly with the lush green hillside meadows. You ride over deep gorges, past turquoise mountain lakes (where you can swim in one) and picture-perfect villages.

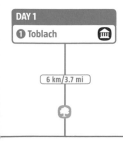

DAY 1

❶ Toblach 🏛

┌── 6 km/3.7 mi ──┐

Before setting off on your route from the train station in ❶ **Toblach,** a visit to the **Drei Zinnen Nature Park visitor centre** *(May–Oct Tue–Sat, July/Aug also Sun 9.30am–12.30pm and 2.30pm–6pm | Via Dolomiti 31 | www.grand hotel-toblach.com)* **situated straight opposite the station** will prepare you for your Dolomites experience. **Head west along the Bahnhofstraße and turn left in front of the SS 51 bridge.** The Höhlensteintal (Val di Landro) spreads out in front of you with the majestic Cristallo mountain range at the end. **After cycling straight along the valley for a while,** you will pass a **2** **military cemetery,** a memorial to the front lines during World War I. Continue on this cycling path for 12 km/7.4 miles until you see the spectacular panorama of the three distinctive battlement-like peaks of the Drei Zinnen (Tre Cime di Lavaredo). **You arrive at the** **3** **Dürrensee (Lago di Landro) shortly after,** a surprisingly warm lake despite its high altitude position (1410 m/4625 ft) and a perfect spot for a quick refreshing dip.

Rest **at the lake** for lunch at the **Ristorante Lago di Landro** *(closed evenings | tel. 04 74 97 23 99 | Budget)* with its tasty authentic cooking and delicious cakes. You are now ready **to tackle the highest section of this route, the 1530 m/5019 ft high** **4** **Passo Cimabanche. Your route now takes you past three small lakes and over a bridge crossing the deep gorge of the Felizon River. A short while later you will reach** **5** **Cortina d'Ampezzo** → p. 54, where you can spend the night in the bike-friendly **Hotel Des Alpes** *(32 rooms | Via La Verra 2 | tel. 04 36 86 20 21 | www.hoteldelespescortina.it | Moderate)* and relax by treating yourself to a hydro massage.

Before jumping on the saddle again, take the opportunity to soak in the spectacular summit view by taking the **Freccia nel Cielo cable lift up to the** **6** **Tofana di Mezzo** → p. 54 at an impressive 3191 m/10,470 ft. **Back in** **7** **Cortina d'Ampezzo, you will join the cycling path again on the Via Cantore which you follow for approx. three quarters of an hour until you reach the** **8** **Albergo Ristorante Dogana Vecchia** *(daily in high season | Via Calvi 31 | San Vito di Cadore | tel. 04 36 89 90 23 | al bergodoganavecchia.com | Budget)*. Here it is worth trying the homemade *casunziei,* the traditionally filled pasta from the Dolomites region.

2 military cemetery
5 km/3.1 mi
3 Dürrensee
5 km/3.1 mi
4 Passo Cimabanche
12 km/7.5 mi
5 Cortina d'Ampezzo
DAY 2
8 km/5 mi
6 Tofana di Mezzo
5 km/3.1 mi
7 Cortina d'Ampezzo
10 km/6.2 mi
8 Albergo Ristorante Dogana Vecchia

In touching distance – the distinctive peaks of the Drei Zinnen Mountains

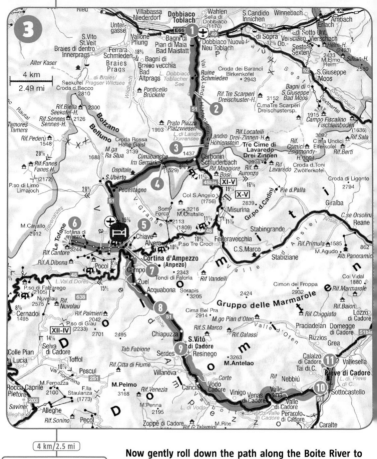

3

9 San Vito di Cadore ☕

4 km/2.5 mi

20 km/12.5 mi

10 Pieve di Cadore 🏛

4 km/2.5 mi

11 Calalzo di Cadore

Now gently roll down the path along the Boite River to **9** **San Vito di Cadore**. Cadore is the name of the valley which cuts through the Dolomites along the Boite and Piave rivers; it is known worldwide as the birthplace of *gelato*. Good enough reason to treat yourself to a generous portion of *gelato artigianale* at the "Ice King" *Il Re del Gelato (Corso Italia 17a)*. The next stop on the tour is **10** **Pieve di Cadore** which once specialised in the production of glasses, home to the original eyewear museum **INSIDERTIP** Museo dell'Occhiale *(July/Aug daily 10am–6.30pm, Sept–June Tue– Sat 9.30am–12.30pm and 3.30pm–6.30pm | Via Arsenale 15 | www.museodellocchiale.it)*. **From here it takes under 30 minutes to your final destination of** **11** **Calalzo di Cadore.**

4 THE MOUNTAINOUS REGION OF ABRUZZO

START: ❶ Teramo
END: ⓫ Guardiagrele

4 days
Driving time
(without stops)
8–10 hours

Distance:
➡ approx. 340 km/210 miles

COSTS: approx. 400 euros for 2 people (petrol, admission costs and accommodation, not including food)
WHAT TO PACK: sturdy shoes, sun protection and rainwear, swimwear

Explore the rugged mountainous region of the Apennines, a unique landscape of breath-taking beauty. This route takes you along winding roads through the Abruzzo National Parks and the Maiella mountain massif with its rich wildlife. You also have the chance to stroll through picturesque villages and try local specialities.

From ❶ Teramo the main road SS 80 goes through the wild Vomano Valley. The journey to **❷ Prati di Tivo** is accompanied by impressive views of the Gran Sasso mountain peaks. **Park up here and on the Via Prati Bassi take the path left (at the Agriturismo dei Prati),** through a dense forest and then past the mountain face of the Corno Piccolo. **This two-hour (there and back) walk** takes you to the natural beauty of the **Rio Arno waterfall.** Have you worked up an appetite from walking? Then head to the **❸ Antica Locanda** *(closed Wed | Via Vicolo Stretto 1 | tel. 08 61 95 51 20 | www.anticalocanda.eu | Budget–Moderate)* **in the idyllic alpine village of Pietracamela** and order a *timballo abruzzese,* the local lasagne-like dish made with crêpes. **The route continues past the vast Lago di Campotosto encompassed by mountains and the smaller, picturesque Lago di Provvidenza over the Passo delle Capannelle (1300 m/4265 ft).** Enjoy the fantastic panoramic views from this height. You will reach **❹ L'Aquila → p. 106** by evening, the perfect time to take a stroll around the Abruzzo capital through its attractively lit *centro storico.*

After exploring the city, buy a *panini* filled with peppers and pecorino cheese from **Panippo** *(Viale Croce Rossa 24–26)* which you can picnic in the **Parco del Sole** at

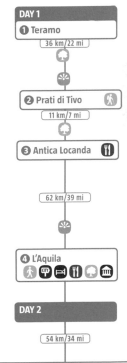

DAY 1

❶ Teramo
36 km/22 mi

❷ Prati di Tivo
11 km/7 mi

❸ Antica Locanda

62 km/39 mi

❹ L'Aquila

DAY 2

54 km/34 mi

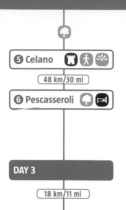

⑤ Celano 🏛️🚶‍♂️🎿

48 km/30 mi

⑥ Pescasseroli 🛏️🍽️

DAY 3

18 km/11 mi

the pretty **Santa Maria di Collemaggio** Basilica. **Continue over the high plains of the Parco Naturale Sirente-Velino to⑤ Celano** with the mighty **Castello Piccolomini** *(Tue–Sun 9am–7.30pm)*. Take a walk along the fortress walls for its fantastic views. **The road now climbs up to the Passo del Diavolo and on to ⑥ Pescasseroli → p. 111**, the **Abruzzo National Park's** visitor centre. The tour agency **Ecotur** *(Via Piave 9 | tel. 08 63 91 27 60 | www. ecotur.org)* organises evening tours to listen to the howling of wolves.

If the "among wolves" guided tour has left you wanting to know more about this species, **stop at Civitella Alfedena**

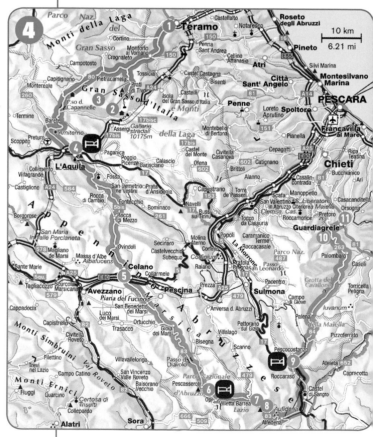

DISCOVERY TOURS

and visit the **❼ Museo del Lupo Appenninico** *(daily 10am–1.30pm and 3pm–6.30pm | Via Santa Lucia)*. Then go for a refreshing swim in the Lago di Barrea, at the beach of **❽ Lido di Gravara** *(June–Sept daily 9am–8pm | SS 83 km 62 | lagravara.altervista.org)*. In the evening, you will reach the Baroque town of **❾ INSIDERTIP Pescocostanzo**, "one of Italy's prettiest villages". Spend the night at the B&B **La Rua** *(6 rooms | Via Rua Mozza 1–3 | tel. 08 64 64 00 83 | www.larua.it | Budget)* with views of the surrounding mountain range.

The SS 84 and the winding SP 214 take you to the Maiella national park with the **❿ Parco Avventura Majella** *(mid March–June Sat/Sun 10am–7pm, July/Aug daily 10am–8pm, Sept–Nov Sat/Sun 10am–4pm | Piana delle Mele | www.parconaturalemajella.it)* where you can try climbing, swinging and balancing your way around the tree canopy tour over suspension bridges. Quench your appetite **at the nearby ⓫ Guardiagrele** → p. 110. This pretty location is famous for its pastry *sise delle monache,* the **Pasticceria Lullo** *(Via Roma 105)* offers a particularly delicious version. Those looking for a suitable souvenir should head to the **INSIDERTIP Bottega Artigianale** *(Tue–Sat 10am–12.30pm and 5pm–7.30pm, Sun 10am–12.30pm | Via Roma 76)* owned by Stefania Santone who sells colourful ceramics.

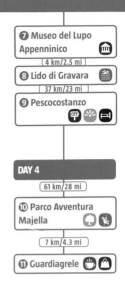

5 HIGHLIGHTS ON THE GULF OF NAPLES

START: ❶ Naples	3 days
END: ❶ Naples	Journey time by boat (without stops) approx. 3 hours
Distance: 🚢 around 100 km/62 miles	

COSTS: approx. 450 euros for 2 people (all transport costs, admission costs, two nights' accommodation, not including food and drink)
WHAT TO PACK: sun protection, sturdy shoes, rucksack

IMPORTANT TIPS: Ferries from Sorrento to Naples may be cancelled due to bad weather. If so, take the Circumvesuviana railway as an alternative

The legendary dream island of Capri, the beguiling coastal resort of Sorrento, the World Heritage Site of Naples: discover the fascinating natural beauty and cultural heritage of the Gulf of Naples on this multi-faceted tour.

DAY 1

❶ Naples

34 km/21 mi

❷ Marina Grande

0.5 km/0.31 mi

❸ Capri

6 km/3.7 mi

❹ Anacapri

4 km/2.5 mi

❺ Capri

Set out in the morning and catch the ferry from the Molo Beverello port in ❶ Naples leaving behind you the splendid view over the hills of Vesuvius and the chaotic cityscape. **It takes approximately 50 minutes to reach the port of ❷ Marina Grande** on Capri where you can jump on the **funicular** to the main town of ❸ **Capri** and the charming **Piazzetta Umberto I.** Stroll along the Via delle Botthege and the noble Via Vittorio Emanuele full of designer boutiques to the **Giardini di Augusto** *(daily 9am–7.30pm)*. The gardens offer a fantastic lookout point to Capri's iconic landmark, the Faraglioni rocks. Just a few metres away in the perfume laboratory **Carthusia** *(Viale Matteotti 2d)* you can purchase Capri's famous floral scent. Then proceed to the **Ristorante Panorama** *(daily | Traversa Lo Palazzo 2 | tel. 08 18 37 52 90 | www.panoramacapri.com | Expensive)* for tasty Caprese cuisine and the namesake view.

Dedicate the afternoon to exploring one of the island's prettiest sights, the precariously perched **Villa San Michele** *(daily 9am–1 hour before sunset | Viale Munthe 34 | www.villasanmichele.eu | Moderate)* on the steep cliffs in ❹ **Anacapri** with its fantastic panoramic view and magical garden. **From the piazzetta in Capri to the Piazza Vittoria bus stop in Anacapri, the journey takes just ten minutes there and back by bus. The last section is on foot along the Via Capodimonte.** Spend the night in ❺ **Capri** at the **INSIDERTIP Capri Wine Hotel** *(10 rooms | Via Provinciale Marina Grande 69 | tel. 08 18 37 91 73 | www.capriwinehotel.com | Expensive)* surrounded by vines.

"Benvenuti a Napoli": the Castel Nuovo welcomes visitors at Naples' port

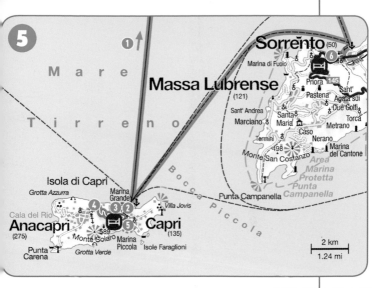

⑥ Sorrento → p. 142 straddles the cliffs picturesquely and is surrounded by lemon tree gardens. **It takes just 25 minutes to reach by ferry. The bus will then take you to the Piazza Tasso where you can stroll along the Via San Francesco to the Villa Comunale,** a park offering fantastic views over the Gulf of Naples. Just a short walk away is the **Trattoria Emilia** *(daily | tel. 08 18 07 27 20 | www.da emilia.it | Budget)* located directly at the waterfront **in the idyllic fishing port of Marina Grande.** Use your afternoon to walk along the old town alley **Via San Cesareo** lined with souvenir shops and delicatessens. Don't miss out on trying the homemade *gelato al limone* at **Raki** *(No. 48)* and limoncello liqueur at the **Limonoro** *(No. 49)* liqueur factory.

Now ferry back to ① Naples → p. 137, where you are welcomed by the impressive **Castel Nuovo** at the port. **From the Piazza Municipio, take the underground line 1 to Piazza Dante,** both fascinating **artwork stations on the Metrò dell'Arte. Head along the Via Port'Alba/ Via San Sebastiano to the** old town with its many artisan arts and crafts shops. The underground of Naples, **Napoli Sotterranea,** is particularly worth visiting, and don't forget to try a piece of authentic Neapolitan pizza *a portafoglio* – to take away.

SPORTS & ACTIVITIES

Few other European countries can claim the geographical diversity of Italy: towering Alpine mountains (up to 4000 m/13,000 ft), large lakes, gently rolling hills, rugged terrain and more than 8000 km/4970 miles of coastline. Correspondingly, the choice of sports and activities is very diverse.

The trendsetter is the "fitness and fun" industry on the Adriatic around Rimini and Riccione, the California of Italy. The wide sandy beaches are ideal for beach volleyball. Many bathing areas focus on health activities, with gyms, sport programmes and beach competitions. The many mountainous regions, whether Alps or Apennines, offer a range of outdoor activities, from paragliding to rafting, ski or mountain bike tours.

CYCLING

Cycling is a popular sport in Italy and at the weekend the cyclists hit the roads in large groups. Although there are very few cycle tracks, there are loads of brochures with proposed tours. In the towns, especially those in the Po Valley, such as Milan, Ferrara, Ravenna and Mantua, you can hire bikes in many hotels or at the station and use them to **INSIDER TIP** explore the restricted traffic zones of the old town centres. Popular mountain bike areas are the Finale area in Liguria and the Tuscan Emilian Apennines. You will also find rental bikes in the seaside resorts, for instance along the Adriatic, for tours in the Po Delta nature reserve or along the beach promenades. Helpful

From cycling to diving and skiing: Italy's geographical diversity is reflected in its wide selection of outdoor activities

websites include *www.bicitalia.org* (cycling routes) and *www.albergabici.it* (cycle-friendly accomodation); *www.pedalitalia.it* is a digital library of cycling routes.

DIVING

The coastal areas particularly suited to diving are in Liguria around the peninsula of Portofino and on the coastal section of the Cinque Terre. A good spot is along the upper Adriatic, the craggy Trieste coast near Castello di Miramare.

Further south in the Marche, divers flock to the rocks of Monte Conero near Sirol. In Lazio the San Felice promontory of the Circeo nature protection area near Sabaudia is popular with divers. The Isole Tremiti archipelago is a highlight in the south, also the tip of the heel at Santa Maria di Leuca as well as the sea off the peninsula of Isola di Capo Rizzuto and at Scilla on the Strait of Messina. A fascinating experience is in Campania, a dive in the INSIDER TIP grottoes of Palinuro and off the Sorrento Peninsula – or you can dive down to the INSIDER TIP ruins of the Roman villas on the seabed off Baia not far from Naples.

GOLF

The Italians caught golf fever some time ago, and there are lovely courses around the country (e.g. in *Val Ferret* in Aosta Valley). *www.greenpassgolf.com* provides detailed descriptions of the courses.

HIKING

You can walk through Italy from north to south on the *Sentiero d'Italia* trail. There are good connections along the entire Alpine chain from the Aosta Valley via South Tyrol to the Carnic Alps in Friaul. Uncrowded hiking trails pass over the Piedmontese Alps and down to the Ligurian Sea *(www.mountainzones. com)*. The mountainous coastal area of Liguria offers stunning hiking trails through verdant Mediterranean maquis, with breathtaking views of the sea. The marked hiking routes in the mountains of *Monti Sibillini* national park, between Umbria and the Marche, offer a spectacular scenic experience. That is also true of the ★ *national parks* of the Abruzzo and the Monte Pollino between Calabria and Basilicata, Sila and Aspromonte, all stunning mountain-scapes. The tourist offices can help by providing the addresses of experienced mountain guides and of organised group tours. The mountains also offer new hiking trails with historic themes, e.g. the pilgrimage route *Via Francigena* from the north to Rome, the Apennine crossing along the German-American frontline in the Second World War, the *Linea Gotica,* or walking in the footsteps of St Francis of Assisi through central Italy.

MOUNTAINEERING & ROCK CLIMBING

The entire chain of Italian Alps offers challenging climbing tours, especially those with summits of 4000 m/13,120ft in the Aosta Valley. *Vie ferrata*, protected climbing routes with iron hooks, ladders and wire cables, pass through the Dolomites and make it possible even for non-mountain climbers to scale the precipices. Arco on Lake Garda and Finale Ligure with cliffs above the sea are popular freeclimbing sports.

THERMAL SPAS

Italy's renowned spa resorts offer diverse treatments, some of which have been popular since ancient times, ranging from mineral waters, mud baths, speleotherapy, drinking cures to hay bathing. The most well-known thermal spa regions include the Euganean Hills, the natural hot springs in Tuscany and the island of Ischia. Although the volcanoes of the Euganean Hills are extinct, there is still geothermal activity in the region which accounts for the large number of thermal springs in exclusive spa resorts such as *Abano Terme, Montegrotto Terme* and *Battaglia Terme.* Thermal mud baths are a speciality; the micro-algae in the mud help to treat arthritis and rheumatism. Roman legionnaires were the first to apply mud bath treatments. Tuscany is also an international health and wellness destination with ancient volcanoes, thermal spring waters and geothermal activity. Alpine air is not the only effective treatment against allergies, the underground INSIDER TIP *speleotherapy centre in Prettau* also helps allergy and asthma sufferers to relax. Since the turn of the last century, the spa resort of Merano has been welcoming guests, today in the modern thermal springs centre *(www.termemerano.it)* designed by architect Matteo Thun.

WATER SPORTS

The top destination for water sports fans is Lake Garda, where the winds in the northern section make it popular with surfers. But there are also surfboard rental companies in all of the tourist areas along the coast and in the large holiday resorts. The Ligurian coast is particularly popular, especially around Albenga and Noli, the Conero on the Adriatic as well as the Lazio coast near Sabaudia and Fregene. Sailing is possible all along the coast, and there are plenty of marinas.

WINTER SPORTS

The entire Alpine range has an established infrastructure. Most of the larger Alpine ski resorts offer a snow park for the snowboarders and freestylers, or ice palaces for the ice skaters. You will find beautiful cross-country skiing trails in the valley of Gran Paradiso in the Aosta Valley, in South Tyrol, in Trentino and in the Carnic Alps. There are also good ski areas further south, e.g. in the Apennines along the Abetone massif around Sestola or further south in the Abruzzo near Pescasseroli. The best place to go for ski tours in unspoilt countryside is the Piedmont Maritime Alps (e.g. the Maira Valley).

The northern area of Lake Garda is a popular destination for windsurfers

TRAVEL WITH KIDS

Italy in the summer with the children promises warm Mediterranean waters, wide sandy beaches on the Adriatic or in the south and – especially along the northern Adriatic – large water and amusement parks.

Many hotels offer a discounted price for children and almost all restaurants have a menu with smaller portions. Children may also enter the larger state museums free of charge. Find especially family friendly hotels here: *www.italyfamilyhotels.it.* For an active family holiday try INSIDER TIP exploring the lagoons along the northern Adriatic in a comfortable houseboat: the 160 km/100 mile *Idrovia Veneta* waterway connects the spectacular Venice Lagoon with the quiet lagoons of Marano and Grado with their rich birdlife and lidos: *www.leboat.co.uk.*

THE NORTH-WEST

ACQUARIO DI GENOVA ●
(187 D5) (*ሙ D4*)
Italy's most exciting, species-rich and popular aquarium with sharks, penguins and underwater worlds is located in Genova's old harbour. *July/Aug daily 8.30am–10pm, March–June and Sept/Oct Mon–Fri 9am–8pm, Sat/Sun 8.30am–9pm, Nov–Feb Mon–Fri 9.30am–8pm, Sat/Sun 9.30am–9pm | 25 euros, children (aged 4–12) 15 euros | Porto Antico | Ponte Spinola | www.acquariodigenova.it*

Ötzi, the glacier mummy, stone monsters in the Baroque park, long-nosed Pinocchio and dripstone caves: all perfect for the little ones!

THE NORTH-EAST

MUSEO ARCHEOLOGICO DELL'ALTO ADIGE IN BOLZANO (188 C2) *(ɰ F2)*

"Ötzi", the well-preserved, world famous, 5300 years old mummy from the Similaun glacier, has found his final resting place in Bolzano. There are also special family rates at selected times. *Tue–Sun, July/Aug and Dec also Mon 10am–6pm | 9 euros, children 7 euros, under 6 free | Via Museo 43 | www.iceman.it*

PO VALLEY AND LAKES

ACQUARIO DI CATTOLICA LE NAVI (189 D6) *(ɰ H5)*

The futuristic architecture from the 1930s resembles a fleet; located on Cattolica beach, it is home to an aquarium with lots of different species of fish. *Easter–mid June, 1st half of Sept daily 9.30am–4.30pm, mid June–Aug 10am–9.30pm, mid Sept–easter only sparsely, mostly Sat/Sun 9.30am–4.30pm | 20 euros, children 1 m–1.40 m (3 ft–4.6 ft) 16 euros |*

Piazzale delle Nazioni 1a | www.acquari odicattolica.it

AQUAFAN IN RICCIONE
(189 D6) *(ØØ G5)*

There is one attraction after another along the Adriatic coast, one of which is this enormous water park. *June–mid Sept daily 10am–6.30pm, longer on selected evenings | two-day ticket 28 euros, children 1 m–1.40 m (3 ft–4.6 ft) 20 euros | Via Pistoia | www.aquafan.it*

AQUALANDIA IN LIDO DI JESOLO
(189 D3) *(ØØ G–H3)*

Offering cascades, slides, rafting tours and Caribbean landscapes, this aqua park is regarded as the most spectacular in Italy. *End May–mid Sept daily 10am–6pm | 31 euros, children 1 m–1.40 m (3 ft–4.6 ft) 27 euros | Via Michelangelo Buonarroti 15 | www.aqualandia.it*

GARDALAND NEAR PESCHIERA DEL GARDA (188 B3) *(ØØ F3)*

Italy's most famous amusement park is based on the Disneyworld concept. *Easter–mid June and mid–end Sept daily, Oct Sat/Sun 10am–6pm, mid June–mid Sept daily 10am–11pm | 39.50 euros, children (under 10) 35 euros, reduced online rates | www.gardaland.it*

MIRABILANDIA IN RAVENNA
(189 D5) *(ØØ G4)*

This enormous funfair is regarded as the main competitor to Italy's most famous one, Gardaland. *Varying opening times, see website | two-day ticket 34.90 euros, children 1 m–1.40 m (3 ft–4.6 ft) 28 euros, reduced online rates | SS 16, km 162 | www.mirabilandia.it*

INSIDER TIP **GIUSEPPE MEAZZA STADIUM IN MILAN** (187 D3) *(ØØ D3)*

If there is no game on, you can look round Italy's largest football stadium. A museum showcases the success story of local rivals Inter and AC Milan. *Daily 9.30am–6pm | 17 euros, children (aged 6–14) 12 euros | Via Piccolomini 5 | Entrance Gate 14 | www.sansirotour.com*

CENTRAL ITALY

PARCO DI PINOCCHIO IN COLLODI
(190 A1) *(ØØ F5)*

Statues of characters from the story of little Pinocchio, set in beautiful gardens. *March–Oct daily 9am–sunset, Nov–feb Sat/Sun 10am–sunset | 13 euros, children (aged 5–14) 10 euros, Nov–Feb 12/9 euros | Via San Gennaro 3 | www.pinocchio.it*

INSIDER TIP **PESCATURISMO ON THE TUSCAN COAST** ✪ (190 B3) *(ØØ F7)*

The Italian fisherman Paolo Fanciulli fights for sustainable fishing and against trawling by inviting guests on board his boat at the port in *Talamone* to spend a day fishing. *Easter–Oct. | half-day tour incl. antipasti 60 euros, children 14 and under 40 euros, full-day tour incl. breakfast and lunch with the catch of the day 100/60 euros | tel. (English) 33 57 06 96 03 | www.paoloilpescatore.it*

ROME AND THE APENNINES

BIOPARCO IN ROME ✪
(190–191 C–D4) *(ØØ G8)*

In the verdant vegetation of this nature reserve on the northern end of the Villa Borghese park, you will find Siberian tigers, apes and rare turtles. The zoo engages in species conservation. *Daily 9.30am–5pm, Easter–Oct until 6pm | 16 euros, children 1 m/3 ft–12 years 13 euros | Piazzale del Giardino Zoologico 1 | www.bioparco.it*

In all shapes and colours: air balloons for sale in Rome's municipal park Villa Borghese

CASINA DI RAFFAELLO IN ROME
(180–191 C–D4) (⌂ G8)

In the urban park Villa Borghese, children (aged 3–10) can run about, play and make things in this beautiful large children's activity centre. *Tue–Fri 9am–6pm, Sat/Sun 10am–7pm | 7 euros | Viale della Casina Raffaello/Piazza di Siena | www.casina diraffaello.it*

PARCO DEI MOSTRI IN BOMARZO
(190 C3) (⌂ G7)

In a dense forest, the "monster park" on the edge of Bomarzo near Orte in north Lazio is home to bizarre and eerie, weathered stone monsters from the 16th century. *April–Aug daily 8.30am–7pm, Sept–March 8.30am–sunset | 10 euros, children (aged 4–13) 8 euros | www.parcodeimostri.com*

RAINBOW MAGICLAND IN VALMON-TONE-PASCOLARO (191 D4) (⌂ H8)

Disney-style amusement park just outside Rome near the motorway to Naples: an enormous funfair with fun pools, wonderland, entertainment and evening parties. *Varying opening times, see website | 29 euros, children 1 m/3 ft–14 years 24 euros | www.magicland.it*

SOUTHERN ITALY

DRIPSTONE CAVES

Inside the many mountains covering Italy's boot are some of the largest dripstone caves in Europe, subterranean chambers full of shimmering crystals that have an enchanting beauty. Among the most spectacular caves are in the mountains of Cilento in Campania the *Grotte di Castelcivita* ((192 B5) (⌂ K9) | *tours March–Oct daily 10.30am, noon, 1.30pm, 3pm, April–Sept also 4.30pm and 6pm | 10 euros, children (aged 6–12) 8 euros | www.grottedicastelcivita.com*). In the boot heel in Apulia the *Grotte di Castellana* ((193 D4) (⌂ M9) | *varying opening times, see website | short tour 12 euros, children 6–14 years 10 euros, long tour 16/13 euros | www.grottedi castellana.it*).

FESTIVALS & EVENTS

FEBRUARY/MARCH

Carnival is celebrated in Piedmont's Ivrea with a food fight, the *Battle of the Oranges (www.storicocarnevaleivrea.it),* in Venice with spectacular masquerades, and in Viareggio with satirical floats depicting political leaders.

MARCH/APRIL

Poignant Easter processions, especially impressive are the *Good Friday processions* in Taranto (Apulia), Sorrento (Campania) and Chieti (Abruzzo), as is the resurrection in Sulmona (Abruzzo) on Easter Sunday: INSIDER TIP *La Madonna che Scappa in Piazza*

MAY

Medieval festival *Calendimaggio (www.calendimaggiodiassisi.com)* at the beginning of May in Assisi with parade and concerts 15 May: ★ *Corsa dei Ceri (www.ceri.it)* in Gubbio (Umbria): three teams race huge statues of the village's patron saints up Mount Ingino – spectacular!

MAY/JUNE

Maggio Musicale Fiorentino (www.operadifirenze.it): international music festival weeks in Florence

Corpus Christi: *Procession* and colourful carpets of flowers, e.g. in Bolsena and Genzano near Rome, in Spello (Umbria) and in Campobasso (Molise)

MID JUNE–MID SEPT

Ravello Festival (www.ravellofestival.com: First-class concerts; unique: the INSIDER TIP concert at sunrise

END OF JUNE–MID JULY

Festival dei Due Mondi (www.festivaldispoleto.com) in Spoleto with theatre, dance and music events

END OF JUNE–END OF AUGUST

INSIDER TIP *I Suoni delle Dolomiti (www.isuonidelledolomiti.it):* awe-inspiring concerts on mountain meadows below the peaks of the Dolomites of Trentino
The world famous *Opera Festival* in Verona's Roman arena

JULY

Neapolis Festival (www.neapolis.it), rock-pop festival in Naples in mid July

2 JULY AND 16 AUGUST

Palio di Siena: Italy's most famous and – for reasons of animal welfare – controversial horse race on the beautiful piazza

Carnival processions, medieval tournaments and top-class music festivals: Italy is in a festive mood all year round

MID JULY

Pescara Jazz (www.pescarajazz.com) and *Umbria Jazz (www.umbriajazz.com)*, two of the best among the numerous jazz festivals

★ *Arezzo Wave Love Festival (www.arezzowave.com):* for five days the best bands of new rock-pop trends play in Arezzo

AUGUST

A vast array of events all month, such as gourmet festivals and on 15 August, *Ferragosto,* a fantastic firework display In the last week, international street *buskers (www.ferrarabuskers.com)* entertain in the squares in Ferrara.

SEPTEMBER

● *Trasporto della Macchina di Santa Rosa:* in honour of their patron saint, 100 men carry a 30 m/98 ft tower through the medieval streets of Viterbo on 3 Sept
INSIDER TIP▶ *Napoli Pizza Village (www.pizzavillage.it):* Giant pizza party on Naples' promenade.

OCTOBER

Barcolana (www.barcolana.it): thousands of sailboats take part in Europe's largest amateur regatta in the beginning of October in the Gulf of Trieste in the northern Adriatic.

NATIONAL HOLIDAYS

1 Jan	*Capodanno*
6 Jan	*Epifania*
March/April	*Pasquetta* (Easter Monday)
25 April	*Liberazione* (Liberation Day)
1 May	*Festa del Lavoro*
2 June	*Festa della Repubblica* (Republic Day)
15 Aug	*Ferragosto*
1 Nov	*Ognissanti*
8 Dec	*Immacolata Concezione* (Immaculate Conception)
25 Dec	*Natale*
26 Dec	*Santo Stefano*

LINKS, BLOGS, APPS & MORE

www.italia.it/en/home.html Italy's official portal for tourism is packed with information about the different areas as well as plenty of practical information to help you organize your trip. You can also click on an interactive map of Italy and make a virtual tour of some of the main towns you wish to visit

www.italia-magazine.com Italia is an online magazine with tips on travel, holiday homes, Italian cooking and even information about buying a property

www.angelsfortravellers.com Locals based all over Italy post their own personal tips and answer travellers' questions on their home city

www.spottedbylocals.com Experience many of Italy's cities like a local with insider tips for Rome, Milan, Venice, Florence and Turin. App download available

www.parlafood.com The personal blog of Rome-based American food historian, sommelier and journalist Katie Parla with lots of great insider tips about her personal favourites: restaurants, pizzerias, wine bars, ice cream shops, and bakeries

www.partyamo.com You can get to know people living or staying in Milan using this network portal. People meet regularly for an aperitif, a game of badminton or brunch on Sunday

instantlyitaly.com/blog Cinzia wants to be "your insider in Italy". She tells you lots of helpful things about the Italian language, Italian lifestyle, books every Italian has read, and so on

www.thelocal.it/20160212/tourist-types-youre-likely-to-meet-in-italy-which-one-are-you Typical tourist types roaming the streets of Italy

anamericaninrome.com/wp Natalie from California lives in Rome and knows everything about what to do and where to go in the city as well as in the rest of Italia

Regardless of whether you are still preparing your trip or already in Italy: these addresses will provide you with information, videos and networks to make your holiday even more enjoyable

www.learnitalianpod.com A free on-line resource that teaches Italian grammar, pronunciation and practical Italian phrases for use in everyday situations through the means of pod-casts that you can download

www.youtube.com/watch?v=tzQuuoKXVqO Very funny five-minute clip by Italian comic artist Bruno Bozzetto showing you in what ways the Italians are different from the rest of the Europeans

VIDEOS

vimeo.com/33976434 In this video, Francesco Paciocco presents his impressions of Milan – people, squares, visual angles, moods, moments – in a wonderfully dense and not touristy sequence of combined images. An excellent video town portrait

www.youtube.com/watch?v=BwcyMgWLZVw With this short portrait of Naples and Campania, the city of Naples has won the Universiad 2019, the world's biggest sports event for students

www.italia.it/en/media/video.html This link on the Italian national tourist board website, ENIT, provides informative videos on many of Italy's regions and cities

www.youtube.com/watch?v=46ZXI-V4qwY The history of the Roman Empire in 20 minutes – great to freshen up that knowledge from school

AroundMe A free app as a travel companion, which locates your exact position via satellite and displays the nearest hotels, restaurants, banks, pubs, etc.

APPS

Italy Guides iPad and iPhone apps with city guides in English to guide you around many of Italy's cities

Google Translate Free Google app used to translate photographed or spoken text. Useful for getting yourself understood on holiday

TRAVEL TIPS

ARRIVAL

If you are travelling to Italy by car from the UK, an attractive route is via Dijon to Chamonix and then through the Mont Blanc Tunnel into the Aosta Valley. Alternatives to the tunnel are the Grand St Bernard Pass or the 17 km/10.5 miles St Gotthard tunnel from Switzerland. Coming from Germany and Austria the route would be via the Brenner Pass motorway in the Italian South Tyrol. There are also numerous passes (some subject to toll), many of which cannot be used in the winter. In the summer, they offer spectacular views, but require considerably more travelling time.

There are direct rail connections to Italy via France, Switzerland or Germany and Austria: www.raileurope.co.uk and www.fsitaliane.it/homepage_en.html. You can also travel to Italy by train on the Eurostar and TGV – and it is a comfortable and inexpensive alternative (www.seat61.com). The average travel time from London to Milan is nine hours. In the main holiday season, it is essential to reserve a sleeper cabin bed or even just a seat well in advance.

A cheap alternative: travelling by Eurolines coach from London to Florence, Milan, Rome, Naples and about 15 other Italian cities. www.eurolines.co.uk/en/destinations/italy

The main international airports in Italy are: Bari, Bologna, Florence, Genoa, Milan, Naples, Pisa, Rome, Trieste, Turin and Venice. British Airways (www.britishairways.com) offer regular flights from the UK to Italy and you can also fly direct with Alitalia (www.alitalia.com) and with low coast airlines such as Easy Jet (www.easyjet.com). In North America the following airlines all have direct flights to Rome: Delta Airlines (www.delta.com) from New York, American Airlines (www.aa.com) from Chicago and Air Canada (www.aircanada.com) from Toronto.

RESPONSIBLE TRAVEL

It doesn't take a lot to be environmentally friendly whilst travelling. Don't just think about your carbon footprint whilst flying to and from your holiday destination but also about how you can protect nature and culture abroad. As a tourist it is especially important to respect nature, look out for local products, cycle instead of driving, save water and much more. If you would like to find out more about eco-tourism please visit: www.ecotourism.org

CAR HIRE

Car rental companies have offices at all the international airports and the bigger train stations. You will pay about 50 euros a day for a small car, or from about 300 euros per week. Enquire about special holiday and weekend rates. It is usually cheaper if you book in advance.

CUSTOMS

UK citizens do not have to pay any duty on goods brought from another EU country as long as they are for private consumption. The limits are: 800 cigarettes, 400 cigarillo, 200 cigars, 1 kg smoking tobacco, 10 L spirits, 20 L liqueurs, 90 L wine, 110 L beer. Travellers from the USA, Canada, Australia or other non-EU countries are allowed to enter with the following tax-free amounts: 200 cigarettes or 100 cigarillos or 50 cigars or 250g smoking tobacco. 2L wine and spirits with less than 22% vol. alcohol, 1L spirits with more than 22% vol. alcohol content. Travellers to the United States do not have to pay duty on articles purchased overseas up to the value of $800, but there are limits on the amount of alcoholic beverages and tobacco products. For the regulations for international travel for U.S. residents please see *www.cbp.gov*

DRIVING

A driving licence and vehicle registration documents are obligatory, the green insurance card and international travel cover are recommended. The speed limit in built-up areas is 50 km/31 mph, otherwise 90 km/55 mph, on motorways 130 km/80 mph or when it is raining 110 km/68 mph, on dual carriageways 110 km/68 mph. Novice drivers have to drive slower for the first three years after gaining their licenses: 100 km/h/65 mph on motorways and 90 km/h/55 mph on dual carriageways. Even during the day, you have to put your headlights on when driving outside of towns. The legal blood alcohol limit is 0.5 (0.0 for novices!). You have to have high-visibility jackets for the driver and passengers in the car.

Except for a few stretches in southern Italy, you have to pay tolls on all the motorways. Dual carriageways *(superstrade)* are free of charge. In order to avoid queuing at the toll stations, you can pay with all major credit cards. *www.autostrade.it* is a useful website which can help you calculate toll fees *(pedaggio)* and find out about the latest traffic reports.

Many of the city centres are pedestrianised; you have to buy tickets to use most parking bays. You can buy scratch parking tickets and magnetic parking cards at kiosks and tobacconists. Cameras are increasingly being used to monitor the streets going into the pedestrianised town centres, called *Z.T.L. (zona traffico limitato)*. Your hotel will help by provid-

CURRENCY CONVERTER

£	€	€	£
1	1.17	1	0.85
3	3.50	3	2.56
5	5.86	5	4.26
13	15.24	13	11.09
40	47	40	34.11
75	88	75	63.96
120	141	120	102
250	293	250	213
500	586	500	426

$	€	€	$
1	0.94	1	1.06
3	2.82	3	3.19
5	4.70	5	5.32
13	12.22	13	13.83
40	37.60	40	42.55
75	70.50	75	79.78
120	113	120	128
250	235	250	266
500	470	500	532

For current exchange rates see www.xe.com

ing you with a vehicle pass. When smog levels are particularly high, towns may prohibit cars in emission classes 1, 2 and sometimes even 3, as well as older diesel vehicles without a particle filter. This is indicated on large displays on the streets into the town. Drivers of the vehicles in question have to leave them outside the centre and continue with public transport; in most cases there is a P+R system. The centre of Milan is an ⊘ environmental zone "area C". Cars with a Euro 0 (petrol-driven vehicles) and Euro 0, 1, 2, 3 emissions standards (diesel vehicles) are generally prohibited from entering Area C zones. You can buy an admission permit for all other vehicles which must be activated by midnight on the following day at the latest. More information can be found at *www.comune.milano.it/areac.*

Petrol stations sell *super 95* or *gasolio* (diesel). Except on the motorway, they close at lunchtime (12.30pm–3pm) and on Sunday, but there are many self service machines.

INTERNET & WIFI

UK EMBASSY IN ROME
Via XX Settembre 80/a | tel. +39 06 42 20 00 01 | www.gov.uk/government/world/ organisations/british-embassy-rome

US EMBASSY IN ROME
Via Vittorio Veneto 121 | tel. +39 06 46 741 | it.usembassy.gov

EMERGENCY SERVICES

Emergency call *(pronto soccorso)* free from every public telephone:
– Police *tel. 113*
– Fire brigade *(Vigili del Fuoco) tel. 115*
– Ambulance *tel. 118*
– Breakdown service *tel. 80 3116,* with international mobile phone operators

8 00 116 800
– European emergency number *tel. 112*

INFORMATION

ITALIAN STATE TOURIST BOARD (ENIT)
– *1 Princes Street | London W1B 2AY | tel. +44 20 7408 1254*
– *686 Park Avenue | New York, NY 10065 | tel. +1 212 245 56 18*
– *69 Yonge Street, Suite 1404 | Toronto ON M5E 1K3 | tel. +1 416 9 25 48 82; www. enit.it*

HEALTH

At hospitals or the local health authority ASL *(Agenzia Sanitaria Locale)*, European residents should present their European Health Insurance Card EHIC. Additional travel insurance is advisable and for non-EU residents essential. Remember to ask for receipts for any treatment that you have to pay for, so that you can apply for a refund from your own health authority upon your return home. The ambulance emergency services *(pronto soccorso)* are generally swift, good and uncomplicated.

INTERNET & WIFI

There are internet cafés everywhere (2–6 euros/hr); in the larger towns, you will also find cafés with WiFi access. That also applies for most of the hotels, many of which at least offer wireless Internet connection in the bar, reception and lounge area, some free of charge, some by means of a fee password from reception. The same is also true of the waiting and bar areas at airports and at larger train stations as well as some motorway service stations, especially in the north. The municipalities of Rome *(www.roma wireless.com)*, Verona *(www.turismovero*

na.eu) and Milan *(info.openwifimilano.it)* have especially many free WiFi hotspots. Community websites provide information about free WiFi for both locals and tourists.

MONEY & CREDIT CARDS

Banks have ATM cash dispensers *(bancomat)*. Almost all hotels, petrol stations and supermarkets and most restaurants and shops accept major credit cards.

MUSEUMS & SIGHTS

Closing times are indicated in this guide, but the ticket office often closes earlier. The admission price ranges from 4–10 euros, occasionally with an additional charge for reservations. The state museums *(musei nazionali)* are also free of charge for EU citizens under 18; young adults aged between 18 and 25 only have to pay half price.

Admission to all state-owned museums is free on every first Sunday of the month. You can buy online tickets for all the major museums and most popular sights; for some attractions, such as Leonardo da Vinci's "The Last Supper" in Milan, tickets must be bought in advance. Take advantage of this service to avoid hours standing in queues. It is also worth inquiring about the tourist cards available in many Italian cities which offer discounts on museum visits and the free use of public transport.

OPENING TIMES

Convenience stores are usually open weekdays from 8.30am to 12.30pm/1pm and from 4pm/5pm to 7.30pm. Although retailers and boutiques in smaller towns close for lunch, supermarkets and department stores stay open all day until 8–9pm, most are open even on Sundays. All shops close one afternoon in the week. Shops and boutiques in tourist resorts often stay open until late in the evening and on Sundays. Churches are usually open from 8am to 12 noon and from 3pm to 6pm.

BUDGETING

Coffee	£1–£1.30/$1.35–$1.68	*for a cappuccino at the bar*
Ice cream	£1.75/$2.25	*for one large scoop*
Wine	from £2.65/$3.35	*for a glass at the bar*
Museums	£3.50–£8.80/$4.50–$11	*for admission*
Petrol	c. £1.36/$1.75	*for 1L Super*
Beach	from £12.30/$15.70	*Daily rental for sunshade and lounger*

PHONES & MOBILE PHONES

The international dialling code for Italy is *+39;* the area code is part of the number and must always be dialled (including the zero). Dial *+44* for calls from Italy to the UK and *+1* from Italy to the USA and Canada. Mobile numbers start without a zero.

To make calls from a foreign mobile telephone it is cheaper to use an Italian prepaid card. They are sold in tobacco shops for 5–10 euro. For frequent callers it is worthwhile buying a rechargeable SIM you can then have an Italian number and the charges for incoming calls are dropped.

POST

Post offices are generally only open in the mornings. The cost of sending letters (max. 20g) and postcards within Europe is 1 euro (at the time of going to print). Letters and parcels to be sent abroad should have a blue "by airmail/via aerea" sticker which is available from kiosks or post offices together with stamps.

PRICES

At the bar, an espresso will cost you about 1 euro, but if you sit down at a table or on the terrace to drink it, it may well cost you twice as much or even three times as much.

PUBLIC TRANSPORT

Trains and buses are relatively inexpensive. The trains are more punctual than their reputation, but often crowed. In addition to the Italian railway *(www. trenitalia.com*, there is also the fast and comfortable private railway Italo *(www. italotreno.it)*. Up-to-the-minute information on delays is provided by the service Viaggiatreno *(www.viaggiatreno.it* and as a smartphone app). The high-speed train services Frecciarossa, Frecciargento and Frecciabianca connect the larger cities and you need to reserve seats in advance to travel on them. Regional trains operated by regional operators will bring you to smaller towns and more remote areas, e.g. with Trenord to the Lombard valleys or with Ferrovie Sudest through the Salento region of Apulia.

You have to stamp your train ticket in the yellow machines on the platform before boarding the trains. Up-to-date information (in Italian only) on scheduled strikes

WEATHER IN ROME

	Jan	Feb	March	April	May	June	July	Aug	Sept	Oct	Nov	Dec
Daytime temperatures in °C/°F	11/52	13/55	16/61	19/66	23/73	28/82	31/88	31/88	27/81	21/70	16/61	12/54
Nighttime temperatures in °C/°F	4/39	5/41	7/45	10/50	13/55	17/63	20/68	20/68	17/63	13/55	9/48	5/41
☀ Sunshine hours/day	4	4	5	7	8	10	11	10	7	6	5	4
☂ Precipitation days/month	8	9	8	8	7	4	2	2	5	8	10	10
≋ Water temperature in °C/°F	14/57	13/55	13/55	14/57	17/63	21/70	23/73	24/75	23/73	20/68	18/64	15/59

☀ Sunshine hours/day ☂ Precipitation days/month ≋ Water temperature in °C/°F

(sciopero) is available on the Italian transport ministry website *(scioperi.mit.gov.it)*. You can take bikes on many of the local trains (supplement 3.50 euros). Cities such as Rome, Milan and Naples have underground trains and large bus networks.

TIPPING

Don't be too stingy: waiters, chambermaids, porters etc. get a five to ten per cent tip – providing you were satisfied with their services.

WEATHER, WHEN TO GO

The holiday resorts are all hopelessly crowded in August. Prices hit the roof and you will often be forced to book half-board. Whilst the towns and museums are relatively empty during the summer, they burst at Easter and over long weekends. A good time to go is May/June and September/October, although a lot of hotels close at the end of September. You can check the weather online at: *www.tempoitalia.it*

WHERE TO STAY

AGRITURISMO

An increasing number of farms in Italy are renting out rooms, holiday flats and pitches for motor homes and tents. They are often elegantly restored country homes, which are priced accordingly. One excellent website with many illustrated offers is: *www.agriturist.it.* Other good websites: *www.agriturismo.org.uk, www.agriturismo.it,* for holidays on farms in South Tyrol *www.roterhahn.it,* ○ organic farms *www.agriturismibiologici.net.*

BED & BREAKFAST

There are numerous listings for private accommodation at attractive rates on the following websites *www.bbitalia.it/en/* and *www.bed-and-breakfast-italy.com*

CAMPING

You can find useful information about the best campsites at *www.camping.it/english*

HOLIDAY HOMES

You can find details of properties by contacting the local tourist board or by browsing *www.italia.it/en/home.html* and *www.homelidays.co.uk.* A good website for holiday homes in southern Italy is *www.nonsolocasa-italy-travel.com/.* Good accommodation is also available at *www.cilento-travel.com/en.html.* You can read about a nice selection in Tuscany at *www.holidayhomestuscany.com.* The renovation and redesign of private accommodation in old villages, hamlets and old town districts into holiday accommodation is referred to as *albergo diffuso*: *www.alberghidiffusi.it.*

HOTELS

In the tourist areas by the sea or in the mountains, you often only get rooms with half or full board during the high season – and the prices rise sharply in July/August. The Lega Ambiente (Italy's environmental organisation) lists a whole range of particularly environmentally friendly hotels: *www.legambienteturismo.it.*

HOSTELS

Youth hostels, Backpacker hostels and cheap hotels are listed under *www.aighostels.it/en, www.hostelsclub.com* and *www.hostelworld.com/hostels/italy.*

USEFUL PHRASES ITALIAN

PRONUNCIATION

c, cc	before e or i like ch in "church", e.g. ciabatta, otherwise like k
ch, cch	like k, e.g. pacchi, che
g, gg	before e or i like j in "just", e.g. gente, otherwise like g in "get"
gl	like "lli" in "million", e.g. figlio
gn	as in "cognac", e.g. bagno
sc	before e or i like sh, e.g. uscita
sch	like sk in "skill", e.g. Ischia
z	at the beginning of a word like dz in "adze", otherwise like ts

An accent on an Italian word shows that the stress is on the last syllable.
In other cases we have shown which syllable is stressed by placing a dot below the relevant vowel.

IN BRIEF

Yes/No/Maybe	Sì/No/Forse
Please/Thank you	Per favore/Grazie
Excuse me, please!	Scusa!/Mi scusi
May I...?/Pardon?	Posso...? / Come dice?/Prego?
I would like to.../Have you got ...?	Vorrei.../Avete...?
How much is...?	Quanto costa...?
I (don't) like that	(Non) mi piace
good/bad	buono/cattivo/bene/male
broken/doesn't work	guasto/non funziona
too much/much/little/all/nothing	troppo/molto/poco/ tutto/niente
Help!/Attention!/Caution!	aiuto!/attenzione!/prudenza!
ambulance/police/fire brigade	ambulanza/polizia/vigili del fuoco
Prohibition/forbidden/danger/dangerous	divieto/vietato/pericolo/pericoloso
May I take a photo here/of you?	Posso fotografar La?

GREETINGS, FAREWELL

Good morning!/afternoon!/ evening!/night!	Buon giorno!/Buon giorno!/ Buona sera!/Buona notte!
Hello! / Goodbye!/See you	Ciao!/Salve! / Arrivederci!/Ciao!
My name is...	Mi chiamo...
What's your name?	Come si chiama?/Come ti chiami
I'm from...	Vengo da...

Parli italiano?

"Do you speak Italian?" This guide will help you to say the basic words and phrases in Italian

DATE & TIME

Monday/Tuesday/Wednesday	lunedì/martedì/mercoledì
Thursday/Friday/Saturday	giovedì/venerdì/sabato
Sunday/holiday/ working day	domenica/(giorno) festivo/ (giorno) feriale
today/tomorrow/yesterday	oggi/domani/ieri
hour/minute	ora/minuto
day/night/week/month/year	giorno/notte/settimana/mese/anno
What time is it?	Che ora è? Che ore sono?
It's three o'clock/It's half past three	Sono le tre/Sono le tre e mezza
a quarter to four	le quattro meno un quarto/ un quarto alle quattro

TRAVEL

open/closed	aperto/chiuso
entrance/exit	entrata/uscita
departure/arrival	partenza/arrivo
toilets/ladies/gentlemen	bagno/toilette/signore/signori
(no) drinking water	acqua (non) potabile
Where is...?/Where are...?	Dov'è...?/Dove sono...?
left/right/straight ahead/back	sinistra/destra/dritto/indietro
close/far	vicino/lontano
bus/tram	bus/tram
taxi/cab	taxi/tassì
bus stop/cab stand	fermata/posteggio taxi
parking lot/parking garage	parcheggio/parcheggio coperto
street map/map	pianta/mappa
train station/harbour	stazione/porto
airport	aeroporto
schedule/ticket	orario/biglietto
supplement	supplemento
single/return	solo andata/andata e ritorno
train/track	treno/binario
platform	banchina/binario
I would like to rent...	Vorrei noleggiare...
a car/a bicycle	una macchina/una bicicletta
a boat	una barca
petrol/gas station	distributore/stazione di servizio
petrol/gas / diesel	benzina/diesel/gasolio
breakdown/repair shop	guasto/officina

FOOD & DRINK

Could you please book a table for tonight for four?	Vorrei prenotare per stasera un tavolo per quattro?
on the terrace/by the window	sulla terrazza/ vicino alla finestra
The menu, please	La carta/il menù, per favore
Could I please have...?	Potrei avere...?
bottle/carafe/glass	bottiglia/caraffa/bicchiere
knife/fork/spoon/salt/pepper	coltello/forchetta/cucchiaio/sale/pepe
sugar/vinegar/oil/milk/cream/lemon	zucchero/aceto/olio/latte/panna/limone
cold/too salty/not cooked	freddo/troppo salato/non cotto
with/without ice/sparkling	con/senza ghiaccio/gas
vegetarian/allergy	vegetariano/vegetariana/allergia
May I have the bill, please?	Vorrei pagare/Il conto, per favore
bill/tip	conto/mancia

SHOPPING

Where can I find...?	Dove posso trovare...?
I'd like.../I'm looking for ...	Vorrei.../Cerco...
Do you put photos onto CD?	Vorrei masterizzare delle foto su CD?
pharmacy/shopping centre/kiosk	farmacia/centro commerciale/edicola
department store/supermarket	grandemagazzino/supermercato
baker/market/grocery	forno/ mercato/negozio alimentare
photographic items/newspaper shop/	articoli per foto/giornalaio
100 grammes/1 kilo	un etto/un chilo
expensive/cheap/price/more/less	caro/economico/prezzo/di più/di meno
organically grown	di agricoltura biologica

ACCOMMODATION

I have booked a room	Ho prenotato una camera
Do you have any... left?	Avete ancora...
single room/double room	una (camera) singola/doppia
breakfast/half board/	prima colazione/mezza pensione/
full board (American plan)	pensione completa
at the front/seafront/lakefront	con vista/con vista sul mare/lago
shower/sit-down bath/balcony/terrace	doccia/bagno/balcone/terrazza
key/room card	chiave/scheda magnetica
luggage/suitcase/bag	bagaglio/valigia/borsa

BANKS, MONEY & CREDIT CARDS

bank/ATM/pin code	banca/bancomat/ codice segreto
cash/credit card	in contanti/carta di credito
bill/coin/change	banconota/moneta/il resto

USEFUL PHRASES

HEALTH

doctor/dentist/paediatrician	medico/dentista/pediatra
hospital/emergency clinic	ospedale/pronto soccorso/guardia medica
fever/pain/inflamed/injured	febbre/dolori/infiammato/ferito
diarrhoea/nausea/sunburn	diarrea/nausea/scottatura solare
plaster/bandage/ointment/cream	cerotto/fasciatura/pomata/crema
pain reliever/tablet/suppository	antidolorifico/compressa/supposta

POST, TELECOMMUNICATIONS & MEDIA

stamp/letter/postcard	francobollo/lettera/cartolina
I need a landline phone card/ I'm looking for a prepaid card for my mobile	Mi serve una scheda telefonica per la rete fissa/Cerco una scheda prepagata per il mio cellulare
Where can I find internet access?	Dove trovo un accesso internet?
dial/connection/engaged	comporre/linea/occupato
socket/adapter/charger	presa/riduttore/caricabatterie
computer/battery/rechargeable battery	computer/batteria/accumulatore
internet address (URL)/e-mail address	indirizzo internet/indirizzo email
internet connection/wifi	collegamento internet/wi-fi
e-mail/file/print	email/file/stampare

LEISURE, SPORTS & BEACH

beach/bathing beach	spiaggia/bagno/stabilimento balneare
sunshade/lounger/cable car/chair lift	ombrellone/sdraio/funivia/seggiovia
(rescue) hut/avalanche	rifugio/valanga

NUMBERS

0	zero	15	quindici
1	uno	16	sedici
2	due	17	diciassette
3	tre	18	diciotto
4	quattro	19	diciannove
5	cinque	20	venti
6	sei	21	ventuno
7	sette	50	cinquanta
8	otto	100	cento
9	nove	200	duecento
10	dieci	1000	mille
11	undici	2000	duemila
12	dodici	10000	diecimila
13	tredici	½	un mezzo
14	quattordici	¼	un quarto

ROAD ATLAS

The green line indicates the Discovery Tour "Italy at a glance"
The blue line indicates the other Discovery Tours

All tours are also marked on the pull-out map

Exploring Italy

The map on the back cover shows how the area has been sub-divided

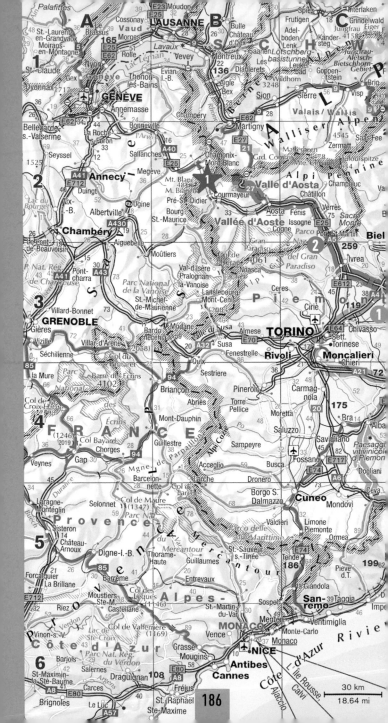

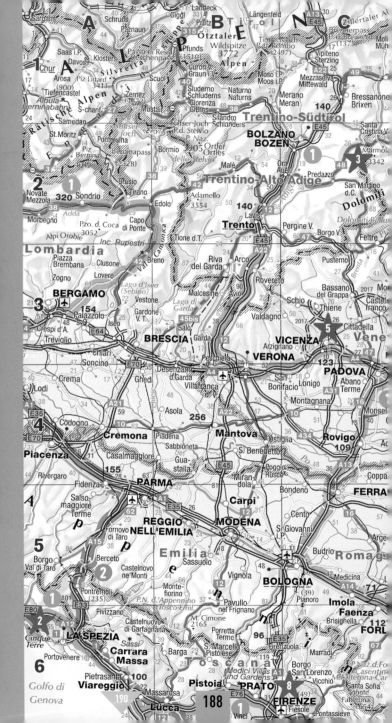

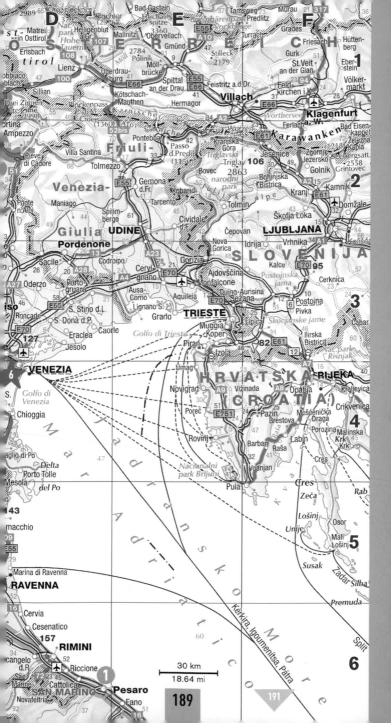

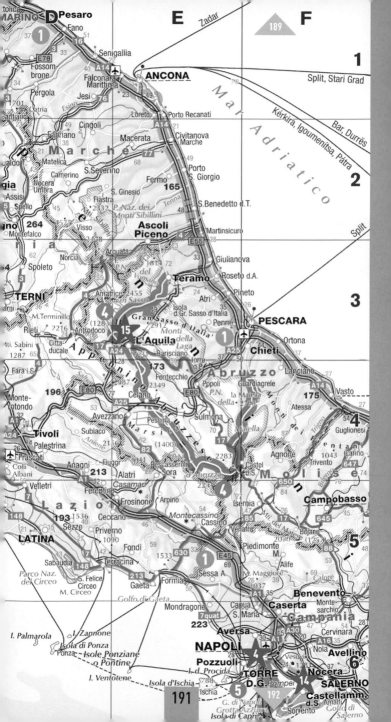

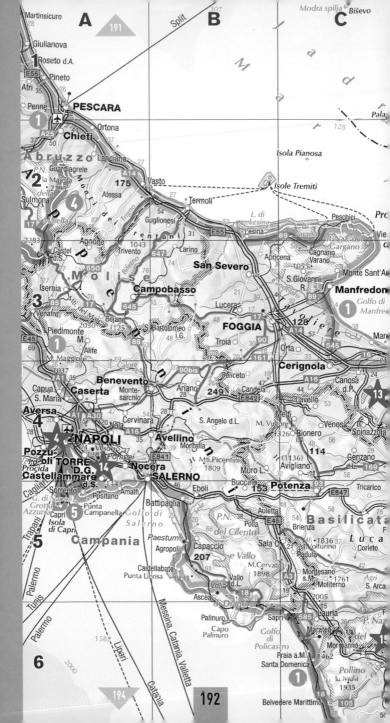

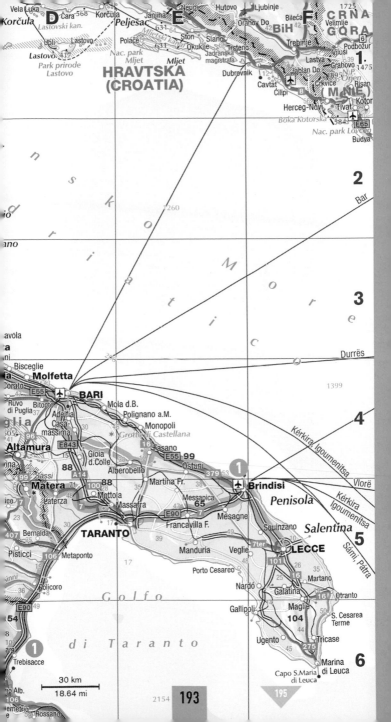

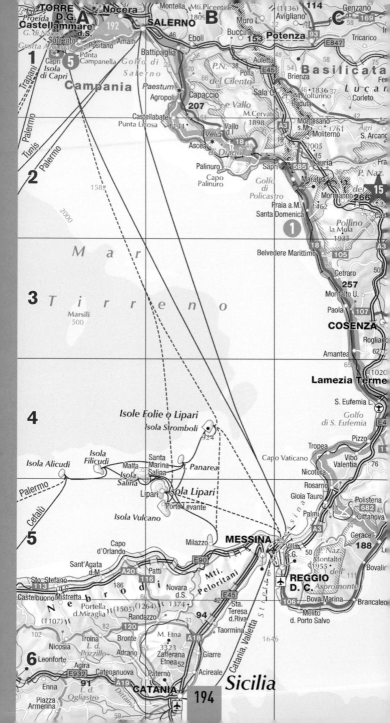

Autobahn, mehrspurige Straße - in Bau Highway, multilane divided road - under construction		Autoroute, route à plusieurs voies - en construction Autosnelweg, weg met meer rijstroken - in aanleg
Fernverkehrsstraße - in Bau Trunk road - under construction		Route à grande circulation - en construction Weg voor interlokaal verkeer - in aanleg
Hauptstraße Principal highway		Route principale Hoofdweg
Nebenstraße Secondary road		Route secondaire Overige verharde wegen
Fahrweg, Piste Practicable road, track		Chemin carrossable, piste Weg, piste
Straßennummerierung Road numbering	E20 11 70 26	Numérotage des routes Wegnummering
Entfernungen in Kilometer Distances in kilometers	**259** 130 129	Distances en kilomètres Afstand in kilometers
Höhe in Meter - Pass Height in meters - Pass	1365	Altitude en mètres - Col Hoogte in meters - Pas
Eisenbahn - Eisenbahnfähre Railway - Railway ferry		Chemin de fer - Ferry-boat Spoorweg - Spoorpont
Autofähre - Schifffahrtslinie Car ferry - Shipping route		Bac autos - Ligne maritime Autoveer - Scheepvaartlijn
Wichtiger internationaler Flughafen - Flughafen Major international airport - Airport	✈ ✈	Aéroport importante international - Aéroport Belangrijke internationale luchthaven - Luchthaven
Internationale Grenze - Provinzgrenze International boundary - Province boundary		Frontière internationale - Limite de Province Internationale grens - Provinciale grens
Unbestimmte Grenze Undefined boundary		Frontière d'Etat non définie Rijksgrens onbepaalt
Zeitzonengrenze Time zone boundary	-4h Greenwich Time -3h Greenwich Time	Limite de fuseau horaire Tijdzone-grens
Hauptstadt eines souveränen Staates National capital	**OSLO**	Capitale nationale Hoofdstad van een souvereine staat
Hauptstadt eines Bundesstaates Federal capital	**Nancy**	Capitale d'un état fédéral Hoofdstad van een deelstat
Sperrgebiet Restricted area		Zone interdite Verboden gebied
Nationalpark National park		Parc national Nationaal park
Antikes Baudenkmal Ancient monument	∴	Monument antiques Antiek monument
Sehenswertes Kulturdenkmal Interesting cultural monument	★ Chambord	Monument culturel interéssant Bezienswaardig cultuurmonument
Sehenswertes Naturdenkmal Interesting natural monument	★ Gorges du Tarn	Monument naturel interéssant Bezienswaardig natuurmonument
Brunnen Well	⌣	Puits Bron
MARCO POLO Erlebnistour 1 MARCO POLO Discovery Tour 1		MARCO POLO Tour d'aventure 1 MARCO POLO Avontuurlijke Routes 1
MARCO POLO Erlebnistouren MARCO POLO Discovery Tours		MARCO POLO Tours d'aventure MARCO POLO Avontuurlijke Routes
MARCO POLO Highlight	★1	MARCO POLO Highlight

INDEX

This index lists all towns and destinations featured in this guide.
Numbers in bold indicate a main entry. Castles, palaces, caves etc. are also listed.

INDEX

WRITE TO US

e-mail: info@marcopologuides.co.uk

Did you have a great holiday?
Is there something on your mind?
Whatever it is, let us know!
Whether you want to praise, alert us
to errors or give us a personal tip –
MARCO POLO would be pleased to
hear from you.
We do everything we can to provide the
very latest information for your trip.

Nevertheless, despite all of our authors'
thorough research, errors can creep in.
MARCO POLO does not accept any
liability for this. Please contact us by
e-mail or post.

MARCO POLO Travel Publishing Ltd
Pinewood, Chineham Business Park
Crockford Lane, Chineham
Basingstoke, Hampshire RG24 8AL
United Kingdom

PICTURE CREDITS
Cover photograph: huber images: A. Saffo
Images: Artissima: Elena Biringhelli (20 centre); DuMont Bildarchiv: Bernhart (59), Spitta (171, 173), Wrba (66/67, 79);
R. Freyer (flap left, 170); R. M. Gill (82); R. Hackenberg (60); Hangloosebeach: Luca Valentini (21 bottom); huber-imag-
es: G. Baviera (90/91), U. Bernhart (70), Borchi (8), A. Capone (132), G. Cozzi (184/185), L. Da Ros (76), H. G. Eiben (112),
O. Fantuz (52/53), Gräfenhahn (9), Hallberg (115), S. Kremer (106/107, 138/139), M. Rellini (84/85, 93, 94), Ripani (99),
M. Ripani (49, 119), A. Saffo (1, 122/123), G. Simeone (105), R. Spila (111); © iStockphoto/lazortech (20 bottom); M.
Kirchgessner (flap right, 25, 100); H. Krinitz (31, 50); N. Kustos (103); Laif: Celentano (108, 165), M. Gumm (124, 127), F. Heuer
(117, 131), G. Knechtel (89), B. Steinhilber (5, 146/147), Zanettini (172 top); Laif/contrasto: L. Pesce (27); Laif/hemis.fr: D. Tondini
(86); Lookphotos: F. M. Frei (2), J. Greune (155), K. Johaentges (140), S. Lubenow (160), D. Schoenen (40), U. Seer (20 top),
A. Strauß (152); Lookphotos/age fotostock (143); mauritius images/imagebroker A. Friedel (3); mauritius images: I. Boelter
(14/15), F. Lukasseck (17), M. Schindler (7), J. Warburton-Lee (81); mauritius images/age: R. Sala (6), J. Wlodarczyk (34/35,
64); mauritius images/age/Clickalps SRLs (39); mauritius images/AGF: A. Calvino (33), U. Ratti (63), V. Valletta (32/33, 47,
73); mauritius images/Alamy (11, 22/23, 68), D. Soulsby (169), J. Wlodarczyk (43); mauritius images/CuboImages: M. Gravili
(75); mauritius images/CuboImages (30 left); mauritius images/Cultura: S. Delauw (30 right, 32); mauritius images/Cultura/
Lost Horizon Images (12/13); mauritius images/foodcollection (4, 28/29); mauritius images/imagebroker: M. Braito
(162/163), mauritius images/imagebroker/Bildverlag Bahnmüller (166/167); mauritius images/John Warburton-Lee: F.
Iacobelli (137); mauritius images/Pixtal/WE111838 (44); mauritius images/Realy Easy Star/Alamy: T. Spagone (36, 128);
mauritius images/robertharding: (144/145), N. Clark (19); D. Renckhoff (56); M. Schulte-Kellinghaus (170/171); T.
Stankiewicz (54, 135); M. Strobel (172 bottom); Vesuvio Trekking (21 top); H. Wagner (10, 96, 121)

2nd Edition – fully revised and updated 2018
Worldwide Distribution: Marco Polo Travel Publishing Ltd, Pinewood, Chineham Business Park,
Crockford Lane, Chineham, Basingstoke, Hampshire RG24 8AL, United Kingdom. E-mail: sales@marcopolouk.com
© MAIRDUMONT GmbH & Co. KG, Ostfildern
Chief editor: Marion Zorn; Author: Bettina Dürr; editors: Stefanie Buommino and Stefanie Claus; editor: Nikolai
Michaelis; Programme supervision: Stephan Dürr, Lucas Forst-Gill, Susanne Heimburger, Nikolai Michaelis, Martin
Silbermann, Kristin Wittemann; Picture editors: Gabriele Forst, Stefanie Wiese
What's hot: wunder media, Munich; Cartography road atlas & pull-out map: © MAIRDUMONT, Ostfildern
Design cover, p. 1, cover pull-out map: Karl Anders – Büro für Visual Stories, Hamburg; interior: milchhof:atelier,
Berlin; Discovery Tours, p. 2/3: Susan Chaaban Dipl.-Des. (FH)
Translated from German by Sarah Trenker, Susan Jones; editor of the English edition:
Margaret Howie, fullproof.co.za
Prepress: writehouse, Cologne; InterMedia, Ratingen
Phrase book in cooperation with Ernst Klett Sprachen GmbH, Stuttgart,
Editorial by Pons Wörterbücher

MIX
Paper from
responsible sources
FSC® C124385

DOS & DON'TS ✊

A few tips to help you avoid the typical tourist mistakes in Italy

DO BE VIGILANT

You must keep your **eyes** open for pickpockets on public transport. When you are wandering through the town, always keep your handbag and camera on the side away from the street. The safest method is to wear a waist bag. At the hotel, you should ask if there are guarded garage facilities.

DON'T BUY FAKES

Even if you are an avid bargain hunter: do not buy anything – Gucci handbags, Louis Vuitton purses – from the street hawkers. If caught, there are high fines.

DON'T ORDER PASTA AS A MAIN COURSE

It might be all right to fill up on a plate of pasta in a cheaper restaurant or tourist trap and then simply pay and go. In better-class restaurants, however, there is an unwritten law against this. In Italy, pasta is a *primo piatto* and is followed by a main course of meat or fish. If you need a snack, a sandwich – *a panino* – or a couple of tramezzini at the bar are a good idea.

DO DRESS APPROPRIATELY

In Italy it is expected that appropriate clothing (no shorts, no skimpy tops) be worn in churches and places of worship. It is also best not to walk around talking and taking photographs while religious services are in progress.

DO BE PATIENT

In Italy – especially in the south – you will discover that the Italians have a completely different concept of time. This often means that you seem to have to wait for no particularly good reason. On the other hand, people have a lot more time and that can result in some very nice encounters and sometimes lead to some wonderful solutions to your problem.

DON'T ORDER ANYTHING WITHOUT ASKING THE PRICE

In many cases, it is advisable to ask the price in advance, e.g. before you take a taxi, when you make a room reservation, before having your car repaired, or when ordering a Tuscan steak, *fiorentina,* where prices are often indicated per 100 g *(etto)*.

DON'T PICK LEMONS OR FIGS

Especially in southern Italy, you will often pass gardens with trees full of figs, lemons and oranges. You should resist the temptation to pick them, rather wait until you meet someone at the farmhouse or working in the orchard and then you can ask permission. The people are usually all too proud of their products and happy to give away a few pieces of fruit.